SPECIAL EDUCATION

SPECIAL EDUCATION: POLICY, PRACTICES AND SOCIAL ISSUES

edited by Len Barton and Sally Tomlinson

Harper & Row, Publishers
London

Cambridge
Hagerstown
Philadelphia
New York

San Francisco
Mexico City
Sao Paulo
Sydney

British Library Cataloguing in Publication Data

Special education.
   1. Exceptional children – Education
   I. Barton, Len   II. Tomlinson, Sally
   371.9   LC3965

   ISBN 0-06-318199-1
   ISBN 0-06-318200-9 Pbk

Printed and bound in Great Britain
at The Pitman Press, Bath

CONTENTS

6 Special Education

FOREWORD

by David Lane

For long special education has been a cul-de-sac well set off from the mainstream of educational inquiry, sociological study and political concern. The essays in this book all share a common ground in seeking to open up the subject of 'special' education to wider intellectual discussion and criticism.

The neglect of the special school population is in itself surprising when contrasted against the intellectual energy, political agitation and financial support given to other underprivileged minority groups. What is often described as the 'handicapped' population is not small: quantitatively, the mentally and physically impaired population is as large as the black population in Great Britain.[1] It is also noteworthy that the incessant debate in the United Kingdom over comprehensive education has largely excluded from its purview the child with 'special' educational needs (if such are defined as those at the lower end of the intelligence range, or of impaired physical performance or having behaviour problems). On the other hand, the advocates of comprehensive education are adamant in their claim that the 'special' educational needs of the bright pupil are not so special after all and could be met in ordinary schools. Section 10 of the 1976 Education Act, it is true, did advocate the education of all children in ordinary schools; but even this Act, with the caveats which it attached, was not implemented.

A distinguishing feature of those children defined as 'mentally handicapped' – the largest constituency of special schools – is their inability to articulate their own needs, making them a 'silent minority'. This book addresses itself to how their needs may be best met and, in doing so, questions established practice. Traditionally, the guardians of the handicapped – disabled of limb and enfeebled of brain – have been the medical profession (in its physical and its psychological branches). In the twentieth century, the legitimacy of a medical approach has been called into question.

It has been recognized that, while the causes of physical or mental functioning may be analysed physiologically, the treatment which may be offered is limited in its medical dimension. And attention has shifted to the nurture rather than the nature of those defined as 'handicapped'. The educational and caring professions have each staked a claim in the rehabilitation and upbringing of this group. In Britain, institutional changes have followed in the wake of enlightened thought. In 1970 mentally handicapped children were given the right to education: the health authorities have been displaced by the educational ones as a frame of reference for children ascertained as having special educational needs – in plain language, what the practitioner calls the educationally and physically subnormal.

Outside the field of education, various exposures of malpractice in mental hospitals have acted as a catalyst to the philosophy that the mentally handicapped should be cared for 'in the community' rather than in medically oriented institutions. (See *Report of the Committee of Enquiry into Mental Handicap Nursing and Care* (the Jay Report) Cmnd. 7268–1, 1979, and *Better Services for the Mentally Handicapped* Cmnd. 4689, 1971.) These developments have led to other practices which in turn are called into question by the contributors to this volume, and in so questioning, the contributors add their own particular sociological perspective to the debate about policy. The question is often posed by the contributors as to whether the professional expertise which is being brought to bear on the children designated as in need of special education is not yet another, and perhaps more insidious, form of containment, control and labelling of this group of children.

What then can a *sociological* as opposed to an educational or medical approach add to our understanding of special education? Sociology is an analytical and a critical discipline. It is analytical in the sense that it has a theoretical perspective: it takes as its subject matter the recurring relationships between human beings – which are manifested in various social groups and institutions, each having goals, beliefs, structures and social effects. Sociology is not then concerned with individual physiology or personality as such, but considers the effects of various forms of organization (informal and formal) on the individual. Hence rather than, as is the case with educational psychology, focusing on the needs and dispositions of the individual child, the sociologist insists that they must be seen in conjunction with the social structures (family, peer group, classroom, school, and educational, industrial and class systems) in which the child is enmeshed. Sociology, again like other disciplines, has generated a number of different, and sometimes conflicting, paradigms of the social world and these are represented in this volume.

This focus on social structures does not lead the sociologist to deny, as is sometimes wrongly assumed, the importance and relevance of the findings of medicine and psychology. The genetic facts about, say, Down's syndrome, and its physiological effects on the process of learning may well be established by medical and psychological sciences. The sociologist, however, would point out that the opportunities society holds out for learning and living are socially conditioned and the environment that the child finds itself in *also* has an effect on his or her levels of learning, behaviour and attainment. While the genetic character of Down's anomaly may set limits to the learning of a child, social behaviour is determined not only by a child's given individual drives but also by the acquired experience and the models to which he or she is exposed and is expected to conform.

The subject matter of special education has been the handicapped child. It is a measure of progress that Warnock does not use this phrase, but prefers the terminology of children 'with special educational needs'. This is indeed a welcome change. The difficulty here is in defining membership of this group and how selection, screening and testing will be carried out. The question is posed by many of the contributors here as to whether the new forms of selecting out and making special provision for certain groups of children will lead to greater stigmatization of some of them rather than the intended opposite.

Sociology is a 'critical' discipline. By 'critical' it is implied that sociologists examine practices as they are rather than as they were intended to be by their advocates. Sociological research often shows that the outcomes of policy are not as beneficial to the recipients as claimed by practitioners. Also, if examination shows that results do not fit the stated intentions of the policy-makers, this becomes not only a challenge to the policy but also to the legitimacy of the decision-makers and the practitioners. (See Coleman, 1978, pp. 692–693.) There is then a debunking element in much sociological discourse which has a discomforting effect on the authorities. A 'critical' approach also involves a positive involvement in social change, in influencing policy; it calls for an understanding of the world as a condition for changing it. What then does this approach call for in the field of special education? While the individual contributors to this volume specify in more detail policy implications, I would like to outline just four areas of further study.

Firstly, some of the essays point to the political context in which education is set. In Britain the 'consumers' of services in special education have fewer rights than do others in mainstream education. Reports and other data on which allocation is made are not available to the parents or guardians of the 'special' child. In the United States and some European countries the testimony of professionals is open to study and question by their clients and due process of law is often invoked to claim equal rights for the handicapped (and for their parents and guardians).

The study of the process of special education might benefit from a critical analysis of professionalization. This concept refers to not only the skills and knowledge which professionals bring to their work but also to the power they wield over their subjects. (For an appreciation in the field of medicine, see Friedson, 1974.) Hence the definition of need for the 'special' pupil does not take place in a political vacuum. The requirements of the consumer are often defined by professionals who also have a 'need' to provide services and to whom structural change may present a threat. Townsend (1974) has shown the ways in which the structure of health and social services effectively balks the implementation of ministerial policy towards the adult handicapped. Sociologists might focus on the bureaucratic structures which enable or effectively prevent the implementation of policy. Clearly, the local bureaucracies and field workers – in the form of local education authorities and educational psychologists – have considerable discretion in the ways that they interpret and implement policy.

Secondly, one might pose questions as to the relationship between the class structure and recruitment to special education. Why is it that such large proportions of ESN(M) children come from the lowest socio-economic groups? (See H. Birch et al., 1970.) Also it would be interesting to study how the relative status of groups with special educational needs becomes translated into financial priorities of the state and how different types of industrial society (communist, social-democratic, liberal and conservative) define, and react to, those with 'special educational needs'.

Thirdly, one might raise the issue of the effects of the various arrangements for education in different societies. Comparative study is a major component in sociological method and study of experience, notably in Scandinavia and the United States, may help to define 'good practice' in the field of special education. One needs not only to compare the effects of 'normalization' on academic competence and social acceptance, but also to consider the quality of services provided and the social effects on those adjudicated to be in need of special education.

Finally, the sociological study of special education has a wider relevance than that centred on the selection of pupils and organization of the curriculum and on the study of what goes on in the school. One may also ask: 'Education for what?' How does educational provision lead to the acceptance, rejection or a 'special place' for the 'special child' by society at large? This is perhaps one of the most important potential contributions that the sociologist might make. Education, as we all know, is not just an end in itself, for children have to leave school to live in the community. Unless the community accepts the 'special child' as a person with something to contribute, his or her life will remain incomplete. Seen in this context, the purely psychological concerns of testing, measuring, grouping, and the provision of special education to meet special needs at present appears to be peripheral to the future needs of the children of our concern.

Notes

1   The survey by Harris et al. (1971, p. 178) of impaired adults (over sixteen years) in Great Britain estimated a population of some three million, the majority of which were physically handicapped. This research is generally held to underestimate the number of handicapped and impaired persons.

References

Birch, H. et al. (1970) *Mental Subnormality in the Community*, Williams & Wilkins

Coleman, James (1978) 'Sociological analysis and social policy', in Bottomore, T. and R. Nisbet *A History of Sociological Analysis*, Heinemann

Friedson, E. (1974) *The Profession of Medicine*, Dodd, Mead

Harris, A.L. and J.R. Buckle (1971) *Handicapped and Impaired in Great Britain*, OPCS, HMSO

Townsend, P. (1974) 'The political sociology of mental handicap: a case-study of policy failure', in Boswell, D.M. and J.M. Wingrove *The Handicapped Person in the Community*, Tavistock

INTRODUCTION: A SOCIOLOGICAL PERSPECTIVE

by Len Barton and Sally Tomlinson

This book has been produced in response to a need – articulated more and more by people who work or have an interest in special education.[1] The need is to acquire wider social, historical and political perspectives on the policies, practices and processes that make up the special education system. It is also produced as part of the more general movement for openness and accountability on the part of those involved in educational and welfare systems in our society.

All the contributors to this book have become convinced that current debates and dilemmas in special education will be widened and clarified by the introduction of alternative – particularly sociological – perspectives. They have sensed some anxiety and dissatisfaction on the part of policy-makers, professionals, practitioners and students, as well as some academics, that the psychological, medical and pedagogic perspectives which currently dominate in special education are not completely satisfactory. In particular they are concerned that people are being asked to accept as unproblematic what are in fact very debatable notions and practices.

It must be acknowledged that there are a number of difficulties inherent in producing a book of this nature. Firstly, given the variety of professionals, practitioners and interested parties who work in, or have contact with, special education, the book seeks to address a wide and diverse audience. It attempts to interest practitioners, academics and lay people, hopefully, neither trivializing issues to the point of academic dissatisfaction nor presenting them in such abstract terms that practitioners are alienated and the whole enterprise becomes 'just another brick in the wall'. We hope the book contains sufficient provocative and stimulating ideas to provoke discussion among a variety of people. If it does it will have done a major service to special education, which is an area where debate is often muffled and disputes resolved by swift recourse to 'experts'.

Secondly, there is the possibility that a book of this nature will be taken as a destructive critique, negatively criticizing the important work done by those involved in special education. We do recognize that very many people working in special education care deeply about their work and the welfare of the people they deal with. What we hope the book will contribute to is the kind of attitude in which commonly accepted or orthodox interpretations of events, issues and practices become open to doubt and examination. There are sufficient grounds for believing that a great deal of what happens in special education does rest on shaky and controversial ground and it is right that the issues should be more openly debated.

This leads to a third difficulty which is that, while sociological perspectives can provide different frames of analysis within which special educational issues can be examined in terms of their fundamental *social* nature, they cannot claim to produce quick, easy answers or neat formulae to guide practitioners or inform policy-makers.[2] As Rex has noted:

> Sociology does not render the exercise of moral and political judgements unnecessary. It makes clearer what the practical choices are, but thereafter the choice lies with men as political individuals and political groups.
> (Rex, 1973, p. 15)

Sociology can help to clarify issues, stimulate debate, provide models and theories on which to base understanding and thus render the moral and political judgements of people more informed, and as such we think it has a valuable contribution to make.

A final difficulty concerns the meaning of 'special education'. This is an umbrella term that is often used to include all categories, provisions and practices relating to the handicapped. In this book we use it to refer to state provisions for the ESN(M) and (S) and maladjusted pupils and adults. Our reason for such a restriction is that in this country sociological interest has concentrated on these areas. We are not denying the importance of the physically handicapped and sensory handicapped, nor of the influential role of voluntary or independent schools within special education, and we hope that future sociological research will include these in their areas of concern.

The emphasis in the book is on understanding special education as a social process in a social context. This involves asking questions about power, social control and resource allocation. Who has the power to define certain children as 'in need' of a special rather than a normal education, and thus affect the lives and futures of particular children and their families? Until recently the prevailing notion that the special education process was a purely humanitarian, caring process undertaken solely in the interests of children has precluded much questioning of the powers vested in professionals and practitioners to affect the lives of the 'special' children they assess and teach. But it is now necessary and possible to examine the social, moral and political judgements which are made when powerful experts decide who is normal or special, or is handicapped or has special needs. Ian Kennedy[3] in the 1980 Reith Lectures has drawn attention to the questions of freedom and responsibility which are involved in making judgements and decisions about others. At what point, he asks, does 'caring become controlling'?

A major aim of this book is to go beyond the notion of caring, without denying that most people involved in special education do care very deeply about their work – to examine the consequences of policies, practices and decisions, which may on occasion be 'controlling'.

With the introduction of the Warnock Report, the Government White Paper on Special Education and proposed new legislation (1978, 1980 and 1981), issues relating to present and future policies and practices within this complex, expanding sphere of the educational system are increasingly becoming matters of concern and debate.

It is important to understand that the handicapped are among a number of groups who are competing for scarce resources that include financial, material and human support and understanding. Thus they are part of political and ideological struggles over who gets what, how and why. Unlike many of the other groups, they are not in a position to plead their own cause or are not treated seriously when they do.

Adding to this dilemma is the fact that despite the advances made at the social, educational and technological levels of society, ignorance, prejudice and stigmatization, particularly of the mentally handicapped, is still prevalent to the degree that some people are prepared to maintain that:

> Only in a few instances has the 'otherness' of mentally handicapped people been valued positively or respected.
> (Ryan and Thomas, 1980, p. 13)

We are not suggesting that there has been no improvement in the attitudes or interest of many people in society, but rhetoric often supersedes practice. The problem is that the labels that are used to refer to the handicapped tend to envelop them so that other aspects of their person are hidden or even denied. These definitions and the interpretations associated with them are the products of powerful groups who have the ability to impose them and, as Ryan and Thomas have pointed out:

> . . . never are they the expression of a group of people finding their own identity, their own history.
> (Ryan and Thomas, 1980, p. 13)

Those professions that have historically dominated the thinking and practice in this sphere of human experience are not beyond criticism. For example, one of the most powerful means for excluding the handicapped from society has been the medical profession. People are defined as 'sick' or in need of 'treatment' and ways of explaining their behaviour are influenced greatly by medical ideas.

In the recent Reith Lectures, Ian Kennedy challenges some of the sacred assumptions underpinning ideas and practices in medicine. He argues that 'illness', while involving the existence of certain facts, also entails a *judgement* of these facts. Medical practice is

> . . . above all, a *political* enterprise, one in which judgements about people are made. (our emphasis)
> (Kennedy, 1980, p. 600)

and, in a discussion about the criterion upon which judgements about abnormality are made, he goes on to argue that:

> The point is clear. What is the normal state against which to measure abnormality is a product of social and cultural values and expectations. It is not some static, objectifiable fact.
> (Kennedy, 1980, p. 600)

In this sphere, medical judgements have always performed a powerful ideological function, and coupled with the realization that these professionals are also the gatekeepers to various forms of institutional care, their power must not be underestimated. Their clients are often on the receiving end of a decision-making process, without understanding the nature of that process, or the grounds on which decisions have been made and their rights in such circumstances.

Another powerful influence has been the judgements of educational psychologists. Beliefs about the existence of innate or heritable intelligence and the use of suitable tests that will allegedly measure intelligence are still evident in the practices of educational psychologists and teachers. However, there have been some movements towards a more progressive approach to the education of children with 'special learning difficulties'. There are educational psychologists working in local authorities who are becoming more critical of psychometric assessments. Apart from the difficulties and criticisms that can be identified and made about the nature of such tests, educational psychologists are given a mandate for defining 'needs' and what constitutes 'competency'. The assessments or tests involve the psychologist in a process of judgements that are not neutral and, by reducing interest to the level of the individual's ability, motivation, as well as personality, they

> effectively render the task of psychology as one of technical diagnosis.
> (Esland, 1976, p. 261)

This tends to mask the inherently political nature of this work and reduces or denies the importance of the question: 'Whose interests are being served by these diagnoses?'

In both the illustrations we have given of the influence of dominant perspectives, we are not trying to maintain that there is a conspiratorial or sinister role on the part of members of such professions; they may act quite unwittingly and the consequences of some of their decisions and actions may be unintended. However, this does not detract from the importance of attempting to understand these practices and assessments in terms of power and vested interests.

The sociological imagination

Sociological writings cannot of course directly change social situations. The exercise of practical, political and moral judgements is the prerogative of the social participants themselves. But sociological perspectives can make clear what the value assumptions are of the people who have power to determine the life-chances of others and in whose interests the decisions they make are actually made, and what the consequences of these decisions are. Our perspective is based on a desire for social justice and change, one which will see the amelioration of those ideas and practices in which people have little or no control, but which have far-reaching effects in terms of the quality of their lives. So, we are interested in the nature of power in our society, and how particular people or groups exercise power and influence, as well as how change comes about.

We are sociologists who have an interest in and concern for the policies, practices and individuals in the area of special education. We believe sociological approaches are necessary because the notion that professionals are solely engaged in 'doing good' to weaker groups is not the whole story. Each of the professional groups involved in assessing, referring or teaching have their own vested interests, areas of competence and very real power over their 'clients'. A crucial factor is that these children, adults and parents often have the least say and influence on a number of important decisions on what happens to them and are subject to the most pressure, persuasion and coercion, sometimes quite overt, other times subtle, of any group in the educational system.

Much of what happens in social life is the product of power struggles and vested interests. The task and promise, according to C.W. Mills, is to develop a 'sociological imagination' which makes a distinction between:

> Troubles [which] occur within the character of the individual and within the range of his immediate relations with others; . . .

and

> Issues [which] have to do with matters that transcend these local environments of the individual and the range of his inner life.
> (C.W. Mills, 1970, pp. 14–15)

This will be a practical tool and will help people to grasp the inter-relationship between history and biography, personal troubles and public issues, including labelling, diagnosis, referral and treatment. These have important relationships to social structures, ideologies and the processes of social and economic reproduction.

Sociological interest in special education will therefore include an analysis of (a) the nature and inter-relationship between how categories and classification systems are created, maintained and changed, including the consequences of such events for the participants involved; (b) the processes of school life, including interactions between the major participants during their everyday encounters; (c) the social construction of knowledge, examining who defines what counts as valuable knowledge and why; (d) the relation of special education to the rest of the educational system and the wider society, including the economic and political features of the system.

This type of analysis raises a number of important questions that need to be seriously examined. For example:

In whose interests did special education actually develop – was it more in the interests of the mainstream system which was provided with a 'safety valve'?

Are the interests of expanding groups of professionals and practitioners in special eduction served by the discovery of more and more children with 'special needs' and what will be the result of current resource cuts that conflict with these interests?

Is there a need to control handicapped children as just another problem group in society, making them productive if possible, dealing with them as cheaply as possible if not, and legitimating them as unemployable in a time of high unemployment?

Has the curriculum of special schools remained ambiguous because of this dilemma? Why, when the education system has spent a hundred years categorizing children out into a special system, is there now a debate over integration?

Or, at the level of the interactional, interpersonal spheres of experience:

What are the aims and processes involved in labelling and categorizing children?

What sorts of teacher-pupil interactions and negotiations, or psychologist-child interactions, take place in special schools and clinics?

What kinds of knowledge are passed over, or withheld, in special schools?

What are the experiences of children in special schools?

Sociological analyses of these questions should be characterized by their willingness to explore the relationship between people's commonsense understandings, assumptions, and the constraints of wider structural features of the world in which they live. The contributors to this book have made an initial attempt to begin to grapple with some of the questions.

Existing social-problem-based traditions in special education

The early days of special education provision were marked by questions such as: how many? what sort of problems? and, what to do about them? The type of research undertaken tended to be based on social surveys, which included samples of the population, the use of various forms of questionnaires, with an overall interest in statistical, quantifiable data.

Interest was focused on the position and role of the handicapped in society. Hence, there developed a literature on the social problems created by defects and handicaps (Gunzberg, 1973; Mittler, 1979), the families of handicapped children (Tizard and Grad, 1961) and the place of the handicapped in the community (Boswell and Wingrove, 1979), and most strongly, the employment prospects of those who had passed through special education (Collman, 1956; Jerrold and Fox, 1968). The employability of the handicapped has been an over-riding concern from the time of the Egerton Committee (1889) to the Warnock Committee (1978), and gives a strong clue to one of the functional needs of an industrial society – that of ensuring that as many members as possible be productive.

Tredgold, in his textbook on *Mental Deficiency* (1908), was able to include a chapter on 'Sociology', which consisted of a discussion of numbers of 'aments' (defectives) and the social problems they presented in terms of employability, reliance on public assistance, crime, illegitimacy and other 'vices' and the prevention of mental deficiency by segregation and sterilization. He considered that the report of the Royal Commission on the Feeble Minded (1908) made 'the first important contribution to the sociology of mental deficiency'. Since it documented possible numbers of defectives, the survey tradition has persisted in special education, because knowledge of the extent and distribution of handicapping conditions is regarded as essential in order to calculate resources and provision. Thus, Lewis's investigation for the Wood Committee (1929) makes a further estimate of 'defectives' and the Isle of Wight Survey (Rutter, 1970) carried on the survey tradition by estimating that 16 percent of children in their middle school years had one or more 'handicaps'. The Warnock Committee used evidence from the Isle of Wight Survey, Rutter's ILEA Study (Rutter, 1975), the National Child Development Study (Kellmer-Pringle, 1966) and their own specially commissioned study (Laing, 1976) to arrive at their recommendation that:

> Planning for children and young people should be based on the assumption that about one in six children at any time and one in five children at some time during their school career will require some form of special education provision.
> (Warnock, 1978, p. 41)

The Warnock Committee thus relied on the social survey tradition to help them reach this conclusion.

It is interesting to note that each survey during the twentieth century has progressively discovered *more* people, adults and children, with defects, handicaps and special needs, and this quite obviously relates to the extended definitions of these categories. As Rutter remarked:

> How many handicapped children one finds in a survey will depend largely on the criteria of handicap adopted.
> (Rutter, 1970, p. 6)

It might appear that some handicaps are easier to define than others, but this is not necessarily so. Ballantyne, in his book on deafness, maintained that:

> There is no really satisfactory definition of degrees of deafness.
> (Ballantyne, 1977, p. 3)

and went on to note that one of the most reliable estimates of the deaf population comes from a government survey in 1947 designed to estimate the number of hearing aids required by the population. If the definition of deafness is a problem, how much more difficult to define is, say, a maladjusted or an autistic child. McMaster's brief chapter on the contribution of sociology is one of the few books which has attempted to discuss a *Theory of Mental Handicap* (McMaster, 1973) and provides a good example of the social problem approach. According to McMaster, the two social units which need analysis, as far as mental handicap is concerned, are the family and the special school. But, according to McMaster, the family of the handicapped child needs analysing primarily to discover reactions to the presence of a handicapped child, and the special school needs analysis from the point of view of child management.

Overall, this type of social problem research was characterized by its interest in documenting the extent and types of handicap or special need at the local or national level, as well as a concern for the organization, management and provision for the handicapped or special child. This literature reflected the spirit of the welfare policies of the 1960s and 1970s, including issues relating to the nature and extent of the integration of the mentally handicapped into the community.

Limitations

From our perspective there are a number of weaknesses in this approach. Firstly, it tended to be based on a 'social pathology' model of handicapped people in which the deficiencies of the individual were highlighted and the major interest was in what could be done *to* and *for* such groups. It was assumed that problems could be overcome by strengthening the efficiency and effectivness of those institutions and organizations that were involved in the socialization of the handicapped. Secondly, these researchers tended to take the prevailing 'official' definitions and concerns and incorporated them into their research in a non-problematical manner, thereby bypassing alternative ways of seeing the issues. Finally, much of this literature is marked by its lack of interest in discussing questions of power and conflict. Relations between the professionals involved are often depicted in terms of official interests as being a matter of 'smooth teamwork', or, where problems are identified, the answers are largely seen in terms of strengthening the organization, communications mechanisms or increasing resources.

While he was not specifically referring to the work in special education, we nevertheless feel Eggleston's comment is most applicable:

> It is now possible to see the over-simplification of the earlier sociological view of the world running smoothly, with agreed norms of behaviour, with institutions and individuals performing functions that maintained society and where even conflict was restricted to agreed areas.
> (Eggleston, 1979, p. 8)

New directions: A case study

Over the last ten years the sociology of education has been marked by the increasing number of perspectives that have been introduced into the study of both micro and macro features of the education system and the wider social order. These have brought with them new interests on the part of sociologists, which have been translated into different types of questions and methods of approach (Hargreaves, 1978; Banks, 1978). A great deal of what previously would have been taken for granted or not been a topic deemed worthy of consideration has now become a matter for serious research and discussion. Nowhere is this more evident than in the everyday language of educationalists, which it is alleged contains the taken-for-granted assumptions that legitimate and maintain not only a great deal of the current practices *within* education, but also have far-reaching implications for the nature of the wider social system.

A sociological concern could be an attempt to identify, understand and explain the social construction of terms within special education. For example, the term 'special needs' has become tautological rhetoric. Part of the rhetoric includes attempts to present whatever passes for a 'special' education as a good thing for the child. Thus,

> Special education is simply education which is specially well adapted to meet a child's need.
> (DES, 1965, p. 1)

or

> Special education is, in effect, no more and no less than education which is so well adapted to a child's needs that he is able to develop to his full capacity.
> (Cave and Madison, 1978, p. 12)

Yet despite the benevolence behind this rhetoric, special education is an exclusion from mainstream education. The concept 'special needs' is often used in a mystifying manner, directing attention away from the needs that are actually being served by the expansion of special education. It is an obfuscation of the issue since categorizing or assessing children into special education disguises the reality that they are not wanted in the ordinary schools.

What are the ideologies and beliefs behind the use of the term 'special needs' as a rationalization? The term did not appear to be widely used until the 1960s, and developed alongside liberal child-centred pedagogies. If all children could be described as having individual needs, to recognize certain children as having special needs appeared to be an humanitarian advance on old systems of categorization by defect, disability or handicap.

Special educational treatment, on the basis of defect, became statutory in 1899. It was later defined in the 1944 Education Act (Section 8(2)) as education by special methods appropriate for persons suffering from a disability of body or mind, and could be offered 'in special schools or elsewhere'. By the 1960s, the notion of treatment had been abandoned and special education began to be defined in terms of need. On closer inspection, need usually turned out to be 'provision'. The Association of Special Education devoted its annual conference in 1966 to a discussion of 'What is Special Education', and after ritually noting the needs of the children, devoted the whole conference to a discussion of the provision for specific handicaps.

During the 1970s discussion of need continued to be carried out in terms of provision, culminating in the Warnock Committee's discussion in 1978. Warnock adopted the concept of Special Needs (in capital letters on page 37 of the report) and promised an analysis of the concept. This appeared in chapter 3, paragraphs 3–19 and 3–40, and was again fundamentally in terms of provision: provision of equipment, facilities, resources, curricula, teachers and other professionals.

The unproblematic acceptance of the concept of special needs is probably assisted by the assumption that there is a foolproof assessment process which will correctly examine children and define their needs. But Broadfoot has recently argued that educational assessment is not unproblematic and that, in our society, it is one of the major means of justifying a continual distinction between professionals and practitioners in terms of their power to determine what happens to children (Broadfoot, 1979).

Needs are relative, historically, socially and politically, and those who can define the needs of others, and impose provision, are powerful people. The relativity of needs is well illustrated by a consideration of the needs of the blind in two different centuries. Lord Egerton's Committee in 1889 considered that the major need of the blind was to be taught manual skills, to save them from 'idleness and vice'. Technologists in 1980 consider that a major need of the blind is to see if possible, and 'artificial sight' is being technologically developed (*The Times*, 27 July 1980).

'Special Needs' have become the rationalization by which people who have the power to define and shape the special education system, and who have vested interests in the assessment of and provision for more and more children as 'special', maintain their powers. The rhetoric of 'needs' is humanitarian, the practice is control and vested interests.

Conclusion

For us, therefore, sociological analysis is both necessary and relevant. However, we are aware as Kelman reminds us that the relevance means different things to different people. It is

> . . . a matter of judgement, depending – among other things – on the time perspective used. Some of us are more inclined to think in terms of immediate applications, others in terms of long-run implications and these orientations may lead to different assessments about what is or is not relevant.
> (Kelman, 1970, p. 94)

A sociology of special education can have short- and long-term relevance. For example, it should allow and enable students to question critically the concepts presented to them by other disciplines and from other points of view.

Much of the descriptive literature on the development of special education asks readers to accept that both statutory and non-statutory categories of handicap have gradually developed, through spontaneous evolution, over the last hundred years. Research has begun to show that administrative categories of handicap do not mysteriously develop in an evolutionary manner. Also sociological perspectives can have immediate relevance by making explicit the possible development of psychological or sociological myths of 'intractable causation' (Hargreaves, 1972; Meighan, 1981) by which a child's deficiencies or handicap come to be explained in deterministic terms. Practitioners may regard labels such as 'a low IQ', 'an organic handicap', or 'a rough background' as adequate explanations for a child being in need of special education. Literature that subsumes children in some parts of special education under that familiar intractable group of children, 'the disadvantaged', is helping to create a kind of sociological myth (Tansley and Gulliford, 1960).

Sociological perspectives must go beyond the acceptance of simple 'sociologese' to examine the relationship between ideologies in society and the way beliefs penetrate practice within the school system. As we know so little about the working and functions of teachers, teacher-pupil interactions, the school curriculum and the treatment and experiences of pupils within special schools, a further way in which sociology can be important is by providing us with insights into the processes of school life which will take us beyond rhetoric and into the realities of the everyday world of the participants.

Lastly, sociology should cause us to reflect upon the way in which we help to perpetuate social arrangements, by, for example, our definitions and beliefs about types and categories of children, and by our actions performed on the basis of such beliefs; and how these judgements and actions are not independent of wider ideologies and practices. Thus the 'sociological imagination' enables us to move in and between personal experiences, understandings and problems and those of a much wider nature, including the ideological, political and economic issues of a given society.

Compared with the influence of research and thinking by other disciplines, sociological analysis is seriously underdeveloped in the field of special education.[4] Yet we believe that it is vitally important, for an adequate understanding of the purposes, problems and changes which are taking place, for a sociology of special education to become established. These children and schools must not be viewed in a vacuum, for they are part of a wider social order. A sociological imagination should enable us to move from the individual to the wider society, from the psychological to the political, and to develop an understanding of the relationships between them. This is vitally important for both understanding and explaining personal troubles and public issues associated with special education. As C.W. Mills wrote:

> No social study that does not come back to the problems of biography, of history, and of their interactions within a society, has completed its intellectual journey. (C.W. Mills, 1970, p. 12)

This perspective should influence the way we view these children or adults, what we think are their rights, our role towards them and ultimately the type of society we wish us all to live in and work towards.

The contributors to this book have all attempted to develop new perspectives and explanations on a whole range of issues in the field of special education. However, the book is by no means intended to be definitive – it is to be taken as an exploratory volume. The studies reported here demonstrate that both analytic and empirical work by sociologists are beginning to be undertaken, but much more needs to be done. Similarly, we are only at the beginning of an understanding as to why special education systems develop, in whose interests they develop, and why they expand and change. The book is thus offered as a serious attempt to meet some of these demands at both the theoretical and empirical level.

Notes

1   We are particularly indebted to Geof Sewell, who published a letter in the *Times Educational Supplement* early in 1980, inviting those interested in developing sociological perspectives on special education to contact him. Following replies to his letter, he organized a meeting at Birmingham University in April 1980. This present volume is, in part, the result of the interest and enthusiasm shown by those who attended the meeting.

2   This is not to suggest that there should be no attempt to inform social policy or practitioners. Within the sociology of education, for example, there is a growing demand that research, undertaken from different,

sociological perspectives, needs to be concerned with such issues. (See D. Hargreaves, 1981; G. Whitty, 1981.)

3 Ian Kennedy Reith Lectures, 'Unmasking Medicine', 3 December 1980, BBC Radio 4.

4 We are of course aware that this is not true of all societies. For example, there is a strong tradition of sociological research in this field in the United States and some of our contributors refer to some of this Literature. Nor do we deny the important work of Squibb, Morris and Townsend, but we still maintain that there has been very little sustained sociological research and discussion in this country.

Acknowledgements

We are grateful to Tricia Broadfoot, Tony Edwards, Martin Lawn, Stephen Walker and Ray Woolfe for their comments on an earlier draft of this article.

Although their names remain unknown to us, we would like to thank those referees of the book who offered us encouragement and many constructive ideas. Finally, we wish to express our thanks to Michael Forster and his staff at Harper & Row for their support, patience and marvellous efficiency.

References

Ballantyne, J. (1977) *Deafness*, Churchill-Livingstone

Banks, O. (1978) 'School and society', in Barton, L. and R. Meighan (eds) *Sociological Interpretations of Schooling and Classroom: A Reappraisal*, Nafferton

Boswell, D. and J. Wingrove (1974) *The Handicapped Person in the Community*, Tavistock for the Open University

Broadfoot, P. (1979) *Assessment, Schools and Society*, Methuen

Cave, C. and P. Maddison (1978) *A Survey of Recent Research in Special Education*, NFER

Collman, R. (1956) 'Employment success of ESN pupils in England', in *The Slow Learning Child*, Volume 3

Department of Education and Science (1965), *Special Education Today*, Report on Education, Number 23

Education Bill, January 1981, HMSO

Esland, G. (1976) 'Diagnosis and therapy', in People and Work, DE351 Open University, reprinted in Esland, G. and G. Salaman (eds) (1980) *The Politics of Work and Occupations*, Open University, pp. 251–278

Eggleston, J. (1979) Editor's introduction, in Broadfoot, P., op. cit.

Gunzberg, M. (1973) *Social Competence and Mental Handicap*, Balliere and Tindall

Hargreaves, D. (1972) *Interpersonal Relations in Education*, Routledge & Kegan Paul

Hargreaves, D. (1978) 'Whatever happened to symbolic interactionism', in Barton, L. and R. Meighan (eds) *Sociological Interpretations of Schooling and Classrooms: A Reappraisal*, Nafferton

Hargreaves, D. (1981) 'Schooling for delinquency', in Barton, L. and S. Walker (eds) *Schools, Teachers and Teaching*, Falmer Press

Jerrold, M. and R. Fox (1968) 'Free jobs for the boys', in *Special Education*, Volume 52, number 2

Kellmer-Pringle, M. et al. (1966) *Eleven Thousand Seven Year Olds*, Longman

Kelman, H. (1970) 'Relevance of social research to social issues: promises and pitfalls', in *Sociological Review Monograph 16*, pp. 77–100.

Kennedy, I. (1980) 'We must become the masters of medicine, not its servants', in *The Listener*, 6 November 1980, pp. 600–604

Laing, A. and M. Chazan et al. (1976) Final Report of Research Project on Services for Parents of Handicapped Children, University College, Swansea

McMaster, J. (1973) *Towards a Theory of Mental Handicap*, Edward Arnold

Meighan, R. (1981) *A Sociology of Educating*, Holt Saunders

Mills, C.W. (1970) *The Sociological Imagination*, Penguin

Mittler, P. (1979) *People not Patients: Problems and Policies in Mental Handicap*, Methuen

Report of the Mental Deficiency Committee (1929) (the Wood Report), Board of Education and Control, HMSO

Rex, J. (1973) *Discovering Sociology*, Routledge & Kegan Paul

Royal Commission on the Care and Control of the Feebleminded (1908) 8 volumes, HMSO

Royal Commission on the Blind, Deaf, Dumb and Others of the United Kingdom (1889) (the Egerton Commission) 4 volumes, HMSO

Rutter, M., J. Tizard and K. Whitmore (1970) *Education, Health and Behaviour*, Longmans

Rutter, M. et al. (1975) 'Attainment and adjustment in two geographical areas. The prevalence of psychological disorders', in *British Journal of Psychiatry*, Volume 126, pp. 498–509

Ryan, J. and F. Thomas (1980) *The Politics of Mental Handicap*, Penguin

Tansley, A.E. and R. Gulliford (1960) *The Education of Slow Learning Children*, Routledge & Kegan Paul

The Times, 12 July 1980, 'Blind given hope of artificial sight'

Tizard, J. and N. Grad (1961) *The Mentally Handicapped and Their Families*, Oxford University Press

Tredgold, A.F. (1908) *A Text Book of Mental Deficiency*, Balliére, Tindall and Cox.

Warnock Report (1978) *Special Educational Needs*, Cmnd 7212, HMSO

White Paper (1980) *Special Needs in Education*, Cmnd 7996, HMSO

Whitty, G. (1981) 'Left policy and practice and the sociology of education', in Barton, L. and S. Walker (eds) ibid.

Further Reading

Booth, T. (1978) 'From normal baby to handicapped child', in *Sociology*, Volume 12, number 12, pp. 203–322

Demaine, J. (1979) 'IQism as ideology in the political economy of education', in *Educational Studies*, 5, pp. 199–215

Scott, R. (1970) 'The social construction of conceptions of stigma by professional experts', in Douglas, J. (ed) *Deviance and Respectability*, New York: Basic Books

Squibb, P. (1977) 'Some notes towards the analysis of the social construction of the "less able" or "backward" child', in *Journal of Further and Higher Education*, 1, number 3, pp. 76–78

Torrance, H. (1981) 'The origins and development of mental testing in England and United States', in *British Journal of Sociology of Education*, Volume 2, number 1, pp. 45–60

PART ONE

ANALYTICAL STUDIES

INTRODUCTION

This section of the book comprises a selection of critical reflections on special education. Squibb's structuralist approach – with its emphasis on the social context in which special education operates – provides a timely antidote to the individualizing approach that predominates in this area. He concentrates on the social process of definition and categorization which produces the special child rather than factors intrinsic to the child, and his analysis of percentage increases and decreases of 'handicaps' provides an ironic warning that increases in official categories and descriptions will increase the numbers of children who are defined as handicapped or in need.

Lewis and Vulliamy offer a critical appraisal of certain aspects of the Warnock Report and argue that the Committee have provided the government with an opportunity to increase bureaucratic powers and to rely on administrative machinery to solve social problems. They maintain that current discussions in special education have largely failed to recognize the social and cultural context in which policies and practices operate.

The following chapters give support to the contention that the uncritical employment of professional judgement and 'expert' opinion can often lead to practices of control and coercion of parents and children in which their rights as well as responsibilities are bypassed. Strivens suggests behavioural approaches in special education can be criticized for 'providing a form of discourse which legitimates social control without questioning' and she thus calls for more public scrutiny of the use of such approaches. Macdonald regards assessment in the field of mental handicap as problematic. He maintains that the purposes and methods of assessment need to be placed within a social context and that we need to be aware of the differences between stated policies and actual practices. He introduces the reader to the

Chart of Initiative and Independence which attempts to add the necessary social dimension to the assessment procedures for the mentally handicapped.

Sutton, himself a psychologist, points out that since special education practitioners will continue to 'learn' educational psychology on their training courses, a critical scrutiny of the major perspective on special education is now overdue. He discusses the influence of the ideas of Burt and Piaget, raising issues about ideology, politics and future trends at the level of both presuppositions and practices. Finally, Barton and Moody contribute a critique of the case of parents in special education, with particular reference to the ESN(S) field. They subject the rhetoric of 'partnership, participation and co-operation' to analysis and conclude that too often such language overlooks the difficulties involved in implementing such directives, including the fact that such ideas often contradict other ideologies associated with some of the key professional groups involved.

This section of the book demonstrates that special education cannot be divorced from the wider economic, social and historical context, that politics and power play an important role in the policy, practices and issues within this field of human experience. Decisions within special education are in important ways the products of the beliefs and practices of powerful professional groups and these judgements do not only affect particular children but also their families, friends, relations – in other words, the quality of life of whole groups of people.

CHAPTER 1

A THEORETICAL STRUCTURALIST APPROACH TO SPECIAL EDUCATION

by *Peter Squibb*

Structuralism, teachers and education

Structuralist approaches in the study of education are not popular with teachers and educationalists in Britain (Young, 1971; Squibb, 1973).[1] The assumptions behind structuralism and the implications derived from research based upon them tend to be rejected. The reasons given for this by teachers are various. They range from the charge that structuralism has no practical application in the classroom, that it plays down the role of the teacher as active change agent and innovator, to the generalisation that it is deterministic and/or pessimistic. Critics often end with the blanket condemnation that it is motivated by a subversively political view of society. There may be some truth, sometimes, in some of these assertions. But we do not normally reject a new theory because it produces knowledge which it is uncomfortable to live with any more than we can necessarily reject a new medical drug or technique because it produces undesired side-effects.

Structuralist analysis does produce ideas and insights which are uncomfortable for teachers trained in and committed to a body of educational aims which emphasize individualistic and idealistic values. But it is important to recognize that the structuralist approach is a means not an end; it does not, in itself, comment on the validity of one's beliefs; neither is it a set of values. It is a set of useful analytical ideas about the way social systems (and therefore, educational systems) function. Research and thought based on these ideas can add considerably to our understanding of education. It is up to the individual to reassert his or her values and personal aims as a teacher within the context of the new knowledge and insights gained through the structuralist analysis. It is quite illogical to reject a useful set of tools because we find them uncomfortable to hold when we first pick them up.

Structuralist analysis is useful. In the opinion of this writer it is the most useful perspective there is available for the analysis of society and its institutions. Within the analysis of education it enables us to ask questions which would not occur from other perspectives but, much more importantly, it offers us the prospect and promise of a coherent, rigorous and detached view of educational processes and, at the same time, a number of touchstones and points of reference for the critical analysis of much that goes on in the classroom, the educational system and in educational theory.

In other words the structuralist approach may provide the basis for a coherent description and analysis of the micro and macro processes and structures which make up the educational system, including its theoretical and ideological underpinnings. It is an ambitious attempt to explain the whole educational enterprise but it is in its early days, and its analyses, descriptions and explanations are as yet tentative and suggestive rather than categorical and definitive and they may, indeed, always remain so.

Parts, wholes and essences

The basic idea within all structuralist approaches is that phenomena must be seen as wholes, or parts of wholes. Parts may only be understood within the whole. Wholes are more than the sum of their parts; they are dynamic systems. Just, for example, as a watch is more than the collection of cogs, levers and springs, it is only when the various parts are put together within the system of the watch that the watch exists. And the various parts have meaning only when they are seen as parts of the watch. Structuralism suggests that all things have internal and external relations, structures or sets of laws which govern them and which it is necessary to delineate if one is to begin to understand both part and whole. The notion of system is essential to structuralism. All continuing things are systematically ordered; all the parts interact and are interdependent. Structuralism sets out to expose these interdependencies and interactions. Things only have meaning within their structural interdependencies and interactions and it is only through these meanings they can be explained.

Structuralism, therefore, denies the usefulness of the search for essences, indeed it denies the notion of essence. Essence, God-given, Platonic or genetic, is rejected. The nature of a thing lies in its relationships, internal and external, not in some prior, ideal form or inner essence.

This denial of essence, or at least the denial of essence as the determinant of socially recognized characteristics, has immediate and urgent relevance for teachers and particularly for the teacher of differentially categorized children. Structuralism makes us realize that one feature of modern educational and social thought has been to persuade us that much which is in fact social in origin has come to be seen, and responded to, as though it were natural and that children are often branded and treated as though their characteristics were natural, or of their essence, when, in fact, they are socially posited and socially maintained characteristics. In other words, the categories which are put on children by educational processes operating within the matrix of social structures must be seen as though they are the outcome of those structured processes rather than the objective external recognition of internal essences.

In the case then, of the special child, there is a structuralist imperative to look for the processes which produce the categories rather than to assume that the category arises immaculately from the inner qualities or essence of the child.

This, of course, is to ask for an approach which is fundamentally different from, and indeed opposed to, the approach normally adopted. For, instead of saying 'we need to know more about the child', etc., structuralism tells us we need to know more about the context which produces the assertion that the child is, or has, a problem.

This is not to argue that, for example, there are no such 'things' as autism or dyslexia, or maladjustment, or stupidity, etc. But it does encourage us to recognize two important qualifications to our normal procedures. To emphasize the structural processes and diminish the essence, forces us to see as problematic both the categories which we use so confidently and their widely accepted behavioural correlates.

Some of the categories may be the product of social structural processes and not of objective scientific research and disinterested observation, and some of the behaviours we have learned to expect of those categorized may not be universal or exhaustive. The fact that black children are numerically over-represented in ESN schools, in some areas, may say more about our society and schools than about black children. Similarly it may not be true to say of all low IQ children as, for example, Sir Cyril Burt (1937) did, that 'powers of sustained consecutive thought or original constructive imagination are hardly to be looked for in the backward or dull . . . always their conduct will be swayed more by emotion than by thought. . . .'

Structuralism prompts us to ask a number of questions about such statements made by those occupying positions of influence and power as

Burt occupied. Why did Burt spend much of his life trying to prove the validity of his views by such dubiously scientific methods as we now know he used? And why did he receive such support from the establishment? What structural needs of the social system did his work serve both ideologically and pragmatically? Why did such views as Burt's become the dominant views and why were contrary views so long scorned? How far do such views reflect general educational opinion? Do such views become self-fulfilling, and by what processes?

We will return to further discussion of questions such as these later. Meanwhile we must elaborate more on the assumption of the structuralist approach.

Sociological structuralism

Various forms of structuralism appear in many disciplines but we are concerned not with structuralism in general but with the application of it in sociology where it has long been a major methodological approach. Sociological structuralism derives from a view of society which starts from a concern with the problem of how and why societies survive and function.

In answer to these questions the structuralist approach suggests that the major social systems, for example, the stratification system, the economy, the polity, and the whole complex system of value and idea creation and dissemination, including the churches, the media and the family, will work towards maintaining the existing distributions of power, property, status and income. The education system is articulated with these other systems. There are two qualifications to add to this. Firstly, the functioning of these systems in this way does not imply that there is a conscious intentionality or motivation shared by the individuals involved; systems function as systems. Secondly, there is a continuing debate as to whether education is a dependent or independent variable; the consensus seems to be that normally it is dependent, or, to use a different terminology, part of the superstructure rather than the infrastructure of society.

At its simplest, structuralism invites us to look for the structures which generate the phenomena we are interested in. Therefore, if we are interested in education, or any part of the educational scene, we should look for the relationships and interactions and the similarities and correspondences between educational phenomena and the wider social systems of which they are a part. Structuralist sociology tells us that the education system tends to reflect and reproduce the social system. As Durkheim (1952) has argued:

'Education is only the image and reflection of society. It imitates and reproduces it in abbreviated form, it does not create it . . . education is a collection of practices and institutions that have been organised slowly in the course of time, which are integrated with all the other social institutions, and express them.'

Of course, this 'fit' between education and the rest of society may be less than perfect, there may be structural forces or aspects of cultures which will intervene in the relationship and distort outcomes. The nature of the 'fit' between education and the rest of the social systems therefore depends upon many factors which do not directly concern us here; but the onus is on the sociologist to look for the 'fit'.

Structuralism is itself a meta-methodology, it sets out to look for structures, to elaborate on their working and to explain in structural terms discrepancies which occur when the empirical evidence does not seem to support the theory. Structuralism is a theoretical and not an empirical approach; it is in itself not dependent upon empirical validation, for it implies that empirical data does not necessarily reflect objective truth but is rather a function of structural processes themselves. For example, data is collected and analysed within certain institutional, cultural and theoretical systems. The structures precede the data. This does not mean that structurally derived hypotheses are sustained regardless of the available empirical data but it does mean that the crude and simplistic correlations of much positivistic research are treated with the utmost caution and that different means of testing and grounding theory have been developed. For examples of development along these lines one can look at the work of people like Willis (1977) or Sharp and Green (1976).

The structural approach suggests that where the wider society has the characteristic of a hierarchy in, say, the distribution of power, income, wealth, or status then we would expect the various educational institutions and processes to work in such a way as to, broadly, illustrate, reflect or correspond to these different and differentiating distributions. One would expect there to be schools, colleges, etc., and sets of curricula, teaching methods and relevant ideas which were appropriate for the offspring of the powerful, the wealthy and the esteemed and from the experience of which these offspring would proceed to occupy powerful, wealthy or high-status adult positions and roles.

Similarly one would expect there to be significant differences in the educational experience of low-status, poor or powerless children. This idea is by no means new or revolutionary; Durkheim (1961) argued very early in the twentieth century that education actually does – and morally ought to – prepare children for the social milieu for which they are destined. More recently Talcot Parsons (1959), a leading conservative American sociologist, has approvingly described how the school class in the American system differentiates between children and socializes them in ways appropriate to their future adult roles; he accepts that generally the future roles are predetermined.

What has developed more recently has been the realization that in order to maintain a hierarchically differentiated society both the children and their parents and the teachers and others involved must be led to accept the legitimacy of the process. Children must believe that they are superior or inferior and the teachers must believe in sets of ideas which persuade them of the correctness of the categories into which they put children and the fairness of the various processes, curricular, pedagogical, etc., involved.

Because some children will have to be able to adjust themselves to relatively lowly positions, it makes good, functional sense that they be encouraged to develop attributes and knowledge appropriate to those positions. It is probable that a society would become unstable if lowly children were encouraged to consider themselves as equal to those at the top of the social hierarchy. Equally, if those at the top were not enabled to believe in the legitimacy of their superiority they might not be able effectively to maintain their superiority and privilege.

If one thinks of a slave-based society the validity of this argument becomes apparent; a little more thought is necessary to realize that it is equally true of any society which is differentiated, be it by caste, colour, race, sex, creed or class. If women, blacks, Catholics, aboriginals or any of the numerous 'minority groups' in the world are to be kept as 'minorities', i.e., less powerful or prestigious, then the educational processes they go through must be appropriate and they must be contained within a set of ideas, knowledge and beliefs – an ideology – which legitimates, explains and justifies the processes and their outcomes. This process of legitimation by which phenomena which are in fact social in origin become transformed into 'natural' phenomena are complex and varied. Man's capacity to rationalize that which he wants to believe seems unlimited. Religion, genetics, psychology, anthropology, even sadly, sociology, mythology, the media, common sense, etc., etc. have all been and still are invoked to 'prove' the inferiority of one group and the superiority of another. Blacks do relatively badly on certain tests and are therefore defined as less intelligent so that their inferior status is 'natural'. Women are defined as emotional, irrational, passive, or genetically different so this legitimates lack of privilege and their failure generally to achieve top positions.

Similarly members of lower strata, the working classes, the untouchables in caste societies, and certain races in racially mixed societies, are kept in their 'proper' places by a complex of processes. Powerful among these is education. In Britain, despite the euphoria generated by the postwar social, welfare, and educational changes, it has in recent years become apparent through a vast amount of evidence – the latest being Halsey's *Origins and Destinations: Family Class and Education in Modern Britain* (1980) – that there are still great inequalities and that the education system works to maintain them.

It should come as no surprise, then, to discover that the working classes and other deprived or 'minority' groups are significantly over-represented among 'special handicapped' children or those with 'special educational need'.

But, as we have suggested above, in order for the working of the structures to be accepted and acceptable to the people involved, patterns of beliefs, and sets of norms, have to be established to legitimate and 'explain' the outcomes in non-structural terms.

In other words, groups attempt to establish and preserve norms, and the social structures which these norms uphold, by stigmatizing and dehumanizing those who are perceived as challenging these norms. Wherever society is hierarchic, wherever there are structured differentiations in the distribution of wealth, power or status, legitimating sets of beliefs will be generated to support the differentiations. These beliefs will be upheld both by ordinary commonsense knowledge and by the official high-status knowledge. This high-status knowledge may be that of witchdoctor or priest, guru or intellectual, wizard or scientist. It will necessarily lead to the definition of some people as marginal human beings. Attempts will be made to destroy, remove, reform or cure the offenders. Various processes will be devised by which the abnormality or deviancy will be established or proved, appropriate descriptive labels will be attached and the label will become prescriptive of the response or treatment to be followed. The subject of these processes will normally be sufficiently socialized into the culture of his society to accept the label and response as proper and legitimate; he will therefore acquiecse in his own alienation.

Special education

Special education lies on the margins of a number of things. It is by studying margins that one can, often, more clearly see the characteristics of the non-marginal. Special education, the special child, special teachers, the special curriculum, are all variations upon 'normal' education, 'normal' teachers, 'normal' curriculum; the study of one will illuminate the other.

Special education facilities have been created in response to the definition of certain categories of children as not fitting into the 'normal' categories. At its crudest level children are defined as special when they are seen to exhibit behaviour which teachers are not able to locate within the range of normal behaviour. In one very important sense a child is not special until he has been defined as special. The process of definition emerges within the structures of the school, the classroom, the consulting room, the magistrates' court, or, alternatively, within the structures of the curriculum – its demands and constraints – or within the structures of the interactions between himself and his peers or teachers.

It is helpful to look at standard definitions, or more accurately, descriptions, of the special child. A typical account is that of Kirk (1970) which is taken by Cave and Maddison in their *A Survey of Recent Research in Special Education* (1978) as standard.

> The exceptional child is the child who deviates from the normal or average child (1) in mental characteristics, (2) in sensory abilities, (3) in neuro-muscular or physical characteristics, (4) in social or emotional behaviour or (5) in multiple handicaps, to such a degree that it requires modification of school practices, or special education services, in order to develop his maximum capacity.
> (p. 11)

This illustrates a point of major importance: put at its crudest it means the child who cannot be handled in a normal class by a teacher may well come to be defined as 'special' or, to put it a little less crudely, the child who is seen by the teacher as not being able to achieve normal educational goals within the normal educational experience may be defined as special. The important point is the fact of perception of a child's specialness by the teachers and the initiation of the various processes by which the child becomes effectively defined as special, categorized appropriately and then provided with what is deemed to be the proper educational facilities/treatment.

From a sociological point of view it is not the characteristics of the child which are the centre of interest but the process of definition, for it is this process which produces the special child rather than anything which the child may or may not have within him or her. It is fairly easy to recognize that this is true when one is dealing with behavioural problems – for it is well known that different teachers and others frequently disagree about whether a particular child is 'bad' enough to be categorized as 'special'. Even with some forms of physical abnormality there can be strong disagreement as to whether a partially sighted child, a withdrawn child, a deaf child or a spastic child is sufficiently handicapped to warrant the label.

What is urgently needed is a number of analyses of the actual processes by which children are defined. We need to be able to lay bare the structures which operate at case conferences; to see how conclusions are reached, which evidence and which form of presentation of evidence tends to dominate, which background or implicit assumptions underpin the ideas, attitudes and arguments of the participants. It is in this area that ethnographical research has an important part to play. We can, however, speculate with some confidence that decisions reached will be influenced by factors extraneous to the case. The relationships and interactions of the members of the case conference will depend on many social factors such as external status, past experience, knowledge, qualifications, etc. The outcome of the conference may be seen as a function of the various structures which impinge upon it. Important among these will be the ideologies held by the members, their view of the world, of the nature of man, of the purpose of education and of the child. As all these are basically political views (in the broadest sense), then the decision which results can be seen as a political decision. This realization of the political aspect of the process is strengthened by the recognition that educational decisions involve the use of scarce public resources through governmental institutions. For example, the provision of special educational resources, which is of course the outcome of political and economic forces, not only constrains the decisions of those engaged in the definitional process but must, empirically, influence those decisions.

The special child is then, in a very meaningful sense, the product of structured social forces which become focused in the definitional process. The influence of these social forces is disguised by the use of a variety of purportedly objective or scientific tests and many practitioners come to believe that the artificial world of the test is the real world. Some of the most widespread of all tests are the various forms of IQ tests, those used to give what is thought to be a measure of intelligence and a strong indicator of intellectual and academic potential. The tests rest upon the assumption that there is a 'thing', or at least a number of 'things' constituting a process, which can be accurately measured. It is further assumed that the tests used do in fact measure what they are supposed to measure. The measurement achieved is not only assumed to be accurate in regard to the child at the time of measurement but also to give an accurate prediction of the child's performance in the future.

All these assumptions must be seen to be not only highly doubtful but very problematic in that they raise more questions than they answer. For example, the concept of IQ may be seen as an artefact created in modern industrial society to meet certain economic and social tensions and to serve certain ideological functions. Equally one must remember that 'tests measure what tests measure and nothing else': it is an act of faith to assume that a test measures intelligence, or creativity, or reading age or anything else. It is an even bigger jump to assume that it can measure a non-existent, future quantity of these problematic qualities. Secondly, the validity of testing becomes yet more suspicious if one recognizes that a test score may be a function not of a thing possessed by the child nor of the test itself but rather of the social situation in which the test was taken in that the score may be produced out of the structured interaction between child, test, tester, immediate context and the whole wider social and cultural world in which the child and the test are located.

All this is not to argue that tests are wholly invalid, however. Where the pragmatics of a concrete situation require that selection and differentiation take place, then the IQ tests may be no worse, nor indeed any better, than other methods. More importantly, the use of IQ tests has in some instances led to data which has caused important redefinition of some categories of children. For example, many spastic children were able to demonstrate they had certain skills which the previously held demonology had denied them; as a result it is now generally held that spastics can legitimately be defined as sharing the same range of 'intelligence' as non-spastics. Similarly other forms of handicap have come to be redefined. Indeed we are at the stage currently where we are having to recognize that many of the stereotypical characterizations of various forms of handicap need serious review. This inevitably leads back into the re-examination of the categories themselves.

A look at some figures

The annual statistics for the year 1961 and 1976 of the numbers of children categorized as handicapped provide a useful starting point for a structural analysis.

Before taking a look at them, however, it is necessary to remind ourselves of the need to regard such categories as are listed and the data relating to them not as absolute measures of given phenomena but as the products of complex sets of structures; not only are the categories themselves open to debate but the measures of them are also problematic.

Therefore we must attempt to regard the categories as things to be explained and not just try to explain the variations in the quantities of each at different times although changes in these may assist in the former exercise. The important point is that an analysis which starts with the categories and the statistics is every bit as valid as the more usual exercise which began with the individual special child or the special class.

One normally assumes that the categories include those handicaps which can reasonably be seen to present learning difficulties to the victims. Most of them are physical in nature and the remainder relate to behaviour of one sort or another. Some, but not all, refer to conditions which might lead to risk, to the victims or to others, if they were in normal school situations. The largest numbers, however, refer directly to those who present severe problems to teachers: the maladjusted and the ESN. Warnock in 1976 and the subsequent White Paper of 1980 argued the educational irrelevance of the categories and suggested those involved in special education should be encouraged to think only in terms of the special educational needs of individual children. It is anticipated that legislation will be introduced in 1981 to expedite this. Such a step is to be welcomed for it should weaken the mythologies and old wives' tales still associated with certain forms of disability. From the point of view of the sociologist, however, the provision and publication of the statistics relating to special education does provide some interesting raw material. The ability to compare data relating to different periods does give the opportunity to pose and seek to answer questions arising from changes over time.

The figures for 1961 and 1976 provoke a number of interesting questions.

How, for example, can we explain the changes which have occurred in the various categories between the two dates? In most cases (with the exception of the blind, partially sighted and delicate) there have been increases in the number of children in each handicapped category greater than the increase

Table 1.1 Some official figures of handicapped children, January 1961 and January 1976

	Blind	Partially Sighted	Deaf	Partial Hearing	Physically Handi-capped	Delicate	Malad-justed	ESN	Epileptic	Speech Defect	Autistic
1961	1,474	2,182	3,594	2,013	10,757	12,724	6,033	47,247	903	151	—
1976	1,250	1,387	4,263	5,928	16,037	6,810	20,338	118,355	1,440	2,163	951
% change	−15%	−36%	+19%	+195%	+49%	−46%	+237%	+150%	+59%	+1332%	∞

Total School Population

1961	7,657,600
1976	9,100,633
% change	+19%

Total of handicapped children

1961	87,078
1976	179,932
% change	+107%

N.B. 1. The total figures of handicapped children includes children aged under five; these were:

1961:	286
1976:	1,550
% change:	+442%

The largest gross increase of all is in handicapped under-fives in the ESN category.

1961:	26
1967:	961
% change:	+3590%

2. There was only a single category of ESN in 1961; subsequently the two categories of ESN Moderate and ESN Severe were introduced.

3. There was no statutory category of Autistic children in 1961.

(*Source:* Educational Statistics, HMSO, 1962 and 1977)

in the total population of schoolchildren. In part this can be explained by reference to the fact that structures set up to provide for a given phenomenon will tend towards imperialism or colonization – they will work in ways which will increase their legitimacy and their territory. The greater the proven need for the service, the greater the power, status and career opportunity which accrue to it. Similarly the greater the range and sophistication of the devices used to test for a handicap, the more widely will that handicap be discovered. Factors such as this may explain in part the superficially frightening increase in the number of under-five-year-olds categorized as ESN: from 26 in 1961 to 961 in 1976, an increase of some 3000 percent. This figure greatly exceeds the large increase in handicapped children-under-fives, which increased by some 400 percent from 286 to 1550, but which is nevertheless only explicable in similar terms. For it is difficult to believe that the affluent 1960s and early 1970s did in fact see an *actual* increase in physical handicaps or a fundamental change in the special education needs of the handicapped.

One of the two cases of decrease, that of the blind and partially sighted, is worth some discussion because it is one of the categories to fall. One can only assume, in the absence of other evidence, that in this field where the medical profession rather than educationalists control the diagnostic process the improvement in the various facilities are such that many children can now be helped in ways which were not previously possible. It may also be the case that improved medical facilities and changes in, say, the use of oxygen at birth and in the immediate postnatal period for premature infants has actually reduced the number of children with eye damage.

Interestingly, however, as eyes have improved, ears seem to have deteriorated. A 195 percent increase in those with partial hearing may indicate greater alertness to the problem unaccompanied by a corresponding improvement in appropriate curative or remedial techniques. Maybe the world of the child is harmfully noisier than it was; maybe more children have learned to simulate deafness to escape. Perhaps pop music does pop ear drums. We need to know much more.

The other category to show decline is that of delicate children. This has fallen by nearly a half. Here one suspects that this is an artefact of the statistics and that they are now frequently categorized differently; which of course could mean that many of them are defined as 'normal' and kept in ordinary schools. We know that tuberculosis is now almost non-existent and that there have been dramatic improvements in remedies for asthma and similar debilitating complaints. We cannot, however, discuss the delicate category without reference to that of the physically handicapped which shows a 49 percent increase. It may be that the delicate have merely been transferred to this group and that there have been no significant changes in the composition of the two groups taken together. Whatever the explanations, we need more evidence and knowledge.

Epileptics appear to have increased by 59 percent and those with speech defects by the staggering figure of 1332 percent. This latter figure would be very alarming if it reflects a real trend, for a continuation over a few generations would have most of the population stuttering and stammering at each other.

Even more alarming are the figures for autistic children. From nil in 1961 to 951 in 1976 constitutes an infinite increase. We may all be autistic soon. More seriously, however, how meaningful is it to say that there were autistics in 1961 but they had not been discovered? Are there other categories not yet dreamed of which will be invented/discovered in the future as there have been categories in the past which have subsequently been discarded? Possession by devils was once recognized by the highest authorities as an actual physical thing which could be remedied by physical treatment, usually fatal. What attitude shall we have in a few years' time to the children of the Moonies – will they be handicapped? And can we expect a significant number of alcoholic or drug-addicted children?

The largest categories I have left until last: the maladjusted and the ESN. Not only are they the largest groups but, taken together, they constitute over ⅔ of all handicapped children and contain those subgroups which are the most problematic and difficult to define. They have also increased dramatically since 1961: by 237 percent and 150 percent respectively.

As a group taken together we know that they include the most extreme forms of physical and mental handicap through to the probably highly intelligent hyperactive child for whom subduing drugs are sometimes prescribed. The group also includes the prematurely and precociously sexually active children, and others who have broken various of the norms which are laid down for children. We know that a high proportion of them come from poor, overcrowded, underprivileged, inadequate, criminal, broken, working-class homes and parents. We know also that in many of the cases the process of categorization has started within the normal schools where teachers, for a variety of reasons, have sought to have the child diagnosed as special and removed from the normal class.

In other words the special child may be seen as a product or construct of other forces and structures rather than a special child per se. In so far as he is a deviant who transcends the norms, then sociological deviancy theory can be applied to him. One of the most interesting and startling hypotheses to arise from this is the idea that the relationship between deviancy and the social processes set up to control it are in the opposite relationship to that ordinarily assumed. In other words it has been suggested that it is the control processes which create the deviancy rather than the deviancy which leads to the creation of the remedial or penal process.

Therefore it may be that the special child is the creation of those structured processes which are set up to deal with him. The implication of this is that if we were to destroy the diagnostic and remedial structures we would reduce the incidence of handicapped children. At least the figure suggests that by increasing the structures we increase the number of handicapped children.

Whatever the validity of any of these arguments however, they cannot proceed without much more evidence and data. We need to know not only much more about the structures but also much more about the social characteristics of the children involved. We need to know parental occupation and other referents of social status and position; we need to know regional, racial, sexual and age characteristics. There is some evidence that there are class and ethnic differentials in the distribution of the categories – we need to know the data relevant to this. Without this and much more information much discussion is necessarily futile.

While there are some comparative statistics (UNESCO, 1973), and information on the categories used in other countries, both those which are similar and those with different economies and cultures, there is some evidence that different categories and different criteria of categorization exist elsewhere. The work of psychiatrists like Szasz (1971) in the USA has shown that psychiatric categories can be related to political and other structures. It may not only be the Russians who define as mentally unbalanced those who express certain opinions or who behave in ways which others might define as normal.

Indeed, the more one examines the categories used, and apparent changes in them, the more tempting it becomes to strip them of any scientific or objective validity. One must accept without much hesitation that they tell us little about the educational needs of the child, and less of his potential. One is forced to the position of seeing them as much more the expressions of social and education structures than of children.

Equally and more importantly, one is also pushed to the conclusion that the concept of the special child, in many cases, can be seen in terms of low status within the educational hierarchy. A hierarchy of people necessarily means that some will be forced into the lowest strata and, at the same time, the ideology which legitimates the hierarchy must contain knowledge, beliefs and values which 'explain' the position of those at the bottom. Therefore one can reasonably expect that sets of ideas and appropriate theories, etc. will be produced to 'make plausible' the outcomes of the structural process. The effect of this process will be to deny the potential for development to those in the lowest position while progressively extending it to those above.

Conclusion

I am very much aware that teachers engaged in the daily toil of working with the severely handicapped will, even if they have read to this point, be bitterly dismissing much of my argument, for they will not see its relevance to many of the real children they are responsible for.

Nevertheless I would ask them to stay with me, for it is the major intent of this paper to show how the structuralist perspective and the approaches and attitudes deriving from it may be of real value to our understanding of the wide spectrum of phenomena associated with special education.

Structuralism requires us to challenge assumptions which in practice and in theory are taken as unproblematic. It requires us to attempt to isolate those beliefs about the consequences of a perceived handicap from the physical facts of the handicap. Only in such a way may the Helen Kellers and Christie Browns (1972) be released from the social constraints put upon them which compound their physical inabilities.

It can also significantly open our eyes to the actual obstacles to integration, which are social, political and economic, rather than physical or psychological. At the same time it can make us more aware of the implications for the special child of separation and segregation.

Thirdly, by encouraging us to see special education, and normal education, as parts of the whole social system and functionally contributing to that system it enables us to see the possibility that there may be social answers to educational problems.

Also, within the micro system of the school or the classroom, the structuralist approach enables us to become more aware of the possibility that some of our aims, objectives and practices may be derived not from an objective view of the special child but from values and attitudes which originate in the wider social situation. Although compassion and sympathy may be a necessary *sine qua non* of the special teacher, it may not be the case that these qualities should colour and constrain everything we do with the special child. It may, in fact, be the case that a preoccupation with sympathy (which may be the obverse side of contempt and rejection) will inhibit the development of more effective teaching methods. Nothing may be more destructive than the 'does he take sugar' syndrome.

Possibly the most important effect of the analysis described in this paper is to enjoin the teacher and all those who may be involved in the process of classification to be extremely cautious before they put any label upon any child and to be even more sceptical before making assumptions about ability and potential on the basis of that label. One of the most relevant conclusions for the practising teacher to be drawn from a structural analysis is that achievement is a function of structures and of the expectations which maintain those structures.

A change in expectations may cause a modification of the structures, for the causal relationship is not necessarily all one way, and once the vicious circle is broken, new approaches, new ideas and new teaching techniques may well emerge as a function of the modified system.

At the very least, not only does structuralism encourage us to look for unities and wholes but it also requires us to rethink many of our practices and beliefs in a society which is already showing degrees of significant structural change and related ideological innovation. Perhaps structuralism itself is a function of these forces.

Notes

1 This generalization is based on the author's experience over many years of teaching in schools, on B.Ed. courses, in-service courses and lecturing to mixed groups of teachers and others. Perhaps the most specific case in point is the reaction of some of those teachers who studied the Open University course E202: Schooling and Society, in which the strong emphasis upon a structuralist approach produced problems for tutors and students. It is the author's opinion that individualist and psychological notions have so deeply permeated much educational thinking that perspectives which challenge this cannot be accommodated or even entertained by many in the profession.

References

Brown, C. (1972) *My Left Foot*, Secker and Warburg

Burt, C. (1937) *The Backward Child*, London University Press (1969 edition)

Cave, C. and Maddison, P. (1978) *A Survey of recent Research in Special Education*, NFER

Durkheim, E. (1952) *Suicide*, Routledge & Kegan Paul

Durkheim, E. (1961) *Moral Education*, Free Press

E202 (1977) *Schooling and Society*, Open University

Halsey, A.H. (1980) *Origins and Destinations: Family, Class and Education in Modern Britain*, Oxford University Press

Parsons, T. (1959) 'The school class as a social system: some of its functions in American society', *Harvard Educational Review* Volume 29, number 4, Fall

Sharp, R. and A. Green, (1976) *Education and control*, Routledge & Kegan Paul

Squibb, P. (1977) 'Some notes towards the analysis of the social construction of the "less able" or "backward" child'; *Journal of Further and Higher Education* Volume 1, number 3, Winter

Squibb, P. (1973) 'The concept of intelligence – a sociological perspective', *The Sociological Review* Volume 21, number 1, New Series, February

Squibb, P. (1973) 'The college of education: a sociological view' in *Occasional Papers in Sociology and Education* number 1, ATCDE Sociology Section

Szasz, T. (1971) *The Manufacture of Madness*, Routledge & Kegan Paul

UNESCO (1973) 'The present situation and trends in research in the field of special education', Paris

Young, M. (1971) *Knowledge and Control*, Collier-Macmillan

Further reading

Cosin, B., R. Dale, and G. Esland (eds.) *School and Society*, Open University/Routledge & Kegan Paul, 2nd edition 1977, in particular papers by: Berger, P., Dumont, R., Wax, M., Platt, A., Baratz, S. and Baratz, J.

Department of Education and Science (1980) *Special Needs in Education*, Cmnd. 7996, HMSO, August

Gleeson, D. (ed) (1977) *Identity and Structure*, Nafferton Books

Glucksman, M. (1974) *Structuralist Analysis in Contemporary Social Thought*, Routledge & Kegan Paul

CHAPTER 2

THE SOCIAL CONTEXT OF
EDUCATIONAL PRACTICE:
THE CASE OF SPECIAL EDUCATION

by *Ian Lewis and Graham Vulliamy*

Paragraph 23 of the Government White Paper on special education (HMSO, 1980) opens with the following sentences, which highlight the essential difficulty which special education raises for anyone concerned with the problems of providing an effective educational service for all pupils:

> In one sense every child's educational needs are 'special', because they are peculiar to him and nearly every child from time to time has difficulties which distinguish him from others. Special needs in this very general sense can be met under the law as it stands. What is needed is a further legal framework which pays regard to the special educational needs of that minority of children and young people whose problems are greater or more persistent than those of the generality, and which include not only those difficulties which arise from physical or mental disability but also those which may be due to some other cause. (p. 10)

It will be our contention that in establishing the Warnock Committee to investigate the problem of special educational needs, the DES – whether deliberately or otherwise – continued to do a dis-service to the educational system by maintaining its policy of asking for major reports on only pre-selected sections of that system. In addition, we shall argue that the Warnock Committee, in its report (Warnock, 1978), actively reinforced the problems of this sectarian stance, by constituting its approach to the problem in a one-sided fashion. Thus, we suggest that consideration of the case of special education provides valuable insights into the problems of the workings of the educational system to add to those emerging from other studies following 'the new directions for the sociology of education' (Young, 1971). It further provides an opportunity to examine the structural and attitudinal constraints which prevent the educational system from serving equally well all groups in society.

It is, perhaps, also worth adding at the outset that although we shall be critical of many of the Warnock Committee's recommendations, of the government reaction to them in the White Paper, and of the system within which such reports originate, we shall also attempt to show the good things which emerged and which, had they been effectively treated, might have led to a more significant and beneficial outcome than that which has emerged. In this, the Warnock Report, and the situation of special education, becomes indicative and typical rather than a special and independent entity.

The context of educational reports

We start from the position – established in the 1944 Education Act – that it is the duty of LEAs to make adequate provision for the education of all school-age children in their area in order to further their 'physical, moral, mental and spiritual development'. Therefore any practices, whether attitudinal or administrative, which prevent these aims from being achieved will act to the detriment of pupils.

Bernstein (1970) said of programmes for compensatory education:

> I do not understand how we can talk about offering compensatory education to children who, in the first place have not, as yet, been offered an adequate educational environment.
> (p. 344)

While many children leave schools to join an ever-increasing number of unemployed – and with ever-diminishing prospects of being employed – with few, if any, formal educational qualifications, then it is possible to suggest that 'an adequate educational environment' is still not universally available. The critical question then becomes one of exploring what it is, within the educational system itself, which conspires to produce and reinforce these outcomes.

In this respect it is worth noting that the same Act of Parliament which established free secondary education for all also contained a clause in which the establishment of a permanent advisory council was recommended. This advisory council should have acted as a watchdog over the *whole* of the maintained system of education and advised the Minister appropriately according to any changes in circumstances. However, the established practice of successive Ministers of State has become that of reconstituting separate councils, uniquely invited to follow a limited brief examining only one aspect of the educational system – in isolation from all others. Thus, whilst the education of children between the ages of five and sixteen is legislatively established on a principle of continuity, both its organization and the system of monitoring operate on principles of selectivity and discontinuity.

Each major report – and the roll call is like the Cenotaph in listing martyrs to the larger cause – on sixth forms, secondary schools, primary schools, teacher training, has appeared, shed a little light on one corner of the educational world, and then disappeared from the scene. The analogy with the Cheshire Cat (Carroll, 1865) is most striking. It, too, appeared and disappeared at whim and had apparently disconcerting effects on those on whom its glance fell.

As Ann Corbett (1968) once put it: 'Each Council is a lobby group for its own particular cause.' Hence the overall effects of reports on primary, secondary and sixth-form stages, teacher training – and now special education – are those of setting one part of the education system against another. Energy and argument are dissipated in terms of claims for competing priorities. Each successive report has succeeded in illuminating its small corner of the educational world, predominantly to the exclusion of all others. Such a partial and near-sighted approach results in successive governments doing little to examine critically the whole shape and structure of the range of educational provision. Each report has contributed in its own particular way to exacerbating this problem.

In the case of the Warnock Report, the Committee adopted an approach which blinkered even further the perspective on one section of the educational system. For example, we would mention the underlying – and occasionally explicit – use of a psychological perspective, which sees the problems associated with special educational need as being the result of some kind of 'illness' to which the pupil is subject. This is not surprising when it is recognized that the membership of the Warnock Committee contained no one with any explicitly sociological expertise.

The Newsom Report (1963), on the other hand, failed to examine critically the assumptions on which the selective system of secondary education was based. Consequently it has contributed, through this omission, to the continuation of labelling of types of children established and reinforced by Cyril Burt's now discredited theories which underwrote the Norwood Report of 1943. The comprehensive system of secondary education has thus become, in practice, in many cases, no more than a convenient administrative response to postwar bulges in school population, rather than an alternative system of secondary school organization and pedagogical practice.

Similarly, the Plowden Report (1967), although it broke new ground in commissioning independent evidence, nonetheless only served to confuse the issue of continuity of schooling by juggling with dates of transfer and speculating about the introduction of a further stage of education – the middle school – to intervene between primary and secondary stages.

The overall effect of these diverse studies of discrete areas of the education system unfortunately provides no effective basis for any kind of governmental action whatsoever. There can be, as with the Warnock Report, an argument that 'additional manpower and funds will become available only as the economic situation permits' (para. 70, White Paper, p. 22). Corbett (1968) described this situation succinctly:

> They [governments] have been able to ignore the case by claiming the needs of other sectors. Avoidance has been easier where the councils themselves have not set priorities to their recommendations.
> (p. 3)

People in positions of power thus have an easy escape route should they wish to turn a Nelsonian blind eye on some pressing problem. The Warnock Committee have, like their predecessors, fallen into the hands of the bureaucrats and, in not recognizing this in the framing of their report, they will, like their predecessor committees, also fail to resolve the very problems they were asked to address.

Thus, both by operating the advisory council mechanism in terms of allowing attention to be focused only upon discrete areas of education, and then by using each council's report against the others, any government is able to act or not according to criteria which may be of little relevance either to the area under discussion or to the education system as a whole.

Whilst members of such uniquely constituted councils accept the limitations of their remits, the only significant beneficiaries of these extensive inquiries must be those charged with administering the educational enterprise. Their views, their priorities, their intentions are the only ones likely to escape from any critical investigation. They devise the machinery, they appoint the inquirers, they give the direction and they, alone, determine the action, if any, which shall result. It is small wonder that both the scope for change as well as the evidence for change within the education system is so severely limited.

Before we are charged with adding further support to some kind of conspiracy theory to explain the maintenance of an educational status quo, perhaps two final points should be made. Firstly, the tensions implicit in the structure of government in this country between national and local systems – and these, in particular, have always focused on education since the 1870 Act – make it difficult to ensure agreement on policies and practices in any case. Secondly, during the postwar period, the effects of trying to cater for significant demographic changes – population growth and mobility, now followed by population decline – must give rise to a concern to ensure that administrative priorities (as seen by administrators) take precedence in all areas of decision making.

That administrators – whether in the DES or the LEAs – determine the rules of the game should be taken more as a description of the reality within which educational debate takes place, rather than as indicating any necessary or subversive attempt to maintain an inegalitarian system.

We will now move from a general consideration of the contents of educational reports in this country to a special consideration of the Warnock Report on special education.

Problems of labelling and special educational needs

The Warnock Committee reported in 1978 and made recommendations for the more effective provision for children with special educational needs. Among other things, they urged the redefinition of what counts as being in special educational need; the provision of special courses for all students in teacher training; the setting up of courses for practising teachers and special courses to train some teachers to be responsible for co-ordinating all work with such children; the introduction of new systems for identifying and coping with children in special need.

Some of these recommendations are of undoubted value and will lead to more effective educational provision for many children. However, there are important issues on which we believe the Committee has failed signally to recognize the nature of the problems with which they were concerned. If we look at the theoretical and methodological basis of the evidence submitted in the report, the lack of a sociological perspective is a crucial weakness. Nowhere is this more apparent than in the question of definition of 'special educational needs'. The report rightly castigates the present system of 'categorisation of handicapped pupils by type of disability or disorder' (para. 3.21). It justifies this view on the grounds that 'Categorisation perpetuates the sharp distinction between two groups of children – the handicapped and the non-handicapped – and it is this distinction which we are determined, as far as possible, to eliminate' (para. 3.24).

But, in recommending the abolition of statutory categorization of handicapped pupils, the Committee – on the basis of their interpretations of highly questionable evidence – introduce a definition of special education so all-embracing as to be of little practical value. They suggest: 'It encompasses the whole range and variety of additional help, wherever it is provided and whether on a full or a part-time basis, by which children may be helped to overcome educational difficulties, however they are caused' (para. 3.38). On this basis the Committee feel that somewhere between one-fifth and one-sixth of school-age children will fall into their category of special educational need. However, it is at least open to interpretation that the above definition could apply to all children since they must all, at some stage of their education, encounter learning difficulties of one kind or another. The ways in which the Committee reduce the applicability of their all-embracing definition are tortuous, to say the least.

This whittling down of the all-embracing definition to one which refers to only about 20 percent of pupils appears to rest on the credence which the Committee gives to the wide variety of diverse and differently intentioned, geographically separate and historically distinct surveys on which they base their estimates of numbers. This can be illustrated directly from the great variety quoted in paras. 3.7 to 3.15 of the Warnock Report.

Thus, using the National Child Development Study report of 1976 – based on all children born in the first week of March, 1958 – 3 percent of sixteen-year-olds were found to be in need of special education; 7 percent were receiving special help within ordinary schools because of some form of backwardness, 5 percent because of behavioural problems; and their teachers considered that a further 5.5 percent would benefit from special provision. A comparison of the incidence of behavioural deviance and psychiatric disorder in the Isle of Wight and an Inner London borough in 1970 found rates of 19.1 percent in London and 10.6 percent in the Isle of Wight. However, both these figures emerged as a result of seeking information inter alia by questionnaires from teachers. But, since Cicourel's (1964) seminal work, *Method and Measurement in Sociology*, and in the light of recent developments in the sociology of education, many substantial criticisms have been mounted on the use of the questionnaire as a research tool, particularly in areas where social labelling is involved. To rely on the unexamined definitions which teachers give of their problem pupils is to beg the question.

The report compounds its definitional problem by an implicit theory that neglects the importance of social factors in the causation of 'special educational needs'. Many handicaps are obviously the result of physiological or medical factors, whether congenital or otherwise. Yet education is now, surely, recognized as one of those areas in which the organizational structures of schools, together with teachers' expectations and pedagogies, can create massive learning and behaviour problems for pupils. Thus, Hargreaves's (1967) famous participant observation study of a secondary modern school pointed to the dangers of a rigid streaming system. More recently, Reynolds's and Sullivan's research in South Wales has suggested that the school climate can significantly alter the incidence of pupil problems (Reynolds and Sullivan, 1979).

Willis (1978), too, shows how social factors external to the school must also be considered in any assessment of why pupils either exhibit learning difficulties or become disruptive in school. From participant observation of both the school setting and the factory shop floor, Willis suggests that there is a marked similarity between factory shop floor culture and the anti-school culture that develops among those working-class pupils in school who are destined for factory work. To many teachers the behaviour of these 'lads' is both irrational and counterproductive. Willis argues, however, that from the lads' point of view their behaviour is both rational and functional for the kinds of future factory jobs for which they realistically recognize they are destined. It is this kind of research which sensitizes us to the ways in which pupils define their problems and difficulties. It is unfortunate that such a viewpoint and its implications were not recognized by the Warnock Committee.

There are, it is true, occasional sentences dotted through the report that explicitly recognize that social factors, including the organization of schooling itself, can affect the incidence of children with special educational needs. Yet the weight of all their analysis, and particularly of their recommendations, suggests that they have been blinded to the possibility that learning difficulties or disruptive behaviour in our schools might not primarily be the result of individual pupil disorders. The Committee's definition of what counts as educationally 'sick' suggests that 'illnesses' are psychological rather than social. When the vital influences of teacher labelling are not recognized, it is not surprising that special education provision is seen as the official and commonsense remedy.

The case of black pupils in our schools perhaps illustrates these points most clearly. As the authors of the report *Cause for Concern: West Indian*

Pupils in Redbridge (1978) point out – as only one of the more recent publications concerned with the problems of black pupils in schools – 'although 27 percent of all first year pupils require remedial help, the proportion among West Indian first year pupils receiving such help was 46 percent.' And later, 'West Indian pupils represent 2 percent of the total Borough school population, but at an ESN school 10 out of 120 children were West Indian.' Such descriptions reflect, on a small scale, in one London borough, the situation revealed by Townsend's (1971) study for the NFER.

We do not question the fact that the normal range of educational experience – which appears to contribute as much to generating failure as it does to encouraging educational success – may not be appropriate to such pupils. What is at issue is the nature of the problems which these special pupils are seen to create and on the basis of which proposals can be made for their remedy.

It is certainly plausible that this situation has more to do with the ways in which a white society labels black people (both in everyday terms and in the use of inappropriate psychological tests) than with the deficiencies of black people themselves. Such a case is argued by Coard (1971). More recently, other studies have questioned the basis for referral of black children defined as being in need of special education (see, for example, Tomlinson, 1981). Yet the Warnock Report pays no more than lip-service to such a viewpoint or to any of the evidence on which such an interpretation can be based.

Not only does the report create difficulties through its implicit theory; it compounds these in developing its recommendations in a number of specific areas. For example, the Committee again misuses questionnaire sources in support of their argument for a compulsory component on special education in initial teacher training courses.

Using a survey of teachers' opinions on preparations for primary school teaching in Scotland, the Warnock Report picks out the following results: only 28 percent felt inadequately prepared for teaching handicapped pupils while 61 percent said that the topic had not been dealt with; on the other hand, 58 percent felt inadequately prepared for teaching slow learners while 94 percent said that the topic had been covered in some way in their training (para. 12.5). On this basis the Committee recommend the inclusion, in all initial training courses, of an element dealing with the teaching of pupils with special educational needs. However, the above figures are surely open to numerous alternative interpretations. For example, they could suggest that the provision of a course is itself counterproductive in terms of student preparedness!

If to this is added the consequences of the earlier argument about the reliance on teacher definitions, then we feel that to act on the Committee's recommendations without further detailed consideration is extremely dangerous. Extensive research, as we have suggested above, has indicated that large numbers of pupils are defined as in need of special educational provision because of the so-called problem nature of their behaviour or their attitudes to schools, curricula or teachers. The recent emergence of special units, refuges, withdrawal units and sanctuary units in many urban comprehensive schools is further evidence of the danger of too much reliance being placed on teacher definitions.

Taylor et al. (1979) report that by 1977 there were 239 such units, 199 (83 percent) of which were established in the years 1973 to 1977. They also note that a survey of the units conducted by Her Majesty's Inspectorate of Schools found that there were no clear, accountable procedures either for admission to such units or for returning children from them to normal schooling again. Moreover, the incidence of such units varied widely from authority to authority in ways which appeared to have little relationship to possible numbers of 'difficult' children. Thus, where Liverpool and Leeds had two each, East Sussex had six and Berkshire seven. As Meighan and Barton (1979) have argued, this practice of setting up special units implies an almost exclusively psychological model of the causation of 'problem' pupils: 'Pupils are failing to adjust satisfactorily to schools is the verdict, and the necessary remedy is to modify this behaviour, to replace the unsatisfactory responses by more appropriate social behaviour' (p. 1). And yet a DES survey on behavioural units, published in 1978, identified the problems that such children had in terms as general as 'they find it difficult to accept the normal framework of life and work in schools', which suggests that the problem might lie as much with the 'normal framework' of schools as it does with the pupils.

Thus problems endemic to schools become easily translated to become problems of particular children, and practice suggests that categorization is followed by isolation, rather than eradication of the causes of the problem. Such teacher labelling can all too easily lead to self-fulfilling prophecies, so that pupils come to exhibit those properties which have been assigned to them. Not only that, but other teachers can think pupils exhibit these properties even when they don't. The dangers of institutionalizing these expectations within initial teacher training courses, as the Warnock Report recommends, are pointed to in a paper by Foster, Ysseldyke and Reese (1975). Their title sums up the difficulties admirably: 'I wouldn't have seen it if I hadn't believed it.'

A further point concerns what we believe to be the most damaging of all the Warnock Committee's recommendations: that the designation of children in special need should be based on the introduction of statistical returns to LEAs using files of each pupil. Appendix 3 of the report suggests an outline grid for such files. Pupils are to be rated in terms of categories like expressive language, current intellectual functioning and social and emotional behaviour. Research, however, suggests that this approach is likely to tell us more about teachers' and testers' attitudes and the different cultural and political contexts of the labels employed than about the pupils themselves.

, Thus the Committee has come full circle. Starting by arguing against categorization they employ a wide-ranging definition which, in fact, could relate to all pupils in schools. To get over this difficulty, they use evidence based in substantial part on teacher-completed questionnaires to suggest a limitation to about 20 percent of the school population as really being in need of special education. The Committee should have recognized the inevitability of social attitudes and values involved in the interpretation of their definition of 'special educational needs'. This is especially so when their diagnostic and remedial process starts in the classroom, and continues with detailed medical and psychological designations. An alternative, less fraught with these difficulties, could have taken as a starting point for further analysis the category system of the 1964 Isle of Wight survey, the results of which they use for other purposes. These categories were an IQ of 70 or less; a reading comprehension or accuracy 28 months or more below the child's chronological age; a psychiatric disorder sufficiently marked and prolonged to cause a handicap to the child; and a chronic disorder (lasting at least one year) associated with persistent handicap of some kind.

Even these categories – clear enough in their diagnosis – leave some important questions unresolved in terms of their educational implications. For example, of the 59 children with IQs below 70 in this study, 28 were in ordinary schools and these were less educationally backward than the 7 children with IQs of over 70 who were in special schools. It may therefore be, for example, that there are no specifiable and recognizable educational difficulties which cannot be catered for within the normal classroom if appropriate provision is made. However, if this is the case, then the Committee would surely have been better employed in using their extensive range of visits and the experience of the many practitioners who gave evidence to examine more thoroughly the real questions raised in the published research which they have selectively used. They might have then been able to identify and illustrate examples of good practice, or the provision of appropriate facilities and resources which demonstrably lead to improved educational performance.

But nowhere within the report's extensive coverage can the concerned outsider or involved practitioner find any suggestions about how to improve performance. There is no considered judgement based on reflection and experience, of strategies which hold out prospects of satisfying educational needs. How best, for example, should we deal with the learning problems which result from severe reading disability, severe motor impairment, severe social disturbance, severe antagonism to school authority? In respect to each and all of these, what is the range of difficulties which they create? And, most important, what are the relative merits of different kinds of approaches to these problems?

Had such questions been posed, then the report might have been of direct and immediate benefit. To be left with proposals amounting to the creation of a vast bureaucratic edifice operating without any clear guidance on how to improve present practices, rather than with a series of limited but practical proposals for improving present provision based on descriptions of demonstrable effectiveness, is unfortunate to say the least. If, as Rutter et al. (1979) suggest, the practices of schools and teachers can have a discernible influence on the educational performance and behaviour of all pupils, how much more so must this influence be discernible in the case of those most in educational need. As the research quoted in the Warnock Report implies, it may not be the designation of need or the labelling which is critical, but the actions and reactions of those directly involved – the teachers.

In saying all this we do not wish to be taken to imply that we feel there is nothing of value in the report. Our concern here, however, has been to expose what we believe to be fundamental theoretical weaknesses in the report which have grave implications for some of its recommendations. By seeing the problems simply in individual, psychological or medical terms, the Warnock Committee have begged the very questions they presume to resolve. By making many of their recommendations concerned simply with administrative superstructures, the Committee have not given adequate practical guidance to teachers.

Bureaucracy, rights and proposals

We pointed out, in the first part of this chapter, that the DES not only decided that special education provision should be examined, but they also determined the identity (and thereby limited the focus) of the examiners. The government now proposes to carry out consultations on their reactions to the Warnock Report which are contained in the White Paper (HMSO, 1980). Thus the ring is drawn for the next restricted round of development by those who will be responsible for framing the legislative proposals.

It is, therefore, not surprising to find that the emphasis in the White Paper lies with the administrative proposals made by the Warnock Committee, rather than with any significant attempt to influence good practice. The significant questions raised by the Warnock Committee in rightly rejecting the previous approach based on the identification of mental and physical disabilities have been begged by the DES as they were begged by the Committee itself.

We have already indicated the main shortcomings of the Warnock Committee – both in misrepresenting the evidence it had available, and also in not examining the evidence for good practice available to it through its many visits. We have, further, drawn attention to the general problem of labelling practices in schools and the difficulties which this must raise unless detailed examination is made of those specific educational needs which cannot be catered for within the normal range of school provision.

It is now possible to take the examination one stage further by exploring the reaction of the government to the Committee's restricted range of proposals. Take, for example, the issue of integration:

> The Government takes as its starting point the principle that children and young people who have such [special educational] needs should be educated in association with those who do not.
> (para. 35, p. 13)

This seems to give a clear indication that integration is viewed favourably. However, another section gives an equally clear indication that integration is conditional:

> For some children with special needs association, or full association, with other children is the wrong solution and to impose it would be unfair to the child, his parents, other children and the taxpayer.
> (para. 35, p. 13)

And, again, the following paragraph (36) defined governmental action in terms of repealing section 10 of the 1976 Education Act, which would have given legislative support to the integration principle.

Critical to this approach, therefore, is the definition of who counts as being in really special educational need. The White Paper indicates (para. 23) that the 'concept of special educational needs as it is described in the Warnock Report' will underpin all future action. We have already criticized this definition – its nature and the misuse of evidence from which it is derived – precisely because it clearly does not provide an adequate solution to the very problem which the Warnock Committee highlighted. Taylor et al. (1979) have added weight to this criticism in pointing out that:

> The exact number of such children depends not just on the intrinsic features of their condition but also on the likelihood of recommendations for categorisation being made, and the criteria which are used in that categorisation. Some differences between areas are hardly explicable in terms of objective characteristics of the population.
> (p. 55)

They also use, to substantiate their point, evidence from the surveys quoted in the Warnock Report that 'the scale on which children are ascertained as being in special educational need varies widely'.

Having defined the problem essentially in terms of an 'illness' which requires specialist diagnosis and specialist treatment, it is unfortunate to see that the cumbersome bureaucratic hierarchy recommended by the Warnock Committee forms the basis for the main features of the White Paper.

Because the Committee steered clear of attempting to define the special educational needs which might require some special educational provision, they were left with making recommendations for the compilation of assessment records of all children. These proposals had two further intrinsic flaws and, in the way in which the White Paper proposes to establish them, lead also to a major limitation on the rights of parents – and ultimately of pupils.

Firstly, the Warnock proposals are based on assessing pupils in terms of various areas of functioning – vision, hearing, mobility, physical health, expressive language, language comprehension, specific learning, current intellectual functioning, social and emotional behaviour. Under each heading various degrees of impairment are listed ranging from none to total. The White Paper modifies this approach to incorporate 'those needs which are attributable to a physical, sensory, or mental disability or an emotional or behavioural disorder and which call for special provision'.

In either case we are left with two bases for criticism: one which sees this new approach as scarcely different from that which it is designed to replace – because many of the above sets of categories are based on types of handicap, the very weakness the Warnock Committee itself pinpointed in the old approach. The other categories create problems in terms we have already explored, since they all require someone (in all likelihood a teacher) to start off the process in terms of a label which could as easily result from contextual factors as be an accurate description of a special educational need.

The second flaw emerges in the following paragraph of the White Paper:

> The Secretary of State will prescribe broad rules which will govern the assessment. These will include the requirement that the medical, psychological and pedagogical aspects must each be covered by a qualified person.
> (para. 55, p. 18)

We take this to indicate a further reinforcement of the underlying notion that somehow it is the child who has the 'illness' which must be diagnosed. Nowhere is there any indication that at least a significant proportion of these 'problems' result from factors endemic to the organization and expectations of schooling. This seems to substantiate our earlier contention that what counts as being educationally 'sick' is based on the assumption that these 'illnesses' are medical or psychological rather than social.

Except in those cases in which it can be clearly demonstrated that physical and medical handicap *result* in learning problems – and this cannot be the majority of such cases or else there would not be such widespread agreement on the inefficacy of the previous system of identification – the role of and need for medical experts is clearly limited. The basis for the incorporation of psychological expertise has been rightly criticized by Taylor et al. (1979) as follows:

> There is nothing in the history of psychological testing in this country, from Cyril Burt onwards, which would seem to justify an unqualified acceptance of decisions made by its practitioners.
> (p. 59)

And this only leaves the presence of pedagogical experts to be accounted for. We feel our arguments in the earlier section outlining the way in which teacher labelling often leads to self-fulfilling prophecies have been sufficient to indicate the weakness of reliance on these.

However, not only is it possible to argue that the Committee's actions have played into the hands of the educational administrators – and provided them with evidence to support their actions – it is also possible to see, in these proposed solutions, a further and more subtle danger. This lies in the lack of safeguards of basic human rights for the very people – parents and children – whom these proposals are designed to help.

For example, the White Paper includes the following:

> If the child is two or over, the parents will be required to submit him for the examinations involved in the assessments.
> (para. 55)
>
> The Government agrees with the widely held view that it would be wrong to require full disclosure to parents of the professional reports lying behind the record.
> (para. 59)
>
> Parents often encounter real difficulties in gaining and understanding information about their children's special needs and the nature of possible solutions. . . . the Government looks to local authorities to consider ways in which parents can gain access.
> (para. 61)

There are, of course, (paras. 58 and 59) opportunities established for appeals against any decisions made. However, it is difficult to see how parents are going to be able to make effective use of such machinery. For example, if past evidence is anything to go on, many of these parents will come from unskilled, low education, working-class backgrounds. These parents, as the recent report on inequality of health service provision (DHSS, 1980) has indicated, are often the ones who do least well in all aspects of the supposedly equally available social and welfare services. In addition, of course, they are further shackled by deliberate lack of access to the detailed information on which administrative decisions are based, since they are to be denied access to the professional opinions which underly them. There is surely a significant difference between allowing the possibility of an appeal and allowing that appeal to be conducted – indeed ensuring that it can be so conducted – with both parties on equal terms.

By providing an opportunity for a government to entrench its bureaucratic powers through reliance on administrative mechanisms to solve social problems, the Warnock Committee have provided a basis for the establishment of the unproblematic nature of its own conclusions. Because they failed to grasp the essence of the problem which they rightly diagnosed – and which was reflected in at least some of the evidence they used – the emergence of this White Paper, with its proposed edifice of special education provision, with its blurred incorporation of integration, and its so-called multidisciplinary approach to the definition of need and newly created batteries of 'experts', can only add to educational bureaucracy. This is done at the expense of consideration of the actual problems surrounding the need to cope with any special educational problems over and above those which can be resolved in normal schooling. It also allows the state and LEA machines to take important decisions without effective remedy or accountability. Thus it is clear that the mechanism within which the report emerged is itself a significant contributor to the educational malaise. The case of special education is only the latest in a long line of such inadequate responses to very real problems. This reiterates our earlier point about the limitations of the advisory council approaches to educational problems.

Conclusion

We have argued in this chapter that both theory and practice within the field of special education have been unduly blinkered by a narrow psychologistic and medical focus. Both the decision to treat a section of the educational system as separate and distinct from the wider totality and the decision to label an individual child as in need of special education inevitably involve cultural and political assumptions. The recognition that other societies define deviance or subnormality in very different ways from our own does not, in itself, of course imply a questioning of the validity of our own procedures in the context of our own culture. It might well be as inappropriate for us to emulate some treatments from 'primitive' cultures as it would be to incorporate the Soviet practice of interpreting some political resistance as medical sickness.

However, the relativity of definitions of abnormality *does* require that both theories purporting to explain the incidence of those with special educational needs and policies designed to alleviate such problems recognize the importance of the social and cultural context within which such theories and policies operate. By focusing on the Warnock Report, and the consequent government White Paper, we have argued that recent discussions of special education in Britain have signally failed to do this. Thus we have questioned some of the interpretions of research evidence by the Warnock Committee and argued that the Committee's attempt to redefine criteria of special educational need have been confused and ultimately self-defeating. We have concluded by suggesting that the major recommendations for change made both in the report and in the government White Paper on it are unlikely to resolve those problems which the report has identified.

One of our central points has been that psychological/medical explanations are frequently given for problems that require social solutions. Other writers in different fields have also argued this. Coles (1978), for example, provides an extensive review of validation studies on the ten most frequently recommended procedures used for diagnosing learning disabilities. One of the many methodological deficiencies he finds in them is 'no study examines the teaching and school environment of learning-disabled children to see how the quality of their education might have contributed to, if not actually created, the difficulties they encounter in acquiring basic skills . . . the quality of the instruction these children receive is always assumed to be adequate' (pp. 327–328). He concludes his study by suggesting that: 'By positing biological bases for learning problems, the responsibility for failure is taken from the schools, communities and other institutions and is put squarely on the back, or rather within the head, of the child' (p. 333). A similar emphasis can be found in, for example, Szasz's (1970) work on mental illness and Kamin's (1974) work on IQ testing. Such analyses, however, are conspicuously absent from the paradigm within which research is generally conducted within the field of special education.

Perhaps sociologists themselves should accept part of the responsibility for this neglect, since their incursions into this field have usually been restricted to critiques from the perimeter. What is needed is a direct engagement by sociologists with issues relating to the identification and treatment of children in need of special educational help – a project to which other chapters in this book make an admirable start.

Note

Parts of this chapter first appeared in I. Lewis and G. Vulliamy (1980), 'Warnock or Warlock? The Sorcery of Definitions: The Limitations of the Report on Special Education', in *Educational Review*, Vol. 32, No. 1, and in I. Lewis and G. Vulliamy (1979), 'Where Warnock Went Wrong', *Times Educational Supplement*, 30 November.

References

Bernstein, B. (1970) 'Education cannot compensate for society', *New Society*, 26 February

Carroll, L. (1865) *Alice in Wonderland*, Macmillan

Cicourel, A. (1964) *Method and Measurement in Sociology*, Free Press

Coard, B. (1971) *How the West Indian Child is Made Educationally Sub-Normal in the British School System*, New Beacon Books

Coles, G. (1978) 'The learning-disabilities test battery: empirical and social issues', *Harvard Educational Review*, Volume 48, number 3

Corbett, A. (1968) *Much to do about Education*, Council for Educational Advance

Department of Education and Science (1978) *Behavioural Units*, HMSO

Department of Health and Social Security (1980) *Inequalities in Health*

Foster, G.G., J.E. Ysseldyke, and J.J. Reese, (1975), 'I wouldn't have seen it if I hadn't believed it', *Exceptional Children*, April

Hargreaves, D. (1967) *Social Relations in a Secondary School*, Routledge & Kegan Paul

HMSO (1980) *Special Needs in Education*

Kamin, L.J. (1974) *The Science and Politics of IQ*, Wiley

Meighan, R. and L. Barton (eds) (1979) *Schools, Pupils and Deviance*, Nafferton Books

Redbridge Community Relations Council (1978) *Cause for Concern: West Indian Pupils in Redbridge*, April

Reynolds, D. and M. Sullivan (1979) 'Bringing schools back in', in Meighan, R. and L. Barton (eds) op. cit.

Rutter, M. et al. (1979) *15,000 Hours*, Open Books

Szasz, T. (1970) *The Manufacture of Madness*, Dell

Taylor, L., R. Lacey and D. Bracken (1979) *In whose Best Interests?*, The Cobden Trust

Tomlinson, S. (1981) *Educational Subnormality: A Study in Decision-Making*, Routledge & Kegan Paul

Townsend, H.E.R. (1971) *Immigrant Pupils in England*, NFER

The Warnock Report (1978) *Special Educational Needs*, HMSO

Willis, P. (1978) *Learning to Labour*, Saxon House

Young, M.F.D. (ed) (1971) *Knowledge and Control: New Directions for the Sociology of Education*, Collier Macmillan

Further reading

Readers who wish to explore our arguments in greater detail should take up the appropriate references from the above list which have been highlighted at various stages in the chapter.

CHAPTER 3

THE USE OF BEHAVIOUR MODIFICATION IN SPECIAL EDUCATION: A CRITIQUE

by *Janet Strivens*

Behaviour modification has a very bad public image. To the layman the term seems to conjure up visions of electric shock, nausea-inducing drugs and mind-control; visions which doubtless owe something to the success of the film *Clockwork Orange*. In gatherings of academics and practitioners concerned with the social and behavioural sciences, introduction of the topic is likely to raise the temperature of the discussion alarmingly. It is a subject which arouses strong emotions, and those who claim to use behaviour modification techniques in their practice frequently find themselves on the defensive against their colleagues. When one looks at the charges levelled against the use of such techniques, it is not difficult to understand the strength of opposing reactions; behaviour modification is accused of being dehumanizing, unethical, simplistic, politically suspect and as damaging to the practitioner as to the client (or victim). What seems particularly galling to some critics is the indifference of devout believers to their attacks, reinforced no doubt by a steady flow of interest from teachers, social workers and others in the 'welfare' professions looking for help with their immediate problems. Behaviour modification will not go away despite the criticisms, and its influence may indeed be increasing. It therefore appears as a matter of some importance in the field of special education to reassess the arguments for and against the use of this approach.

The discussion in this chapter rests on the belief that an adequate critique of behaviour modification must be grounded in a careful examination of practice. At the level of theory, where the arguments circulate endlessly, it appears to be the assumption of most protagonists that they are discussing a unitary phenomenon; that is to say, there is no problem over what *counts* as the behavioural approach in practice. Even a cursory acquaintance with the varied use of behavioural techniques in the United Kingdom makes this a highly dubious assumption. Differences in practice are often more striking than similarities, and make uneasy bedfellows of those who would identify themselves with the use of these methods. The use of extrinsic reinforcement to improve academic performance, the policy on punishment adopted within a token economy system, the role of counselling and the involvement of the child in decisions about his or her programmes are typical of the issues which create controversy within the ranks. If this view of the diversity of practice is accepted, it follows that an evaluation of behaviour modification must include attention given to factors peripheral to or outside the model. In other words, what aspects of the model are stressed in practice and which are given less emphasis? What external constraints act on an individual or an institution to define the content and goals of a programme? To say this is not to accept the claim of many behavioural practitioners, following Skinner himself, that behaviour modification is a set of neutral techniques; but neither does it support the opposite view that the implicit moral, social and political assumptions within the model inevitably lead to unacceptable modes of use.

In stressing the need to look more carefully at the practice of those who claim to use this approach, the intention is not to deny the importance of the theoretical issues in the debate referred to above. An adequate critique of practice requires an understanding of these issues, and some of them will be discussed in a later section. First, however, it is necessary to offer a description of the essential features of the model, and an account of what the behavioural practitioner actually does. It follows from what has been said already that this cannot be a neutral description; and while the attempt has been made to make it as general as possible (in the sense that it would be acceptable to the majority of those identifying themselves with this approach), the aspects stressed and examples used inevitably reflect a particular value position.

Essential features of the model

The first essential feature of the model is that behaviour is *learned*. This means that the effect of the environment is always central in accounts of behaviour, though a continuum ranges from those who exclude all other explanatory concepts to those with a relative emphasis on, for example, genetic factors.[1] This stress on behaviour as a learned response to one's environment has the necessary implication that human beings are capable of changing their behaviour in response to changes in the environmental contingencies. In contrast with certain other psychological models of human development, there are no assumptions about a necessary sequence of development of skills or behaviour patterns, nor about the inherent stability of certain forms of behaviour acquired during 'critical' periods of development.

The second feature is that behavioural analysis and change is a *science*. All behavioural practitioners stress the importance of accurate observation and recording. Typically, they count the occurrence of 'target behaviours' within fixed periods of time and make much use of graphs to note and analyse changes. In this way, they claim to be able to monitor the effects of their own interventions, and the treatment programme is open to critical scrutiny by others. Since aims are clearly specified in behavioural terms, there is no mystique in evaluating its effectiveness. In principle the methods are available for use by other practitioners who wish to test the claims made.

The third essential feature is that, in human beings, behaviour is best learned through *positive reinforcement*. The word 'best' here is deliberately ambiguous. Contrary to popular belief, most behavioural practitioners who work with children place great stress on the priority of reward over punishment, and some refuse to use any techniques that might be seen as 'aversive'. This is not merely a way of trying to avoid awkward ethical problems; the claim that punishment is an ineffective means of changing the behaviour of human beings is central to Skinnerian versions of the model (Skinner, 1948, 1953).[2] When it is used there may be two justifications offered: it serves a discriminatory function (that is, it helps to clarify to the child what is defined as appropriate and inappropriate behaviour); and by temporarily inhibiting the display of certain behaviour, it allows other patterns to be developed, through positive reinforcement, which are incompatible with the former behaviour and may come to replace it.

This third feature may be regarded as the most controversial; however, all three are important in understanding the process of designing a treatment programme. Practitioners may differ in the degree of their awareness of the theoretical assumptions which underpin the guidelines they follow in programme design. In training manuals, the tendency is for considerable stress to be laid on the underlying model, and the terminology in which it is expressed. The material is often presented in the form of a self-instructional programmed text, to reinforce the message. It might be assumed in consequence that those who learn to use behavioural techniques also acquire a degree of sophistication in their understanding of the theoretical assumptions of the model; this would at least be seen as desirable by those involved in training.

Programme design: what does the behaviour modifier do?

Specification of target behaviour

In her first encounter with a new case, the behavioural practitioner is likely to classify the problem in one of two ways: either the child is *lacking* certain skills, or the behaviour patterns that do exist are *'inappropriate'*. In the first case her task is to teach new behaviours, in the second it is to replace inappropriate with appropriate behaviour. Her first step is to define the goals of her treatment programme in terms of the behaviours she wants the child either to develop or to desist from. In the first category, the development of motor skills and physical dexterity often plays an important part. Typical goals of a programme could be the ability to dress without help, including the management of buttons, zips and laces; the competent handling of knives, forks and spoons; the ability to play ball-games to a standard acceptable to other children. For a child who appears to have difficulties in maintaining interpersonal relations, a programme might be designed to increase the amount of eye-contact and encouraging signals such as smiling that the child uses in conversations. Some academic skills could be included as target behaviours. In many cases, the specification of desirable skills which the practitioner is aiming to develop will go hand-in-hand with the attempt to reduce the occurrence of other behaviour; for example, a programme which rewards the child for not bullying other children is likely to include an attempt to make friendly and co-operative interaction with the peer-group more rewarding for that child. If bizarre or 'disruptive' behaviour seems to have a positive function for the child in attracting attention, a programme to reduce such behaviour should provide alternative means for the child to gain attention. It is often the case when using programmes to decrease disruptive and 'off-task' behaviour in classrooms that the child begins to find the work intrinsically more satisfying as more time is spent 'on task', and this should be the teacher's main aim.[3]

Recording of baseline data

When attempting to eliminate certain behaviour patterns, it is essential to have a period of careful observation to establish the incidence of the behaviour. At the same time the immediate antecedents and consequences of the behaviour's occurrence will be noted. (The observation of antecedents, behaviour and consequences is sometimes referred to in training manuals as the behaviour modifier's ABC.) In skills training, the observer will want to note the occurrence of situations in which the skills could be developed, and whether there are already rudimentary skills possessed by the child which could be built upon.

Planning of a programme

At this point the practitioner's experience, judgement and imagination play a crucial role. She must change the contingencies surrounding the child's behaviour, which typically means what happens immediately after the behaviour, although immediately preceding events may also be important. She must also make these changed contingencies highly explicit to the child. Beyond these minimal requirements, a well-designed programme includes the following criteria:

a   A programme is 'developmental' – at the beginning reinforcement may be concrete in order to make explicit the changed contingencies, but over a period of time external rewards must be phased out. It is also developmental in the sense that a total change in behaviour is not to be expected at once; steps are built in which are judged to be within the child's capability at any time.

b   Linked to the point above, the emphasis should always be on success. At any stage of the programme the child should be receiving rewards signifying successful achievement. As far as possible, lapses are ignored and the required behaviour noticed and approved. When this proves impossible, a 'Time-Out' procedure is often adopted. This generally means that the child is removed, or asked to go, to a room away from other children and adults for a specified period, usually a few minutes. The intention is to remove the reinforcement of others' attention or any other stimulation in the original situation. There should be nothing unpleasant or aversive about the 'Time-Out' situation other than the removal of these satisfactions; thus, if bodily removal is necessary, it should be done as calmly and gently as possible. However, it seems that children can readily accept the 'Time-Out' routine and even use it themselves as a means of controlling outbursts of rage or temper. In these cases, putting the head down into folded arms on a desk may be sufficient as 'Time-Out.'

c   Concrete reinforcement should be accompanied by a demonstration of pleasure and approval from the adult involved in the programme. This can be surprisingly difficult for some teachers, and parents, who have become accustomed to hostile relations with the child. A separate programme may be needed for the adult to increase the incidence of words of praise, smiles or hugs in response to approved behaviour.

d   If possible, the child should be involved in the design of the pro-gramme. This has several advantages; the programme designer stands a good chance of finding out what the child finds rewarding, the child gets a clear idea of what behaviour is required and can be involved in monitoring his or her own progress. Many programmes can be represented in an attractive visual form on which the child can make the relevant entries. It is also important for the child to be able to hold the adult to the conditions of the programme; on this principle the use of *contingency contracts* has developed. These are written contracts drawn up and signed by the child and any adults concerned, often the teacher or parent and the practitioner as overseer (see Brooks, 1974).

Implementing and evaluating a programme

Again careful recording is essential at this stage. Implementation and evaluation are combined here because the programme may be revised at any stage if the child is not succeeding. Failure of the child to achieve the targets set at different stages is, as a matter of principle, seen as a fault in the design of the programme. As the child gets nearer the target, the programme is gradually withdrawn until the behaviour appears to be maintained by 'natural' contingencies. These may of course have changed themselves; the child who no longer bullies may find more children ready to be friendly, parents are more willing to spend time with a child who no longer throws constant tantrums.

Behaviour modification as a total environment: the token economy

Behaviour modification programmes are used to work with individual children or families outside institutions. They also can be, and often are, used in conjunction with other methods within institutions, if a behavioural programme is thought to be appropriate for a particular child. However, where the behavioural approach has been adopted as the philosophy of the whole institution, it is possible to operate a *token economy*. Again, this is a term which covers a variety of practices, but minimally it implies that all children in an institution are subject to a system where tokens can be earned for specified behaviour, and traded in for a range of desired goods or activities which are held available. (A 'token' often means a stamp on cards which the children carry around with their own name on, a method which helps to circumvent illicit trading or extortion.) This does not necessarily result in a 'blanket' regime aimed at standardizing behaviour; on the contrary, where the institution professes *educational* aims, it is most important for individual programmes to be planned for and with each child in the system. This can impose a great strain on staff, who need to be aware of the different kinds of programme in operation with different children. To take an extreme example, while one child might be on a programme to increase the period of time spent concentrating on a task without disturbing others, another child who tends to be withdrawn and socially isolated might be earning tokens when he initiates contact with other children. In fact, since children learn very quickly how the system operates, staff can expect to be reminded if they fail to notice when a token is earned. In practice, token economies in special schools frequently have two functions in that they are used both to back up the general rules of institutional life and to provide help in the design of individual programmes.

To run a successful token economy system it is essential to have a committed staff who understand the system and are prepared to take on the extra burdens of constant reassessment and monitoring. The system is easily sabotaged where one or two members of staff are in disagreement or unenthusiastic about its operation. This raises questions about the selection and training of staff in special education, which will be taken up in the final section, together with a number of other problems and criticisms concerning token economies.

The case against behaviour modification: some theoretical issues

Behaviour modification has been characterized here as a process of planning guided by certain principles and assumptions. This emphasis on the *process* of designing, implementing, evaluating and modifying a programme tends to stress the role played by the experienced practitioner's judgement and imagination, and the child's own active involvement. Perhaps a more usual presentation of behaviour modification is as a set of techniques and some practitioners might argue that a list of these would provide a full and adequate description of what they do. This is in part a problem of attempting to represent the practice of behaviour modification as if it were a unitary phenomenon, and it has already been suggested that the differences may be more significant than the similarities. However, in discussing the theoretical debate over the use of behaviour modification, the term will be taken to refer to the essential features of the model already listed.

These assumptions clearly derive from that tradition in psychology known as behaviourism; hence it is not surprising that the arguments against behaviour modification are largely attacks on behaviourist psychology. However, it is worth noting that a number of writers (London, 1972; Schweiso and Hastings, 1980) have suggested that the basic principles of behaviourism are largely irrelevant to the practices of behaviour modification, which are developed and refined on the pragmatic basis of what seems to work best in the situation. Furthermore, behaviourism itself is not monolithic, but comprises a number of different strands. There is not space here to review the different versions in any detail, but the following discussion indicates some of the central controversial issues.

The first issue deals with the nature of scientific method and the language of behaviourism. In setting out the methodological principles of their discipline, there is no doubt that the early behaviourists, among whom Watson was perhaps the major influence, operated with a particular understanding of the nature of science. This led to a stress on observable events as the only acceptable data, with related implications of replicability and inter-observer reliability. While the primacy of observables remains a methodological principle, Watson's extreme position is rare, and non-observable 'phenomena' have crept into the vocabulary of many behaviourists as explanatory concepts. The growth of 'cognitive behaviour modification' bears witness to this trend, though undoubtedly there are some behavioural psychologists who reject such a notion as a contradiction in terms.

Nevertheless, behaviourism's early and continuing espousal of a positivist epistemology has laid it open to a flow of criticism from philosophers and social scientists, which has with some justice been transferred to behaviour modification (see in particular Koch, 1964; Chomsky, 1972; MacKenzie, 1972). Training manuals and written reports of cases in journals, the two most common means through which behaviour modification is presented to the outsider, tend to follow clear conventions in language and form. Treatment is seen as an experimental condition; ideally it is assumed that one variable is manipulated in the 'treatment condition' which is applied to the subject. Training manuals tend to stick closely to the terminology of operant conditioning, implying that the ability to use the jargon correctly is a necessary prerequisite to good practice. This insistence on a technical language, combined with a tendency to present the material in the form of a self-instructional programmed text, can be very alienating for the reader. Hastings and Schweiso (1979), in a useful discussion of the effects of the language of behaviourism, note the concern of a number of well-known writers of books on behaviour modification, and conclude that the terminology is not only provocative but actually misleading. The position they take is representative of what Mishler (1976) calls 'the soft-core version' of behaviourism, which is 'more eclectic, less concerned with and constrained by the underlying theory, and open to other approaches'. Mishler himself remains unconvinced by the optimism of that group of behaviourists who claim that a behavioural approach can be used for radical social purposes. He concludes an extended critique, to which Habermas's ideas are central, with this statement:

> If one believes, as I do, that ideas have consequences and that language is not simply a by-product of behaviour but an active and dynamic shaper of the categories with which we see and the alternative practices from which we choose to act in the world, then the critical analysis of assumptions and ideas is important.

Is it possible to avoid or abandon the terminology of behaviourism when describing the practice and procedures of behaviour modification? Hastings and Schweiso cite an interesting study by Woolfolk et al. (1977) which suggests that the actual practice of behaviour modification can be described by a commentator in terms drawn from a humanistic perspective; and that this not only does not do violence to the practice but actually enhances its value to other observers. Heather (1976), admitting the possibility of justifying token economy systems for chronic psychiatric patients provided their aims are explicitly educational, continues:

> However, we do not need the dehumanised jargon of the Skinnerians to explain the efficacy of genuine praise and encouragement; it could also be the case that beneficial effects occur because for once the patients are being noticed and recognised as human beings with needs and aspirations. But, if so, this is a far cry from operant technology. . . .
> (p. 58)

If behavioural practitioners are to continue making claims for the distinctiveness of their approach, this is clearly one issue they must be prepared to take up.

The second issue deals with the determining of behaviour through environmental contingencies. In philosophical terms, behaviourism belongs within the materialist tradition and faces a major problem of such philosophies – can our experience of ourselves as purposive, creative beings be reconciled with an apparently deterministic account of human behaviour? In his critique of Skinner, Mishler (following Bernstein, 1971) contrasts the 'mechanical materialism' of Skinner's operant conditioning model, which he takes as the main theoretical pillar of behaviour modification, with Marx's dialectical materialism, where the concept of praxis is central:

> Praxis refers to man as an active agent in the world, a world that he constructs and transforms, on which he confers meaning, and to which he responds. Behaviour is the analogue in Skinner's lexicon, but it is not equivalent in meaning.

Taking an opposing view, Kolbe (1978) suggests that:

> the real locus of the 'purposiveness' of both operant and reflexive behaviour is neither the organism nor the environment, but the relation or 'exchanges' occurring between them.

Both he and Ulman (1979) provide an alternative interpretation of Skinner's 'radical behaviourism' which, according to Ulman, takes into account phenomenological data such as 'thoughts', 'feelings' and 'consciousness' and 'private events taking place within the skin'.

This debate between American psychologists is interesting because, in basing their defence of the behavioural approach on Skinner's work, Ulman and Kolbe might seem to be adopting one of the hardest positions in the battle. Skinnerism is the main focus of attack in the critiques of Chomsky (1972), Heather (1976) and Creel (1974), to name but a few examples. In this country a more common defence of the behavioural approach against the charges of mechanistic determinism is to point to its growing eclecticism and, in particular, to the integration of cognitive and personality variables into the explanatory framework. This integration of concepts from alternative psychological frameworks may offer something to the 'model-of-man' type of criticism of philosophers such as Chein (1972) and Clarke (1980). Perhaps the most important representatives of this trend are Meichenbaum (1976) and the more recent work of Bandura (1977). Both place great emphasis on the child's ability to represent to himself the contingencies of his situation, to reflect on them and to make choices among alternative courses of action. Language plays an important role in this process, both as a tool used by the child to direct his own actions, and in negotiations between child and adult.

What is the relevance of the controversies discussed here to the practitioner? There is a danger in calling these issues theoretical, in that it allows them to be considered as a realm apart from the practical problems of professional work. However, to understand the different arguments and positions concerning the nature of scientific method and the construction of knowledge, the influence of language on our perceptions of the world and our actions, and the relation between language and cognition is to develop essential tools for the critical examination of values and assumptions embodied in practice. As part of a framework for self-evaluation and reflection they should be seen as a necessary component in the training of all practitioners in the welfare professions. Yet, important as these issues are, they provide only a partial critique; insofar as they spring from traditions of inquiry which are largely philosophical or psychological, there are certain questions which they barely touch upon. In the final section, an attempt will be made to formulate some of the questions raised within special education which urgently require research from a sociological perspective. Such a perspective allows for an analysis of the provision of welfare services, including special education, within a specific social structure, and brings to the fore issues of power and control, resource allocation and competing definitions of social acceptability. In particular, one needs to consider what difference, if any, is made by the psychological orientation of the individual practitioner or institution, when such questions are raised.

The behavioural approach in special education

Schools, staffing and referral

Although the majority of children diagnosed as having 'special educational needs' are catered for within mainstream education (often in special classes or units attached to schools), this discussion will concentrate on special education within institutions designated for this specific purpose. About 2 percent of the school-age population receive their education within 'special schools' which generally specialize in a particular category of need. The categories are defined in the Handicapped Pupils and Special Schools Regulations 1959 (amended) for England and Wales, and the Special Educational Treatment (Scotland) Regulations 1954 for Scotland. The majority of these schools are state-maintained, but a small percentage are voluntary or independent. Specialist provision is by no means evenly distributed among these three types; for example, according to the Warnock Report (1978), in January 1977 the category of maladjusted children accounted for less than 12 percent of the total population of special schools in England and Wales, yet they formed 58 percent of the pupils in independent special schools. Similarly, there is a strong tendency for voluntary schools to cater for the blind and deaf.

In some cases the provision offered by voluntary schools relates to the nature of their endowments and trust deeds. The establishment and special-ization of independent schools is more problematic, as indicated by the somewhat ambivalent comments of the Warnock Report:

> Independent schools . . . have in the past carried out useful pioneering work; and some of them continue to innovate and experiment in the same way as some non-maintained schools do . . . there is however a much greater variation in the quality of individual independent schools and in their approach . . . some individual proprietors appear to view the provision of boarding special education as a commercial venture which should yield a profit. . . .
>   . . . At present, because of the inadequacy of their own provision, local authorities have no choice but to make use of independent schools for placing children . . . particularly those with emotional or behavioural disorders and those with severe learning difficulties who require residential education. (paras. 8.57 and 8.58)

A questioning is clearly implied here and elsewhere in the report of the accountability of the independent and voluntary sector. As long as local authorities remain eager to find places for their 'problem' children, there seem to be remarkably few constraints on the operations of these institu-tions. One potential consequence of such freedom, recognized in the report's comment on pioneering work, is that a more total and thorough implementation of a particular approach becomes possible. It seems to be the case that the majority of those schools which have built up reputations for a distinctive approach, whether on the model of a 'therapeutic commun-ity' such as Peper Harrow or New Barns, for behavioural methods as at Chelfham Mill or more idiosyncratic philosophies, fall within the indepen-dent or voluntary sector. Hanvey (1980), in a discussion of the growth of therapeutic communities, suggests that at least two characteristics of 'suc-cessful' communities are a charismatic leader and 'almost total commitment from staff' who often 'work hours that any self-respecting trade-unionist would disbelieve'. There would seem to be an increased chance of finding both these characteristics outside the state system, in institutions whose heads have greater freedom to choose staff in basic sympathy with their own philosophy, and train them as they see fit. However, this would seem to apply regardless of therapeutic orientation; to run a token economy system as previously described also makes heavy demands on staff commitment and training. Schools within the state system, whatever approach they might wish to adopt, are likely to face much greater problems in recruit-ment, training and turnover of staff. More research into the recruitment of staff into special education, in relation to the different types of school (state-maintained, voluntary and independent) and different therapeutic orientations, would be useful here.

Further problems are raised by the selection and referral of the clients of special education, the children themselves. Questions can be asked at each point of the process, from the initial labelling of a child as having special educational need, through the special categorization of need, to the actual placement within an institution. Of particular interest to this discussion is the allocation of children to an 'appropriate' type of treatment, whether this decision depends on the referral agency or the school's own selection procedures (whether, for example, it sees its treatment as suitable only for children of above-average intelligence). Such policies may conceal important differences between groups of children undergoing different regimes.

Although special schools, even within the state system, may not experience the pressure for accountability in the same way as in mainstream education, their relation to the outside world and to other institutions is likely to have some influence on their policies and practices. Day schools cannot escape awareness of the children's home lives and parental expectations. Residental schools and homes may be more free from the daily balancing of parents' requirements with their own, but the period the child will spend in them is limited; a junior school may feel directly accountable to a senior establishment, whether it be another special school or an ordinary school. No evaluation of practice can afford to ignore these variations in the conditions and constraints under which the institution operates. An adequate critique of the use of behaviour modification in special education would need to consider the type of institution in which it is used, the staff it attracts and the kind of children to whom it is applied, if it is to be of value to other researchers and to practitioners.

Special education as social control

The challenge provided by certain perspectives in sociology to the role of the welfare professions is by now well established, developing from a questioning of the assumptions underlying the labelling of social problems and identification of clients to a re-analysis of the structural relations of the different groups thereby defined. The social controlling function of the 'people professions' (Ingleby, 1974) is linked in recent critiques to the dominance of the conceptual frameworks of psychology (Esland, 1977; Ingleby 1970, 1974, 1980).

Institutions of special education serve a clear function in the removal from the 'normal' state system of problems which interfere with the smooth running of that system. This function conflicts with the professional ideologies of most of the workers in them – teachers, social workers, residential care staff, psychologists. Their definition of their role may emphasize the therapeutic or the educational, depending on training, experience and theoretical orientation; whichever is stressed, both carry implications of a concern to return their pupils to society to play as full a part in it as possible. As a result of these contradictory functions, tensions may arise within an institution: is it run for the benefit of the staff, to minimize problems of management, or for the benefit of the children, to equip them to cope with non-institutional life?

The problem presents itself in rather different ways to those working within the different categories of special school. With children classified as severely educationally subnormal or mentally handicapped, staff may consider that a sheltered environment will always be necessary, and that the greater freedom these children can enjoy through careful teaching of certain skills (such as using buses or telephones, crossing roads, preparing food) brings with it increased risks. To run an institution which is highly regulated and places low demands on the children for independent behaviour may make it much easier for the staff to cope; a real desire to develop the maximum independence for each child immediately increases the staff's responsibility and workload, and places demands on the children to which they may not always respond positively. With children categorized as maladjusted or moderately educationally subnormal, the staff's function as agents of social control may become more salient. Both categories contain an increasing number of children whose behaviour is often disruptive and occasionally violent; staff cannot escape the conclusion that these children are sent to them because ordinary teachers (and parents) cannot handle them, and some resent this as a misuse of their expertise (see, for example, the response to the Warnock Report by the Association of Workers for Maladjusted Children, 1979).

A central accusation against the behavioural approach has been that it provides a form of discourse which legitimates social control without questioning. Clearly, the behavioural model provides no criteria for reflection on the role of the institution. It has been argued, however, that different values may be reflected in the practice of behaviour modification. If the suggestion is correct that institutions may be run for the benefit of the institution and its staff, or for the benefit of the children, a behavioural approach makes this particularly explicit. Token economies lend themselves to be used for smooth management, and it is this aspect which has been emphasized by their critics. Yet it is claimed with equal force that they can be used to provide an experience of a consistent and easily comprehended environment which has been lacking in the lives of many of the children who arrive in special schools. When the things they do have predictable consequences, they can come to experience themselves as having a degree of control over events, and making choices between alternative courses of action becomes meaningful, since adults behave in consistent and reliable ways and can be kept to their promises. Features of a token economy which might be useful to consider in an evaluation of its operation are, firstly, whether the degree of control is graduated, with the expectation that the child's need for structure will be reduced during its stay, and to approximate more closely to life outside the institution; and, secondly, whether the emphasis shifts from programmes aimed at controlling behaviour within the institution to those based on developing skills. Undoubtedly many social skills training programmes are adaptive in the sense that they are designed to help the child win approval from society outside the institution. Yet it is at least open to question whether a teacher attempting to develop control of immediate reaction and alternative strategies of response in an adolescent who typically responds to authority with violence is necessarily functioning as an agent of social oppression. Some skills are required to challenge systems as well as to adjust to them. Since social skills training is an increasingly important aspect of the behavioural approach in special education, it is particularly necessary for practitioners to reflect on the content of such programmes and the reasons why certain skills are regarded as 'appropriate'.

Summary

This chapter has argued that a critique of behaviour modification based solely on the analysis of a conceptual model within academic psychology could be misleading, and of little value to those working, or training to work, in the welfare professions. It has been suggested that the claim to be using a behavioural approach conceals wide variations in the values and practices of different individuals and institutions. In part, this is a question of the emphasis placed on different features of the model; but also, in view of the increasing readiness of practitioners to make use of a variety of techniques and theoretical approaches, and reservations expressed by some over the language of behaviourism, the distinctiveness of the behavioural approach itself may come under question.

If the necessity of basing a critique on the examination of practices is accepted, it is important to clarify the questions to be asked. It has been extremely difficult to evaluate the claims made by the proponents of rival methods and approaches, since their own criteria deriving from the underlying assumptions of different models are incommensurate. Perspectives from sociology have an important function in showing the relations between systems of values and beliefs and the social context in which they have developed, which they both reflect and help to recreate. This has been pursued at the macro level, in critiques of the welfare professions and their supporting ideologies. In special education, the assumptions are starting to be questioned behind both the general and specific categorization of children with 'special educational needs'. However, there is still a strong need to extend the concepts and methods of sociological research to the study of different institutions, both in terms of the creation of institutional cultures and of their role in the selection and labelling of their clientele, the children.

Such questions need to be asked over the whole range of approaches and theoretical orientations in special education; in this respect there seems no reason for differentiating between the behavioural approach and any other. There may be differences in the research problems encountered, in that a distinctive feature of the behavioural approach is said to be its commitment to public scrutiny (at least within the research community) of its methods and results. Such openness among practitioners requires to be demonstrated.

Notes

1   As in the work of H.J. Eysenck, where the concept of 'conditionability', or *inherent* learning capacity, plays an important role.

2   For a demonstration of the opposing views on the effectiveness of punishment within the behaviourist school in psychology, the chapters by Skinner and Solomon in a collection of readings on punishment (Walters, Cheyne and Banks, 1972) make an interesting comparison.

3   An interesting implication of this attitude is that the use of behaviour modification could do something to combat the negative effects of teacher expectations; where no *necessary* assumptions are involved as part of the theory about why a particular child lacks skills, or has acquired inappropriate behaviour, staff may be encouraged to raise their expectations of what is possible. At the least they may be more wary of implicit assumptions about the child's limitations. This would be an

area to note in considering the influence of different theoretical orientations on the labelling of children and attitudes of staff in special education.

References

Association of Workers for Maladjusted Children (1979) 'The implications of the Warnock Report', *Journal of the Association of Workers for Maladjusted Children*, Volume 7, number 1, pp. 3–6.

Bandura, A. (1977) *Social Learning Theory*, Morristown, N.J.: General Learning Press

Bernstein, R.J. (1971) *Praxis and Action*, Philadelphia: University of Pennsylvania Press

Brooks, B.D. (1974) 'Contingency contracts with truants', *Personnel and Guidance Journal*, Volume 52, number 5

Chein, I. (1972) *The Science of Behaviour and the Image of Man*, Tavistock

Chomsky, N. (1972) 'Psychology and ideology', *Cognition*, Volume 1, number 1, pp. 11–46

Clarke, C. (1979) 'Education and behaviour modification', *Journal of Philosophy of Education*, Volume 13, pp. 73–81

Creel, R.E. (1974) 'Skinner's Copernican revolution', *Journal for the Theory of Social Behaviour*, Volume 4, number 2, pp. 131–145

Esland, G. (1977) 'Diagnosis and testing', Unit 21, Open University Course E202, *Schooling and Society*, Open University Press

Hanvey, C. (1980) 'What is a therapeutic community?', *Mind Out*, number 43, pp. 11–13

Hastings, N. and J. Schweiso (1979) 'Practices, prejudices and prospects: behaviour modification and teacher training', *Psychology Teaching*, Volume 7, number 2, pp. 137–141

Heather, N. (1976) *Radical Perspectives in Psychology*, Essential Psychology Series (48), Methuen

Ingleby, D. (1970) 'Ideology and the human sciences', in Pateman, T. (ed), *Counter Course: A Handbook for Course Criticism*, Penguin

Ingleby, D. (1974) 'The psychology of child psychology', in Richard, M.P.M. (ed), *The Integration of a Child into a Social World*, Cambridge University Press

Ingleby, D. (1980) 'The politics of psychology: review of a decade', unpublished

Koch, S. (1964) 'Psychology and emerging conceptions of man as unitary', in Wann, T. (ed) *Behaviourism and Phenomenology*, Chicago: University of Chicago Press

Kolbe, W. (1978) 'B.F. Skinner's radical behaviourism: logical positivism or dialectical materialism?' *Behaviourists for Social Action Journal*, Volume 1, number 1, pp. 29–55

London, P. (1972) 'The end of ideology in behaviour modification', *American Psychologist*, Volume 27, pp. 913–920

MacKenzie, B.D. (1972) 'Behaviourism and positivism', *Journal of the History of the Behavioural Sciences*, Volume 8, pp. 222–231

Meichenbaum, D. (1976) 'Cognitive behaviour modification', in Spence, J.T., R.C. Carson and J.W. Thubaut (eds) *Behavioural Approaches to Therapy*, Morristown, N.J., General Learning Press

Mishler, E.G. (1976) 'Skinnerism: materialism minus the dialectic', *Journal of the Theory of Social Behaviour*, Volume 6, pp. 21–47

Schweiso, J. and N. Hastings (1980) 'The role of theory in the teaching of behaviour modification to teachers', in Wheldall, K. (ed) *The Behaviourist in the Classroom: Aspects of Applied Behavioural Analysis in British Educational Contexts*, Educational Review Publications, University of Birmingham

Skinner, B.F. (1948) *Walden Two*, New York: Macmillan

Skinner, B.F. (1953) *Science and Human Behaviour*, New York: Macmillan

Ulman, J. (1979) 'A critique of "Skinnerism: Materialism minus the Dialectic" ', *Behaviourists for Social Action Journal*, Volume 1, number 2, pp. 1–8

Walters, R.H., J.A. Cheyne and R.K. Banks (eds) (1972) *Punishment*, Penguin

Warnock Report (1978) *Special Educational Needs*, HMSO

Woolfolk, A.E., R.L. Woolfolk and G.T. Wilson (1977) 'A rose by any other name . . .; Labelling bias and attitudes towards behaviour modification', *Journal of Counselling and Clinical Psychology*, Volume 45, pp. 184–191

Further reading

On the use of behavioural techniques in special education:

Brown, B.J. and M. Christie (1981) *Social Learning Practice in Residential Child Care*, Pergamon Press

Ward, J. (1975) 'Behaviour modification in special education', in Wedell, K. (ed) *Orientations in Special Education*, John Wiley and Sons

Yule, W. and J. Carr (1980) *Behaviour Modification for the Mentally Handicapped*, Croom Helm

Kiernan, C.C. and F.P. Woodford (eds) (1975) *Behaviour Modification with the Severely Retarded*, Amsterdam: Associated Scientific Publishers

Macmillan, A. and I. Kolvin (1977) 'Behaviour modification in educational settings: a guide for teachers', *Journal of the Association of Workers for Maladjusted Children*, Volume 5, pp. 2–18

On token economy systems:

Ayllon, T. and N.H. Azrin (1968) *The Token Economy: A Motivational System for Therapy and Rehabilitation*, New York: Appleton Century Crofts

Turton, B.K. and C.E. Gathercole (1972) 'Token economies in the U.K. and Eire', *Bulletin of the British Psychological Society*, Volume 25, pp. 83–87

General:

Bulletin of the British Association of Behavioural Psychotherapy (Back copies obtainable from Dr. R.J. Hodgson, Addiction Research Unit, Institute of Psychiatry, 101 Denmark Hill, London, SE15 8DF.) This has now become a journal, *Behavioural Psychotherapy*, from 1980, Academic Press

Newsletter of the Association for Behaviour Modification with Children (obtainable from J.R. Burland, Chelfham Mill School, Barnstable, N. Devon)

Behaviourists for Social Action Journal (obtainable from Joe Morrow, Psychology Department, California State University, 6000 J. Street, Sacramento, California 95819.)

CHAPTER 4

ASSESSMENT: A SOCIAL DIMENSION

by Ian Macdonald

Introduction

The central concern in this chapter is assessment in the field of mental handicap. While some of the issues raised have broader implications and are developed in other parts of the book, this chapter is addressed to the concerns facing families, workers and mentally handicapped people when and where an 'assessment' takes place. The way in which this is to be done here is first to look at the purposes of assessment, including what tools are used and their inherent problems. Secondly, I examine problems, not only of the tests themselves, but also the social context of assessment, including implications for policy making. Then finally I offer a method of assessment which, perhaps, goes some way to fill some of the gaps, without necessarily replacing other forms of assessment.

In recent years screening during pregnancy and tests at birth have identified certain conditions, for example, Down's syndrome and phenyl-ketonuria (Smith, G. and Berg, J., 1976; Hsu, L. et al., 1973; and Gibb, N., 1959). However, in the majority of cases pregnancy and birth do not lead to an identification of the possibility of mental handicap. In one survey of hospital patients Leck (1967) found no identifiable cause for subnormality in over 70 percent of cases. Aetiology is not easy to establish; even in profound mental handicap known causes do not account for anything like the total population.

Therefore the reason for a detailed or special assessment rarely arises simply from a direct and early medical diagnosis. In the majority of cases an assessment is the result of a *socially identified* problem. That is, for one reason or another, a relationship is unsatisfactory or causing distress: a parent may feel worried that their child is not apparently developing like others they know; a teacher may be worried about a child who is consistently unable to keep up with classmates; a health visitor or doctor may be worried by behaviour during routine visits or surgery. In all cases someone will be concerned that 'something might be wrong'. They will have come to this conclusion by feeling uneasy, in comparison with their expectations. Therefore, a problem precipitates anxiety. Usually the parents will attempt to reassure themselves by reference to friends or relatives. This may lead to them attempting to 'put things right' themselves, by playing more with a child, talking more or deliberately teaching skills. This may also lead to a denial, a refusal to admit anything is wrong (Schaefer, N., 1978) or a belief that help is needed in the relationship. Here professionals and parents may be at odds because of differing views.

The main point here is that the first 'assessment' is made *before* a 'specialized assessment'. This first 'assessment' is based on personal beliefs and expectations about normal parent-child relationships. The extent to which parents feel guilt about their child's possible disability is in part due to a recognition that parents are usually expected to be able to provide the context in which a child should develop 'normally'. Therefore even a semi-formal recognition of a parent's fears may as easily lead to denial, relief, or sorrow that someone else has 'noticed it too'. This is exemplified in the book *Walter* by David Cook (1978); here the headmistress carries out in principle the main elements of assessment: (i) identification of a problem, (ii) comparison with other children, (iii) prognosis and (iv) possible treatment/intervention.

> Your child needs special help, Mrs. Williams . . . the case is beyond us . . . he still wears nappies under his trousers. . . . That's not right for a lad over six years old. It shows no sign of changing. Children can be very cruel they notice such things . . . they'll [the education authorities] write to you with the name of a Special School. You'll get a letter from County Hall.' 'He can't undo his buttons yet; that's all.' Walter's mother turned away from the headmistress.

Although she has known this for some time the formal statement by the headmistress, the explicit confirmation, has robbed Walter's mother of her fantasy of the relationship she might have had with her son, like other mothers:

> Through the window she could see other children being collected by other mothers – boys swinging school satchels, boys with ties and long socks, held up by garters, beneath short trousers which showed the shapes of their clean little bottoms.

Therefore *preceding* the formal, special assessment is a prior set of beliefs about relationships at home, school or work, about appropriate roles and social behaviour which confer status and stigma and an anxiety that the special assessment will show, despite wishes to the contrary, that there *is* something to worry about.

Therefore the assessment cannot only be concerned with identifying the problem within the child, but must take into account the social context, in the knowledge that an easily identifiable cause and prognosis is unlikely.

Purpose of assessment

In her article 'Severely Subnormal Children' Rosemary Shakespeare (1973) puts forward four aims of assessment:

1 General Diagnosis – is there a handicap;
2 Degree of Handicap – the extent of such a handicap;
3 Plan for Training – the best methods to use;
4 Prediction – what can be predicted for adult life.

One of the main problems in assessment is that the tools used to achieve these aims do not achieve all four. That is, whereas some may be useful for one and two, there may well be a split between these and the last two. Also, there is no predictable relationship between these aims and social policy and no clear link between the assessment and the roles of people involved: parents, teachers, psychologists. These emerge more specifically when the plan for training has been formalized. Then it is possible to ascertain whether there is anyone to carry out the programme, and if there is, whether they are, or they regard themselves, as appropriate – professionals or family or volunteers.

Taking a slightly different perspective the purpose of assessment may be seen from several points of view: the purpose for the family, including the mentally handicapped person, the purpose for the assessor (including professional responsibilities and career aspirations), and the purpose for the agencies potentially providing resources; i.e., it will be of concern whether this is a 'medical', 'social', or 'educational problem'. However, to return to the four aims, the first diagnosis is in direct response to a family's needs and is congruent with the need to order experience. That is, the first question is whether the person to be assessed is, or is not, significantly different from others. The 'others' in the assessment procedure are the group that the test was standardized on, rather than known children in the neighbourhood or school. This aspect of assessment, 'general diagnosis', is a *location* of one person, at one point in time, relative to others at relatively the same point in time. Once this location has been established, by the test scores being perhaps equivalent to co-ordinates on the apparent map of normality, so the first fears are dispelled or confirmed. Clearly location alone is insufficient, so the second aim, 'degree of handicap', is attempted. This is essentially to see if the person, while not 'ordinarily normal', is part of another group and can be classified as, for example, severely subnormal. This consequential classification can give the illusion of an alternative normality; i.e., your child is a 'normal', severely handicapped child. The child now belongs to an identifiable group and at least is a member of an apparently known entity. The possible illusion, for the parents at least, is that this subgroup is homogenous in something other than their scores on the test. In the field of mental handicap at least, this is not so evident. Secondly, it may give the illusion that there *are* known consequences, or a clear prognosis. Again this is not necessarily so. Therefore, the crucial step is the link between the categorization and the consequences: the 'plan for training' and 'prediction'. This plan and prediction is also inextricably bound up with current policy and resources allocation since the implication of any plans and actions depends upon the availability of resources. It is the steps between categorization and plans or programmes, and programmes and policy implications, which need examining in terms of the current assessment tools and processes available. In summary the procedure may be represented as shown in Figure 4.1.

Current methods of assessment

Although this section does not attempt a full critique of all methods of assessment (IQ tests alone could fill and have filled volumes), it is important to outline the main types in relation to the problems raised above. For the purpose of this chapter assessment is seen in three types in the field of mental handicap.

1 Cognitive tests, the main being IQ tests;
2 Developmental scales; and
3 Social competence scales.

This does not mean this is the full extent of assessment. So far the discussion has centred around two meanings of assessment: first, that made by families, or non-experts, on the basis of common sense, intuition and/or

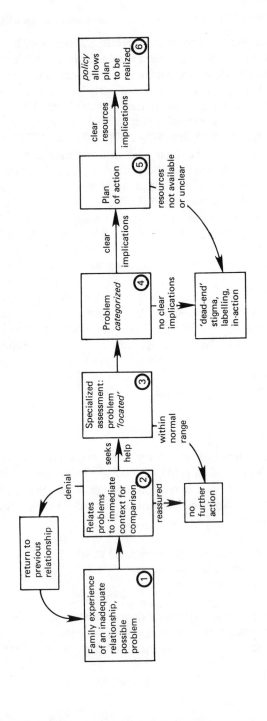

Figure 4.1

social expectations; this assessment usually raises the possibility of assessment of the second kind – 'specialized assessment'. It is the particular methods used in the second kind which will now be discussed.

Cognitive tests

The main intelligence tests used are the Wechsler Adult Intelligence Scale (WAIS), the Wechsler Intelligence Scale for Children (WISC) and the Stanford Binet IQ test. The first problem is one of the testing situation itself. The standardization required to ensure the test is used reliably means a relatively unfamiliar and possibly foreboding context. While many educational and clinical psychologists are undoubtedly aware of this it cannot be discounted, especially when considering that the reason for referral is usually perceived as trying to find out if anything is wrong. The implications of 'failure' for the family and person being tested are crucial, even if they are unclear; indeed, the unclarity may increase the anxiety. Also, many people, particularly young children, are regarded as untestable or simply cannot complete any of the items, and although they score a theoretical zero obviously they do not have zero intelligence.

The 1959 Act defines severe subnormality as 'a state of arrested or incomplete development of mind which includes subnormality of intelligence and is of such nature or degree that the patient is incapable of living an independent life. . . .' There is an inherent assumption of causality or at least a relationship between low intelligence and independent living. While H. Gunzburg (1973) argues that an IQ of below 25 will always mean a person will be socially incompetent, he also cites evidence from Clarke and Clarke (1965) and from his own work (Gunzburg, 1968) that people with IQs even as low as 35 do not preclude successful functioning in the open community. Further, he claims that low IQ scores may be more relevant in a context of academic achievement, i.e., school years, than in later life since the criteria of success are more congruent. Illingworth (1966) attributes some of the poor predictability to an over-reliance on a pass/fail scoring system and the ignorance of qualitative variables.

IQ scores are most used at the location and categorization stages. Scales are standardized on normal children and are based on an assumption that intelligence is normally distributed, which in itself would predict a lower number of mentally handicapped people than there apparently are. Scores calculated by standard deviations from the mean are used in the UK and USA to categorize, usually as borderline, mild, moderate, severe and profound (Heber, 1959). The crucial aspect of this or any other form of categorization, as mentioned above, comes when the implications for placement or training or living are considered. Certainly with all the criticism levelled at taking IQ test scores as inherently meaningful, not least by psychologists using them, other forms of assessment need to be used. However these other tests need not only to be *used* but they must be of at least comparable status to IQ tests to be influential. The campaign by educational and clinical psychologists to be more than test administrators was recognized by the Trethowan report (1977) which also accepted some of the criticisms of the tests themselves. Given that IQ and similar tests (e.g., Merril Palmer, Peabody Picture Vocabulary Test for children) are inadequate on their own, what else is there?

Developmental scales

Of the most widely used scales, Gesell's, Catell's Infant Intelligence Scale or the Griffith's Mental Development Scale, only the Griffith has been developed and standardized on English babies. These scales also, like IQ tests, have been standardized on normal children. As R. Shakespeare (1973) points out, 'the disadvantage of using the normal as a standard is that the subnormal child can never hope to attain the latter levels to which these scales are leading.' Also the particular patterns which may be especially relevant to mentally handicapped people may remain unrecognized. Again like the IQ tests the scales are mainly useful in determining where a child is, that is, location. They are more useful than IQ tests in that they also show what the next stage of development should be. At least this gives some clue to a possible plan of action and the Griffith's scale broadly based on Piagetian concepts gives some clue as to training.

If we return to the original problem, what is to be done, the IQ tests seem of less relevance. The identification, prior to location and categorization and hence prior to the person joining the mental handicap group, usually stems from a *social* problem. A relationship is not as it should be, or is expected to be: a child is not responding. The location and categorization aspects of assessment emphasize an individualistic assumption: that a person *has* an IQ of 55, a person *has* a developmental age of six months. Such assessments, on their own, tend to ignore the social aspect of the problem and the fact that abilities are never demonstrated in isolation but in the context of at least one other person. Further, the *overall* purpose of assessment lies in the completion of the process from identification to resource allocation (see Figure 4.1). The *result* is not just a score, not just an attempt to identify an attribute of an isolated individual, but a decision regarding what rights or resources are to be allocated to the individual and/or the family. The resources are in the form of aids, professional help, financial assistance, premises which are the actual manifestation of the plan or programme. This is the social meaning of the test score. It is equally meaningful if no resources are forthcoming. Consequently, the relationship between test score and resource allocation, while most important socially, is the weakest aspect of most of the tests by themselves. These tests, and forms of assessment, although general by their nature, are used not only to make general statements, but also particular statements to justify decisions concerning the future social life of individuals and their families. This is compounded by an emphasis on reliability and a blurring of validity. For example, despite the arguments concerning the prognosticating value, and simply what an IQ test *does* measure, they are constantly updated, objectified and restandardized. Cicourel (1974) and Roth (1974) point to the absence, in such tests, of a monitoring of the processes actually involved in the testing situation and claim that the products or results of such tests are seen to be individual phenomena (from the individual being tested), although the social consequences are highly relevant.

Underlying a request for a specialized assessment and the consequences of it is the question: how will this person cope in the world, given that he does not seem to be coping as he should? Even the 1959 Act put the emphasis on social abilities: '. . . such a nature or degree that the patient is incapable of living *an independent life*'. Resources, if any, are allocated on a basis of social competence, such as with the Social Security attendance allowance, hostel or hospital placement and social services. Educational resources in special education are likewise not aimed solely at increasing a person's intellectual abilities, but also at improving social competence.

Various research studies, for example, Mundy (1957), point to the development of intellect (increase in IQ score) as a result of environmental changes and Clarke and Clarke (1959) note the effects of environmental deprivation. However there is no agreed scale of deprivation or a deprivation score. Few psychologists now would be satisfied with giving only an IQ score or a developmental scale result; they are increasingly concerned with social competence, how a person relates to others, which means that scales of social competence may become more widely used.

Scales of social competence

The most widely used are the Vineland Social Maturity Scale and the Gunzburg Progress Assessment Charts. The Vineland Scale, designed by E.A. Doll in 1935, was, like the scales above, based on studies of normal children but designed for use with mentally handicapped people. This scale is related to mental ability and, although it includes items like 'uses a pencil for drawing', does not specifically ask for the opportunity available to a person. That is, the scale assumes a general availability of resources, is not entirely clear under what conditions behaviour may occur, and includes culturally specific items, some of which are difficult to score. The scoring also tends to be on a pass/fail basis. Although it is a scale of social competence it does not specify the other end of the relationship (e.g. 'follows simple instructions', but whose? mum or dad? a psychologist? a social worker? teacher? etc.). Shakespeare (1973) criticizes the Vineland Scale because some items depend as much on the parents' attitude as on the child's ability. However this assumes that *social* competence is an attribute of an individual as much as intelligence. This is consistent with Doll's own construction since the scale is designed to give a social age (S.A.) much as the IQ test gives Mental Age (M.A.). It would be useful to know as clearly what the parental attitudes are since *social* competence is dependent on a social *relationship*. That is, if it involves more than one person, it would be useful to know what the other person is doing at the same time.

PAC

Gunzburg's (1960) charts, unlike any forms mentioned so far, do not compare mentally handicapped people with results gained from a normal population. Instead, his Progress Assessment Charts are based upon the skills of a population of mental handicapped people. This means that 'location' has already taken place, as has 'categorization', and that this is progress within a category. As discussed above the process of categorization may mean that a person may be 'normal' relative to their own subgroup, rather than the population as a whole. This 'normality' is what the charts assess. Gunzburg does not claim that the PAC is a quantitative measure of achievement. The 'result' is a chart which indicates an individual's deficiencies in social knowledge and competence and this suggests a plan of action and, by implication at least, the resources required to carry it out. Although not a quantitative measure, Gunzburg has established average achievement levels based on IQ groupings. It is one of the few methods of assessment which has, as part of its design, specific implications beyond location and categorization.

So far two types of assessment have been considered – the initial recognition of a problem and the formalized methods of ascertaining whether a problem exists. In summary the ultimate purpose of assessments carried out by welfare state/voluntary organization assessors is to decide whether a person qualifies for resources. In this way a 'failure', relative to normal results, in most of the above assessment methods *increases* the likelihood of achieving success in gaining resources. Assessment is not merely to locate and categorize a person, but to do so for a purpose. Nevertheless, the most socially powerful tests, IQ and to a lesser extent Developmental Scales, are those least related to specific resource provision. The closest form giving a clear picture of what might be done is the Gunzburg PAC and this assumes that a person has already been designated mentally handicapped. In the Overview to the book *Psychological Assessment of Mental and Physical Handicaps*, P.J. Mittler writes: 'In the past psychologists have tended to confine themselves to assessment' (here called location and categorization) 'and left others to incorporate (or ignore) their findings in whatever was done for the patient or client.'

While such practice is not entirely over, the question remains that, if, as argued above, psychologists are no longer so confined, what else do they use? They may well discuss qualitative issues but there is still a demand for figures. This demand stems both from the medical model where diagnosis is in terms of the attributes of individuals, and where figures tend to be interpreted in terms of absolute rather than relative values. It also stems from power being vested in the person who can define the problem. The professional assessor is in a position to label and categorize, be apparently more familiar with the problem than the presenter or owner of the problem. He or she can then take over the management of the problem from the presenter. However the means of definition, as described above, do not necessarily lead to a clear statement of management, in terms of training or prognosis. The only method that does, the PAC, is the least effective in defining, in terms of a score or a single result. To continue Mittler's argument, 'a change of emphasis in the aims and goals of psychological assessment is bound to effect a corresponding change in the nature of the assessment instruments used and in the whole assessment process.' This change also implies a change in professional role and authority. Professions are not noted for their desire to change practices or power bases, unless it is to increase them (Packwood and Macdonald, 1978). This is of particular relevance since, although categorization may relate in general to some sort of homogeneous grouping, it is the 'borderline' cases on which the results of referral are most contentious and far-reaching.

If the assessors are to widen their repertoire then they will have to question the assumptions that statements about constructs, such as intelligence, are directly relevant when moving from categorization to a plan of action. Mittler calls for an 'inclusion of a person's developmental history, experiences, that have affected his development, home background and environmental variables'. All these variables are not easily, if at all, gained in a standardized testing context or open to fully reliable verification; they are argued out on the grounds of subjectivity. However they are crucial in the person's social world, the world they have lived in and may or may not continue to live in. The apparent difficulty in attaining this information does not make existing traditional methods any better. The point is that the methods which are used to gain statements about locations and categorization do not have well-established behavioural or psychological correlates. It is no longer sufficient to attempt to define attributes of individuals and expect them to predict specific behaviour without reference to social context.

So where and how can the social context be described and what are the relevant aspects to include? The most obvious place to look is not *just* at the one person referred but also at the relationships they are and have been engaged in. This means that the status of the information known to relatives, nurses, teachers, or residential social workers is increased. The assessor is much more dependent on a wider social network to make a full appraisal. Indeed the validation, if not the appraisal itself, lies *in* that social network and the 'assessor' can no longer define, or redefine, the problem based on one-to-one tests using the tools discussed above. Thus, changing procedure means weakening the 'assessor's' power base.

At a wider level this perspective is borne out by the Warnock Report (1978). This report argued that rigid classification of children with significant disabilities or difficulties stands in the way of effective flexible educational provision. It also argued that terms were, far from leading to relevant help, oversimplifying problems and perpetuating stereotypes. With regard to assessment the Committee pointed to the need for assessment within schools, by teachers, i.e., part of their social world, and for only the latter two of five stages to be conducted by 'multiprofession' analysis of a child's special needs. This 'specialist assessment' could therefore be more systematically informed of the child's continuous relationships.

Therefore, there is a need to add a third type of assessment, related to the first (usually by the parents). It is the constant monitoring, evaluation and judgement done by those around the person being assessed. The reason why such assessments have not been included so readily is the lack of organization of this information, the PAC being an exception.

When the original problem arises, when a person is not performing as

well as he apparently might do, parents particularly do not rush for assessment at the first sign of difficulty. A series of events will precipitate actions.
When asked to recall these events it is unlikely that they will recall each and
every one accurately. It would hardly be realistic or desirable for all families
to record precisely everything that went on, including their beliefs and
expectations, just in case they need to recall events if and when a problem
arises. However, in the classroom and in residential care people, teachers,
nurses and residential social workers, are paid not merely to occupy those in
their care for so many hours a day, but also to monitor progress. It is this
information which could be most easily used to enrich the traditional forms
of assessment. This has been decried as being 'too subjective'. The traditional forms are 'objective'; teachers' and other 'face-workers' ' observations are 'subjective'. This need not be so. Let us replace the objective/sub-
jective duality with an explicit/implicit duality. In this way the criterion
becomes whether information can be explicated and put in a form which is
public and testable in the sense of being open to question. In this way
beliefs, expectations, prejudices, observations, opinions can all be included
in assessment, in so far as they can be explicated. This then opens up the
assessment process to include the powerful social forces of role expectations, opinions and values. The object of assessment is thus not an individual's performance in relation to a prepackaged task but a person's
performance in relationships, including what pressure and expectations are
present in the relationships. Therefore a person can be seen not merely in an
apparently neutral context, i.e., with the 'objective' assessor, but in live
social interaction. Therefore both sides of the relationship need to be
described if this is to contribute to a fuller understanding of the problem.
The usual reason for ignoring the 'other side' is that usually the assessor
tries to standardize his or her behaviour, i.e., act in a predictable, prepro-
grammed way as laid down in the manual. An assessment of relationships is
needed because in real life people do not always cope with predictable
environments; indeed the point of including social competence is, in part,
to find out how a person can deal with an unpredictable and changing
environment.

Since ordinarily parents have no need or desire to be formally noting their
relationship with children, or friends with one another, initial referrals will
always be problematic in gaining insight into the history of a social relationship. However there are many people already in care, in hospitals and
hostels, already diagnosed or labelled as mentally handicapped. They are
also assessed, not just on entry, but as part of their lives and to decide when

they may leave. Judgements are made continuously about their daily needs as well as their relevant place in society – in hospital or in the community. Their access to the world and resources is being constantly monitored by staff immediately caring for them. However most of these day-to-day judgements remain implicit while the *specialist* activity of assessment is explicit, for example, in IQ scores, psychiatric diagnosis. Further intuitive judgements may be influenced by stereotype views gleaned or half-learned from the specialist. Tautological explanations are used to maintain status rather than challenge it (for example: 'he does that because he is severely mentally handicapped – severely mentally handicapped people always do that'). This can lead to a resignation coupled with all the pressures of institutionalization which do not question the original assessments (Goffman, 1961). Indeed the specialized assessments gain a status not perhaps even intended by the assessor.

Assessment and policy

Discontinuities in bureaucracies are marked by official procedures. For example, however the informal networks and systems may effect the realities of day-to-day life, the major changes are bound by rules: admission, discharge, appointment of staff, promotion, dismissal, and so on. These discontinuities are essentially bound up with status, i.e., they are about ascribing roles and authority which, despite the influence of informal power structures, remain the public presentation of the organization. For example, although a staff nurse may, in terms of informal influence and power, have more influence in a ward than the ward sister, the public statement is that the ward sister is senior in terms of the organizational structure. Since the discontinuities, as mentioned above, are typified by rules, they are typified by formal procedures. Therefore the 'opinion' of the residential workers or families has less importance, publicly, than a written report containing a formal layout with figures, scores and results of other formal procedures, that is, the specialized assessments. These assessments therefore are bound up with the formal ascription of status for residents or patients. The problem really comes when these formalized procedures bear little relationship to the actual day-to-day life of the relevant organization.

This in turn relates to policy. The formal procedures are part of the *written policy* and history of an organization; that is, they can be seen – in organizational charts, memos, policy documents, minutes of meetings, etc.

This may be separate from the *spoken policy* – what can be heard in and around the establishment, the interpretation of policy – and *enacted policy* – what actually goes on whether written down or not. If these three strands are separate then there will be a considerable degree of alienation, for staff and clients, and a split between authority and power. This is further compounded by formal policies being ambiguous. Kushlick (1975) and Mager (1972) make the distinction between 'a performance' and a 'fuzzy'. With performances you know whether they have been completed or not, with fuzzies you do not. Much of the formal policy of institutions abounds with 'fuzzies', for example, improve hospital morale, improve the quality of life, increase potential. It will never be possible to fully integrate these strands, indeed if this were done the establishment may merely be over-run with specified rules and procedures which may in turn preclude creativity and change. However one of the major criticisms of some of the methods of assessment mentioned above was that they do not relate the assessment to action and in turn policy. That is, not only do they tend to overlook the social context in terms of the immediate environment but also in terms of a wider environment of policy setting.

One way to attempt to integrate these aspects would be to take into account the experience and effect of that environment in the assessment procedure itself. This would entail an explicit statement of the relationships of a resident, for example, between staff and resident, and a statement about the constraints acting on the staff. In this way the staff (in this case, although it could be the family) must be involved in the assessment. There is no doubt that staff in close contact with the mentally handicapped person (Kushlick's category of direct-care staff) are continuously making judgements and assessments which constantly affect the lives of those in their care. What is more doubtful is how much of this social world is publicly recognized in formal assessments, especially when it comes to the major decisions mentioned above. The inclusion of this social dimension has two major problems. Firstly to recognize it may undermine the 'professional assessor's' position and, secondly, it may expose the disparity between the 'public' organization and actual daily life within it.

The Chart of Initiative and Independence (CII) (Macdonald and Couchman, 1980)

There is of course the further difficulty of how this might be done even if it were possible. The CII is an attempt to achieve these aims, and bring the social dimension into a formal, in the sense of explicated, assessment procedure. The CII makes three assumptions. First, that information about the daily relationships between carers and cared for are both crucial and valid parts of the assessment procedure. Second, that this information should be organized in a way that reveals information in terms of who makes the decisions in the relationship and why. Third, that assessment is a continuous process and recording the 'result' is more analogous to a comma than a full stop. The point about recording is not to make an absolute statement but to make public the current state of affairs so that it can be challenged and questioned. Therefore the objective of the CII is to provide a method of assessment for the direct-care staff whereby they can describe the behaviour of a person in their care within a specified social context, i.e., the limits put on that behaviour by, for example, peer-group, staff, policy, *as well as* the person's own inhibitions, physical handicap, illness or dislikes.

This is done by first asking the staff to outline the policy of the residential unit in terms of the level of discretion allowed and required of residents for admission and discharge (the Residential Policy Format). To do this staff must first decide what activities are important. This is no simple task as there may be many different assumptions as to what the unit is concerned with: personal hygiene, social relationships, domestic skills, financial dealings, use of services, leisure, etc. When this is done staff are then asked to look at these activities for individual residents, again specifying the level of discretion, i.e., what they are allowed to do and what they are not, and why not. When this is completed staff must also comment on what they intend to do for the resident, the plan of action (this is the Individual Assessment Format). They then are asked to state the outcome of these action programmes, that is, what the resident might achieve and by when (the Development Programme Format). At the end of the programme *another* individual assessment is recorded which can then be compared with what should have happened and a new plan of action constructed. This continuous process is characterized by not only recording the behaviour of the resident but also the behaviour and the expectations of the staff.

One of the most influential aspects of daily residential life is not just what staff and residents do, but also what staff *believe* residents can do. These beliefs and expectations are not usually recorded as part of a formal assessment. They are seen to be too subjective. However staff will react differently to a person's behaviour according to whether they *believe* the person is doing their best or merely 'being lazy', whether they have 'hard evidence' for this belief, or prejudice, or not. These expectations are included in the

KEY	No Opportunity N	Complete Dependency C/D	MODE A	MODE B	MODE C	MODE D	MODE E
LEVEL OF OPPORTUNITY	There is no opportunity available to do this	It is always done *for* him/her	You tell him/her *when* to do this *and* how to do it. It is always under your instructions	You tell them when to do it but then leave them to get on, but later check how it was done	You allow the person discretion to decide when and how to do something but you check *when* it is done and monitor *how* it is done	You allow the person discretion to decide when and how to do something, checking *when* it is done but not monitoring how it is done	You allow the person full discretion and do not check or monitor. You intervene only if requested to do so by the person
BEHAVIOUR	I have not seen the person actually do this recently. If the person refuses to do this activity state this by noting 'R' under N	The person does not achieve goals or plans even when told or shown	The person only does this when told or shown what to do and how to do it	The person only does this when told what to do but can then get on and do it	The person does this activity without being told but *when* and *how* they do this is in a pre-set way	The person does this activity without being told. The *when* is not fixed and others' wishes are tolerated unless they threaten the goal of activity	The person does this activity in a flexible way without being told. They can take into account the needs of others and substitute goals
PRESENT POTENTIAL	There is no opportunity for the person to show any potential	The person does not have the capacity to act on goals or plans even when told or shown	The person can only do this when told or shown what to do and how to do it	The person can only do this when told what to do but can then get on and do it	The person is capable of doing this without being told but *when* and *how* they do this is in a pre-set way	They are capable of doing this activity without being told. The *when* is not fixed and others' wishes are tolerated unless they threaten the goal of activity	They are capable of doing the activity in a flexible way without being told. They can take into account the needs of others and substitute goals

© Macdonald & Couchman Associates

Figure 4.2

CII (under 'present potential' – see Figure 4.2) on the grounds that they can be explicated and separated from observable behaviour. The reason that the staff's behaviour (level of opportunity –see Figure 4.2) is included is not only to make the other end of the relationship clear but also to show where staff limit residents' behaviour for administrative convenience. For example, a mentally handicapped person may be woken up, washed and dressed by staff even though they are capable of deciding for themselves, because it is felt to be the only way thirty people can be sure to have their breakfast and be out of the ward or hostel by 9.30 am.

The 'scale' of discretion is shown in Figure 4.2. Here the range is from no opportunity to where the person is making his or her own decisions and where they only call in help when *they* see fit. The scale itself has relevance to our earlier discussion in which the main concern for parents and staff was the extent to which a mentally handicapped person could make decisions and do things for himself if given the opportunity to do so. These considerations can be made whatever the IQ level or developmental age of the person. The main variations can be made in the choice of activities. For example, one person may be allowed to make decisions about what job to apply for, another only about choosing his socks.

The main point of the CII is that the mentally handicapped person is not seen in isolation. He or she is seen as part of a social reality which includes those in charge of their welfare and the conditions under which they work or live. This does not mean that information is inherently less 'objective' than in other methods of assessment. What it attempts to portray is a social situation and where responsibility for action or inaction lies. In the CII behaviour cannot be explained solely in terms of the inherent attributes of an individual. Further, development depends on specific action being taken which in turn implies the availability of resources. If these resources are not available at least this can be made public and the consequences apparent. In this way policy can be negotiated in the light of 'performances' rather than 'fuzzies'.

Conclusion

This chapter has tried to argue that the 'specialized' assessment of individuals is insufficient in itself because it ignores a wealth of information that is, and could be made, available. Further, that assessment is a continuous process which starts with a felt lack in a relationship and implies the eventual allocation or withholding of resources. Traditional assessment methods are concerned primarily with the location and categorization of people and, while few assessors would now rely solely on such methods when considering action, alternative or complementary methods are needed to represent the social context of the person being assessed.

One such method is the CII. If this or other methods are used then it becomes possible to shift the focus of attention from the individual to the individual in his world. To do so is not an innocent matter as Mittler has noted. It shifts not only the focus of attention but also the focus of power. The specialized assessor is no longer the sole definer of the problem; there are other 'experts' – direct-care staff, families and the person being assessed. Allowing for the social dimension also increases the visibility of all the experts: what are they doing and why? The social dimension need not remain in a vague world of 'subjectivity', excluded from the assessment process, but by being open to explication may become a central part in the understanding of a person's present life and future possibilities.

References

Cicourel, A.V. (1974) 'Assessment of performance – some basic theoretical issues', in Cicourel, A.V., K.H. and S.H.M. Jennings, J.C.W. Leiter, R. Mackay, H. Mehan and D.R. Roth, *Language Use and School Performance*, New York, Academic Press

Clarke, A.D.B. and A.M. Clarke (1959) 'Recovery from the effects of deprivation', *Acta Psychologica*, number 16, pp. 137–144

Clarke, A.M. and A.D.B. Clarke (1965) *Mental Deficiency: The Changing Outlook* (2nd edition; 1st edition 1958), Methuen

Cook, D. (1978) *Walter*, Penguin

Gibb, N.K. and L.I. Woolf (1959) 'Tests for PKU: results of a one year programme for its detection in infancy among the mentally deficient', *British Medical Journal*, Volume II, 532

Goffman, I. (1961) *Asylums*, Penguin

Gunzburg, H.C. (1960) *Social Rehabilitation of the Subnormal*, Bailliere, Tindall & Cox

Gunzburg, H.C. (1968) *Social Competence and Mental Handicap*, Bailliere, Tindall and Cassell

Gunzburg, H.C. (1973) 'Subnormal Adults' in Mittler, P. (ed) *The Psychological Assessment of Mental and Physical Handicaps*, Tavistock

Heber, R. (1959) *Manual on Terminology and Classification in Mental Retardation*, American Association on Mental Deficiency

Hsu, L., E. Dubin, T. Kerenyi and K. Hirschhorn (1973) 'Results and pitfalls in pre-natal cytogenic diagnosis' in *Journal of Medical Genetics*, Volume 10

Illingworth, R.S. (1966) *The Development of the Infant and Young Child* (3rd edition), Livingstone

Kushlick, A. (1975) 'Some ways of setting, monitoring and attaining objectives for services for disabled people', Research report number 116, Paper presented to a conference on 'The Handicapped – Towards Independent Living'; National Committee on Residential Care, Brisbane, Australia, June 19–21

Leck, I., W.L. Gordon and T. McKeown (1967) 'Medical and social needs of patients in hospitals for the mentally subnormal', *British Journal of Preventative and Hospital Medicine*, number 21, pp. 115–121

Macdonald, I. and T. Couchman (1980) *The Chart of Initiative and Independence*, NFER

Mager, H.M. (1972) *Goal Analysis*, Belmont, California, Fearon Publishers

Mundy, L. (1957) 'Environmental influence on intellectual function as measured by intelligence tests', *British Journal of Medical Psychology*, number 30, pp. 194–201

Packwood, T., and I. Macdonald (1978) 'Organisation for the care of the severely mentally handicapped' in Jacques, E., (ed), *Health Services*, Heinemann

Roth, D.R. (1974) 'Intelligence testing as a social activity' in Cicourel, A.V. et al., op. cit.

Schaefer, N. (1978) *Does She Know She's There?*, Harper & Row

Shakespeare, R. (1973) 'Severely subnormal children' in Mittler, P. (ed) *The Psychological Assessment of Mental and Physical Handicaps*, Tavistock

Smith, G. and J. Berg (1976) *Down's Syndrome: Down's Anomaly*, Churchill Livingstone (2nd edition)

Trethowan Report (1977) 'The role of the psychologist in the Health Service' chaired by Professor Trethowan, HMSO

Warnock, H.M. (1978) *Report of the Committee of Enquiry into the Education of Handicapped Children and Young People*, Warnock Report, Cmnd. 7212, HMSO

Further reading

Broadfoot, T. (1979) *Assessment, Schools and Society*, Methuen

CHAPTER 5

THE SOCIAL ROLE OF EDUCATIONAL PSYCHOLOGY IN THE DEFINITION OF EDUCATIONAL SUBNORMALITY

by Andrew Sutton

The Education Act (1944) defined special education as 'education by special methods'. It did not, however, specify the mechanisms by which teachers or local authorities should bring into being or monitor the efficacy of these special ways of working. By the time of the Act a number of social, mental and behavioural sciences had already emerged that could potentially contribute to technologizing the process of education, and willy-nilly over the period that the Act has been in force they have been incorporated into our pluralistic and discretionary state education system at various of its levels. Of particular relevance to the interplay of forces between teacher and pupils, and to the effect of this process upon the very substance of the pupils' mental development, is the collection of psychological insights and techniques grouped under the loose heading of 'educational psychology', which at the present time includes cullings from mental measurement, developmental and social psychology, behaviourism and psycholinguistics, and abuts on to areas outside of psychology itself, such as linguistics, sociology and medicine. Educational psychology has in various manifestations been the longest established wing of psychological practice in this country, being made flesh in local education authorities in the persons of 'educational psychologists'; it has provided a central part of the socialization process of teacher training and an important component of our small national effort in the field of educational research.

Perhaps it is not surprising, therefore, that problems met in the education system are often described and disposed of in primarily 'psychological' terms; for example, problems of attainment become 'learning difficulties', and 'problem children' get referred for detailed individual examination and personal intervention. Only a small proportion of children so identified of course actually meet a psychologist, most will be dealt with by teachers who may be operating within a 'psychological' model of individual diagnosis or pastoral care. The cardinal identifying feature of the term 'psychological' in such a context lies not in the idea of a *science* of behaviour or development, but in the focus upon features within the individual and the individual's immediate environment (particularly the family). Where this intra-individual and non-experimental 'psychology' is practised, not only is it altogether removed from the more specific meanings of psychology as a 'science', it is also distanced by its very nature from the prime requirements of the pedagogic process. Despite the extensive teaching of psychological concepts to teachers, and the now universal employment of educational psychologists by local educational authorities, central government (*via* the Department of Education and Science) takes no formal account of the psychology of education, and has no formally appointed adviser on psychological matters (as it does do in the field of mental health, *via* the Department of Health and Social Security). Perhaps the psychology of education is now regarded as so widely internalized as to require no separate institutionalized existence of its own at the highest levels of politics and administration. Or perhaps at these levels there is a recognition that psychology (as does any other social science) poses questions about education that administrators and politicians would prefer to leave unasked.

If any area of special education is to be regarded as particularly influenced by educational psychology then it is that which concerns those who are increasingly termed 'children with learning difficulties'. For the most part, except in the case of the more severely handicapped, such children are defined largely in 'psychological' terms, and their backwardness or retardation, and their formal processing to special schools or units when it occurs, are nowadays a central role of the local authority educational psychologist. At the time of writing, however, these children remain officially 'educationally subnormal', a category which in both official and popular minds is largely defined in psychological terms. Two specific aspects of this definition will be discussed here, to illustrate the problematical nature of some of that psychology and the way in which it has been used. They relate to the 'upper borderline' of the 'ESN range', and to the very idea that there is unquestionably a range upon which a demarcation has to be made.

'IQ 70'

The educationally subnormal constitute by far the largest single group within the special-school population in England and Wales. This category of educational handicap was brought into being by ministerial regulations following the Education Act (1944), being defined as comprising

> . . . pupils who by reason of limited ability or other conditions resulting in educational retardation, require some specialised form of education . . .
> (*Handicapped Pupils and School Health Regulations*, 1945)

In 1946 the then Ministry of Education published a pamphlet setting forth specific guidelines on how its views on special educational treatment were to be put into practice (Ministry of Education, 1946). A considerable section of this pamphlet (paras. 45–73) was devoted to the new category of the 'ESN'. It explained how the category was to be a very broad one, including not just those children who had up until then been deemed mentally defective, but also all children whose school work fell below that of the average child 20 percent younger. The reasons for retardation would have no bearing upon eligibility for special help: the child's retardation may or may not be related to a general dullness, it may be associated with emotional problems, with factors at home, or with inadequacies within the educational system itself. In all, it was estimated, around 10 percent of the school population would be included (para. 25). It was not of course intended that this vast number of children should go to special schools, though it was thought that in urban areas one-tenth of them (1 percent of the total school population) would ultimately be so placed. In considering which children out of the ESN population should go to special schools, rather than receive their special educational treatment in their ordinary schools, the pamphlet devoted particular attention to the children's relative mental development as indicated by intelligence testing. For example:

> The children for whom the day special school is most appropriate are found among those whose limited ability corresponds with an intelligence quotient of about 55 to 70 or 75. Those with lower intelligence (55 to 60 or 65 intelligence quotient) might all attend, but among those in the group with higher intelligence, more and more other factors have to be taken into account before a decision is made to send a child to a special school.
> (Ministry of Education, 1946, para. 60)

In effect, therefore, given the dominant assumptions of the time, special schools for the ESN were largely to be for those among them whose retardation was 'by reason of limited ability', or at least this factor was the one most clearly emphasized in the official guidelines about selection. They could thus be easily perceived by those responsible for selection ('ascertainment' as it was called) as being predominantly for a similar population to that of the previous schools for the mentally defective, with the proviso that it was now legitimately within the range of professional discretion to send brighter children there too, as long as 'more and more other factors had been taken into account'.

It is not the intention here to focus on the failure of the educational system to fulfil the early intention of providing special educational treatment ('education by special methods') for around 9 percent of the school population within their ordinary schools, nor to pay account to the long and sometimes bitter power struggle between the medical officers and the educational psychologists over who should have hegemony over the ascertainment of ESN children. Suffice it to note that very soon after the generous advice of the 1946 pamphlet the Ministry issued a circular to local education authorities, advising that unless a formal certificate were issued (by a medical officer) children

> . . . would not be ascertained within the meaning of Section 34 and they would not be registered as handicapped pupils, and special arrangements for their education would not technically be known as 'special educational treatment'.
> (Ministry of Education, 1947)

It is hard to regard the above advice as much other than a return to the status quo in the public conceptualization of decisions about who should attend special schools for backward pupils. One aspect of this conceptualization, the idea of an 'ESN range' of intelligence, in particular the 'upper limit' or 'cut-off point' of around 70, is dealt with here. The strange fate of this 'psychological' concept in educational practice over the years since the Act is offered as an illustration of the cavalier way in which educational psychology may be bandied about, even by educational psychologists, with little regard for what its ideas might mean, providing the trappings of 'science' where these might appear advantageous, though honoured largely in the breach when it comes to hard decision making.

The origin of the cut-off point of 'IQ 70' in this country appears to have lain in the work of that most inventive and influential educational psychologist, Cyril Burt. In the second of his three memoranda, presented shortly after the Great War to the London County Council, on the use of psychometric tests (Burt, 1921a), he had dealt in detail with what he regarded as 'the central problem of this memorandum – the line of demarcation for mental deficiency' (ibid, p. 175). He was by then firmly committed to a view of intellectual differences framed in terms of population distributions, and would have liked to have offered a crisp theoretical statement of this demarcation of this group from the normal, based upon mathematical principles. The 'quicksand of subjective judgement' involved in the case-finding and diagnosis of his reference population precluded a definite statement of this type. The point that he would have liked to identify on a linear scale 'wavers like the unsteady needle of a compass; oscillating, for the most part, according to the personal views of each examiner, between −2.5 and −2.0 S.D., points which correspond to mental ratios of 70 and 75 per cent' (ibid, p. 178). To avoid this problem he determined that *'mental deficiency must be treated as an administrative rather than as a psychological concept'* (ibid, p. 178, Burt's italics). At the same time he considered that for most practical purposes mental deficiency in children was to be regarded as a defect 'primarily or solely in intelligence'. He was mindful that *'many children, who might otherwise be transferred to a special (M.D.) school, would undoubtedly receive proper benefit from instruction in the backward classes of the ordinary school, and at the same time escape the unmerited stigma of mental deficiency'* (ibid, p. 179, Burt's italics). To avoid unnecessary transfer of children out of the ordinary schools, on the basis of what he recognized as a wholly undefined diagnosis, he proposed a solution that linked categorization most directly to social provision on a wholly quantitative model.

> The variations from one authority to another are, in present circumstances at any rate, all but inevitable. But under the same local authority the standard should in justice be the same throughout. From this follows yet a further postulate: *for immediate practical purposes the only satisfactory definition of mental deficiency is a percentage definition based on the amount of existing accommodation.* If in the special schools of London there is accommodation for only 1.5 per cent, then to adopt a borderline which, followed out consistently, would cut off nearly 2 per cent, is plainly indefensible. The effect of a personal standard, at variance with available provision, can only be that *less urgent cases of a higher grade that chance to be transferred at an earlier date will forstall more urgent cases of a lower grade that are presented for examination later.* This is no rare occurrence.
> (Burt, 1921a, p. 179, again Burt's italics)

His own local authority at that time provided special school places for 1.51 percent of the school population at the age group at which children were admitted to special school. In that county and at that time, therefore, and according to Burt's criteria, the mentally defective child was most justly to be defined as one in the lowest 1½ percent of the intellectual range for its years. Using his own intelligence test, locally normed, he concluded

> Between the ages of seven and fourteen, out of the conjoint population, ordinary

and special school, the lowest 1.5 per cent will embrace all those who fall below a deviation of 2.6 S.D. This is equivalent to a retardation of 30.6 per cent, or a mental ratio of 69.4 per cent.
(ibid, p. 180)

His borderline would therefore be, in those defined circumstances, a 'mental ratio' (later more generally termed an 'IQ') of 70. Others in different circumstances would have to be similarly specific and, as the technology of testing advanced, further refinements might be expected.

I should add that my formulation of a borderline holds good in the first instance merely for average conditions in an industrial area, such as that which I have been studying. Where environment or stock are better or worse different figures would unquestionably be obtained. In the near future we shall doubtless need separate statements for rural areas and residential areas, and perhaps even for the weaker sex as distinguished from men and boys.
(ibid, p. 179n)

Burt's shape of things to come, in the form of carefully conducted surveys to relate the distribution of intelligence test scores to the amount of special-school provision for specific localities, or even subgroups of the population, was not, however, to be realized. At an administrative level the central research position that he occupied as the 'first educational psychologist' within the LCC was not to be the general rule among those who later bore the title of educational psychologist in the English local education authorities (see Keir, 1952). But, at a much more immediate level, Burt himself appears to have abandoned his own position, that *the only satisfactory definition of mental deficiency is a percentage definition based on the amount of existing accommodation* even before his memoranda on mental testing were published. For in the month of June, 1920, he had conducted a survey of the senior departments of ordinary elementary schools in the city of Birmingham. His data, drawn from a mix of brief individual testing conducted by himself (562 children in all) and of teachers' ratings of mental and scholastic development, were analysed according to crisply defined criteria.

A child's intelligence and attainments are measured most conveniently by expressing his mental age as a percentage of his chronological age. Thus, a child whose mental age is that of a child of 7 (Standard 1) has a mental ratio of $^7/_{10}$ or 70%. In these terms, and upon these grounds, I would regard as backward all whose mental ratio is, on an average, below 85 per cent, and as mentally defective all whose ratio is below 70 per cent. In diagnosing mental deficiency I consider chiefly the child's general level of intelligence as shown, for example, by the

Binet-Simon Scale; and in diagnosing backwardness chiefly his educational attainments.
(Burt, 1921b, pp. 6–7)

In sharp distinction to his proposals to the London County Council (Burt, 1921a), that intelligence test cut-off points should be worked *back*, on an indigenously normed test, from the amount of local provision, Burt's (1921b) near contemporaneous report to Birmingham Education Committee used the same cut-off point and the same norms as in his LCC work, and on their basis worked *forward*, to calculate that in the city's senior elementary departments as a whole 'between two and three hundreds should be considered mentally defective' (Burt, 1921b).

Burt's ability in his later years to produce a precise figure to make an exact point is now well documented and accepted (Kamin, 1974; Hearnshaw, 1979), though whether his earlier work was marred in this way remains to be investigated (Clarke and Clarke, 1980). Burt's '69.4' may have been such a doctoring of figures to support a particular cut-off point, or maybe the about-turn in his arguments between his London and his Birmingham surveys represented a major change of heart or emphasis. Be that as it may, Burt subsequently supported the figure of 'IQ 70' as the arbitrary cut-off point for mental deficiency, certainly in urban areas. He was a member of the immensely influential Mental Deficiency Committee, and contributed substantially to its theoretical viewpoint. In its report (the Wood Report) the Committee adopted the position that

> Speaking generally, it may be said that a person with a mental ratio of between 50 and 70 per cent is probably feebleminded; but to this there are exceptions (Mental Deficiency Committee, 1929, Part I, p. 12)

In the national survey specially commissioned by the Committee, and conducted by Dr. E.O. Lewis, the figure '70' on an intelligence test was adopted as the basis for establishing prevalence figures for the country as a whole.

> . . . in the case of children it seems obviously desirable that the line of demarcation should be drawn definitely above that for adults. We accordingly took our borderzone between 60 and 70 per cent, and so far as a single line of demarcation can be laid down, adopted as an upper limit a mental ratio of 70 per cent (ibid, Part III, p. 52)

Whatever the merits or validity of Burt's carefully argued case to the

LCC, the figure of 'IQ 70', as an important means of identifying a certain group of schoolchildren, had begun to assume a reified existence in professional folklore. Burt's (1921a) arguments about how cut-off points should be derived to meet specific local conditions have not figured in the various subsequent reiterations of this borderline, nor have any other justifications been proposed for its use as a basis for professional clinical judgement. This borderline was reiterated in the Ministry of Education's 1946 pamphlet (which drew heavily upon the Wood Report for its definition of the new category of educational subnormality), though now solely as an IQ, an isolated figure unrelated to the particular test used, to its normative basis, or to the standard deviation involved. Although looking 'scientific' (i.e., a measurement), it was no more meaningful in practice than a statement such as 'a length of 70'. Seventy what? An intelligence test score of sorts was clearly expected, since a space was specified for their results in the recommended form to be completed at the time of ascertainment (Form 2 HP). As late as 1974 the first handbook published in this country in the practice of educational psychology was content to subdivide 'children with learning difficulties' into four subgroups, one of which, the ESN(M), was specifically defined in terms of IQ. . . .

> ESN(M). This term will be used to refer to pupils in special schools or special classes catering for a population with IQs mainly in the range 50/55 to 70/75, though many of such schools or classes will also have some children with higher IQs.
> (Chazan, et al., 1975, p. 175)

No basis was given for quoting these figures as a guideline for practioners to demarcate a concept which elsewhere in the same book was defined as 'a descriptive category rather than a diagnosis' (ibid, p. 23).

The disembodied 'IQs' or 'IQ-ranges' so often coupled with consideration of ESN pupils and ESN schools have been rendered the more unreal by a major technical advance in psychological test construction that began to affect practice in this country substantially from the early 1960s. The tests most used from then on as part of special-school admission procedures, the Revised Stanford-Binet and the Wechsler Intelligence Scale for Children (WISC), had been constructed in the United States in ways that did not involve the still oft-quoted formula

$$IQ = \frac{MA}{CA} \times 100$$

Strictly speaking, neither test produced IQs at all, though their results were stated as though they did, presumably for commercial reasons, and the superficial numerical similarity of the scores masked real differences in norms and construction. When the WISC first appeared the British Psychological Society conducted a pilot study on a representative sample of English ten-year-olds (British Psychological Society, 1955). They found only about 1 percent of the children to lie in the 50 to 70 range, rather than the $2\frac{1}{2}$ percent predicted by the US norms. There were never the resources available to conduct the large-scale study required to establish proper English norms, and the test went into widespread clinical use without them. An attempt to 'calibrate' the Stanford-Binet against the results of English children found 'significant and quite marked differences between American norms and British: users should take this into account. A calibration is urgently needed to make test norms reliable and usable for British populations' (Wright, 1972, p. 32). The test had already been in widespread use for some years, and no such 'calibrations' have since been undertaken. One crumb of consolation was, however, offered to users of the Stanford-Binet in this country: not only was the mean score of the test significantly higher for a British population (say, around 106 instead of 108), so too was the standard deviation (around 18 instead of 16). As a result,

The borderzone for ESN special school (assuming it to be 70±5 for a test with mean 100 and a standard deviation 15) would still be 70±5 (106 − 2 × 18). (Wright, 1972, p. 32)

In other words, the magic numbers would still be produced in very many of the cases where they would be needed, even if it took error compounded upon error to achieve them.

Perhaps in the long run the effects of such sloppiness were not as universally important as they might have been. Certainly many teachers, heads and administrators continued to believe in the ESN as a category of special education for children with IQs below 70–75, and many school medical officers and educational psychologists carried with them into their practice their own personal IQ-ranges of what they regarded as appropriate or otherwise for ESN school admission. Abuses at this formal level, with different professionals in the same local education authority applying their own personal criteria irrespective of all that was going on around them, were what Burt had tried to avoid when he established his personal 'borderzone' for the LCC – though there could have been few instances as extreme as the situation described in one large LEA in the early 1970s (Brindle, 1974), where the figure '60' (tests unspecified) represented the *lower* end of one educational psychologist's IQ-range for ESN schools, and the *upper* end of another's! But did it really matter that much? In most cases it was the teachers in the normal schools that originally picked out who should be put forward for 'ascertainment', and the teachers in the special schools who set limits on what they would take. The medical officers and the educational psychologist who formalized the pupils' transfer to special schooling could serve as a filter, but their 'intuition' or 'clinical judgement' was as likely the determining factor in this decision making as were the results of their laboriously conducted intelligence testing (see Presland, 1970, for the only published account of decision making in this field, in terms of the practitioner's problems in matching the knowledge-base to the reality). Irrespective of the technical merit of professional knowledge, personal professional practice may be conducted according to altogether separate principles. Bloor (1976) has given an illuminating account of such divergence in an area of surgical practice.

Intelligence testing had become associated with placement in special schools for the mentally defective in the distant days shortly after the Great War, and a certain specific guideline for practice began subsequently to be quoted with a general force that was not its original stated intention. Once cut off from its origins, however, a reified figure of 70-ish derived from an intelligence test (it mattered little, apparently, which one) became a sort of fetish in selection for ESN schools, involving vast numbers of children over the years in individual intelligence testing that may have had more a ritual significance than one relating either to psychometric reality or to the actual decision being made. In the event the gatekeepers to the ESN schools made an enormous number of exceptions to the oft-quoted upper limit (see, for example: National Union of Teachers, 1958; Ministry of Education, 1962; William and Gruber, 1967; Birch et al., 1970). There was after all a more pressing imperative within the system than cut-off points in intelligence test results.

> It is sometimes very easy to take advantage of the facilities that do exist for removing a child from a problem situation . . . what happens is that teachers sometimes get quite desperate.
> (Oral evidence to the Select Committee on Race Relations and Immigration, 1974)

Continua

Specific intelligence-testing related issues, such as 'IQ cut-off points' and the role of intelligence testing in 'ascertainment', now seem increasingly distant in time. In many local authorities there are educational psychologists who wholly eschew psychometric assessment for the purpose of special-school selection, as much as for anything else, and indeed there are some who wholly eschew special-school placement. This is not universally the case . . . there certainly still exist educational psychologists all over the country who routinely administer individual intelligence tests to every child that they meet professionally, regardless of the original referral problem, seeing it as the central component of their professional role, and there are certainly very many teachers who still hold the results of intelligence tests in superstitious awe. The public debate, however, has switched from consideration of IQs. Much more important now is the question of 'integration', with its clear implication that the children who were previously deemed 'educationally subnormal' would be better conceived of as part of the whole range of children, rather than being considered or treated as a separate group.

Progressive positions in special education were widely felt to have been given a major official boost by the advisory circular from the Department of Education (1975) which offered new guidelines (and forms!) for 'informal' practices in the placement of pupils in special education. More recently, the publication of the Warnock Report (1978) on 'special educational needs' has crystallized the demands of the progressive special educational establishment for reforms in the structure of special educational provision, and a government White Paper (*Special Needs in Education*, 1980) has indicated at least a partial official willingness to go along with those demands. The Warnock Report had not made much direct reference to psychological research, nor did it discuss the major theoretical issues surrounding the question of the development of handicapped individuals. At the very outset of the report, however, certain underlying 'general principles' were made explicit. Among these was a working assumption which many regard as providing a model or topology to describe not only the educational needs of the handicapped, but also the very nature of handicap itself.

We have been concerned, however, not only with the severely handicapped but with all those children who require special education in any form. The help needed may range from continuous support from specialist services, including an intensive educational programme in a special school for a child with severe and multiple difficulties, to part-time assistance from a specially trained teacher for a child with mild learning difficulties. It is perhaps useful to regard this range of special educational need as a continuum, although this is a crude notion which conceals the complexities of individual need.
(Warnock Report, 1980, para. 1.9)

This 'crude notion', the continuum of need, is an important theme in progressive special-education thinking in this country. At the end of the Warnock Report it re-emerges in the firm recommendation that 'statutory categorisation of handicapped pupils should be abolished' (ibid, para. 3.25 and p. 338). In the education of the educationally subnormal it has already been a practical reality in many schools since the Education (Handicapped Children) Act (1970) brought the severely subnormal into the education system, and into the already very wide category of the ESN. For many special educators the 'integration' of different kinds of special education, both with each other and with normal education, is an ideological tenet as important as was 'genericization' for social workers in the years leading up to the Social Services Act (1970). The White Paper that followed the Warnock Report responded to this widespread feeling. Though fighting shy of a total commitment to the integration principle, the White Paper made a most definite statement about a system that defined different kinds of handicap.

> . . . The government proposes legislation which will do away with the present system of special educational treatment for children ascertained as belonging to a category of handicap.
> (*Special Needs in Education*, 1980, para. 39)

It would seem that, as long as the legislators can get round the tricky question of how to put it into law, the 'continuum of need' will be an important principle in defining and describing the organization of special education in this country for some years to come.

The idea of a continuum has been a longstanding one in English special education, though initially considered to involve factors other than 'need'. The Ministry of Education's 1946 pamphlet had emphasized the quantitative distinctions to be made between children (expressed as IQs) and counselled against qualitative distinctions (based on aetiology and prognosis) when making decisions about who should go to ESN schools (Ministry of Education, 1946, paras. 48 and 61). The very wide-ranging statutory definition of the ESN category, involving pupils retarded educationally 'by reason of limited ability or other conditions', derived from a central principle advanced by the Wood Report which had regarded *all* backwardness as 'a unit problem'.

> . . . we have come to the conclusion that these two groups of children – the mentally defective child who is educable and the child who is dull and backward – can no longer be regarded as separate and distinct entities, but must really be

envisaged as a single group, presenting a single educational and administrative problem.
(Mental Deficiency Committee, 1929, Part I, p. 93)

It is important to remember that the Mental Deficiency Committee had concerns about the retarded that went far beyond how backward children should be placed educationally. Its concerns were also of a much wider political nature, with the least-able being seen as generating the social problems amongst which they often lived, by virtue primarily of their own low ability. Low intelligence was related to poverty, crime, unemployment, etc. in a causal manner. The 'unit problem' in school provision was not, therefore, simply an educational one.

> An intimate relation exists between the two groups of children, the feebleminded and the backward group known as the dull. . . . From an aetiological point of view it is also necessary to emphasise the very close relationship between dullness and the higher grades of mental deficiency. There are cogent grounds for thinking that there is a causal relationship. The dull of the present generation will probably be the progenitors of a large number of the feebleminded children of the next generation.
> (ibid, Part IV, p. 142)

The 'discovery of the moron' and the eugenics scare with which it was associated had been an unforseen by-product of the first intelligence scale developed by Binet and Simon, when its mental ages had been converted to 'mental ratios' or 'IQs'. From the curves of the distribution of intellectual ability which are so commonplace nowadays, but were startlingly unfamiliar sixty to seventy years ago, an unexpected statement had emerged about people and about society.

> It became evident that intellectual inadequacy was not an absolute, all-or-none attribute, as had been previously presumed. There were gradations from the slightest deviation to the most profound state of deficiency. Between the 'average' and the idiot-imbecile stood a huge contingent of 'borderliners' who became known as morons.
> (Kanner, 1964, p. 123)

Burt (1921a) gave widespread academic currency in this country to the way in which this range of ability over-rode in importance the previous qualitative distinction made between the normal and the defective (pp. 174–175), and to the overwhelmingly hereditary mechanism of the transmission of intelligence (pp. 129–134).

This is not to impute that the current integration issue is being argued on eugenicist grounds, but merely to raise the question of the historical roots of the longstanding concern in this country that special education for the retarded should be reformed by blurring possible qualitative distinctions in favour of a continuum of provision. Once raised, this question leads inevitably to another, one that points up the contrast between our own national heritage in this respect and certain conflicting views from continental Europe. What does developmental psychology, surely an essential component of the psychology of education, have to say about continua in development, and in its disorders?

Perhaps the most widely quoted name in any consideration of children's development in this country over the last decade or so has been that of the late Jean Piaget. Piaget was Swiss, and as a francophone was heir to an intellectual tradition altogether unfamiliar to most English-speaking people – structuralism. This amorphous philosophical tradition is distinguished by the common conviction that there is a structure underlying all human behaviour and mental functioning, one that has cohesion, meaning and generality, and can be discovered by orderly analysis (see Gardner, 1976). It is, therefore, altogether different in its approach to natural phenomena from the positivist view that underpins so much Anglo-Saxon thinking. A structuralist analysis of a given phenomenon will include attention to its temporal aspects, and will seek factors which change in response to historical forces. These 'diachronic' aspects may be either 'irreversible', i.e., they move solely in one direction over the course of time, or they may be 'reversible', i.e., they shift from pole to pole and back again. In the investigation of children's mental development this background results not merely in a marked divergence in methodology between Piaget's approach and that of, say, Burt: more fundamentally it has been reflected in an opposition in the respective models adopted to construe the course of development.

> The main difference between Piagetian theory and the theory behind traditional IQ testing is that the latter holds that development is a progressive, continuous process, whereas Piaget's theory argues that development involves frequent repetition and even reversal, with an older child at times doing less well than a younger child on the same task.
> (Bower, 1979, pp. 119–120)

Though Piaget's stages of cognitive development are a part of the common socialization process of all English schoolteachers, and therefore, presumably, knowledge of them constitutes one component of their professionalism, it is to be wondered how much English educationalists are effectively aware of the metatheoretical chasm that separates Piaget's scientific tradition from our own. Aspects of Piaget's psychology, and the works of the Genevan school in general (especially Piaget's and Inhelder's), have been closely associated with progressive ideas in British primary, preschool and special education. In the United States, especially, there has been extensive research relating 'Piagetian' ideas to problems of special education (see Warner and Williams, 1975; Lange and Urban, 1977). Given the high esteem in which such ideas have been held, one ought to inquire about the view of the Piagetian school on the subject of continua in developmental disorders.

The major work in this area was done by Piaget's closest collaborator, Barbel Inhelder (1943). Using the well-known *méthode clinique* on a varied population of retarded children and young adults she demonstrated grades of defect, qualitatively distinct one from the other in terms of their mental operations and analogous to the stages that she and Piaget had described in the development of normal children. Mental retardation did not merely involve different *degrees* of intellectual backwardness, as defined upon some linear scale such as 'mental age' or IQ (as most of her subjects had already been defined). There were also different *kinds* of mental retardation, that differed both from each other *and from the normal*, these differences having important implications for prognosis and therefore for education. The Piagetian school is of course only one part of the, to us, largely unknown body of theory and practice that constitute French-speaking psychology. In that psychology the conflicts of opinion about whether development is primarily a linear or qualitative process have been well aired (see Association de Psychologie Scientifique de la Langue Française, 1956), and the tensions that this engenders in psychological practice are clearly apparent in modern French diagnosis, where psychometric measurement has to accommodate to medico-educational concepts that conceive of different kinds of mental backwardness, with correspondingly divergent educational requirements (Moore, 1973).

If Piagetian psychology had been the *basis* for many of the educational activities that have evoked aspects of that psychology to support and justify them, then it seems reasonable to expect that such activities (and their underlying ideology) would have shown some indication of contact with the wider Piagetian theoretical system. This has not been the general case. It seems rather that the indigenous educational ideology has held primacy, with Piaget's being a high-status name that could be called upon for the purpose of legitimation. Had a Piagetian-structuralist view been more fully incorporated (or even recognized) by educators in their general way of thinking, it is hard to see how a 'continuum of need' could have been stated or accepted with such *unquestioned* authority, as if there could be no other reasonable or responsible view. It also seems that, although specific psychometric issues such as IQ-ranges are no longer a live issue in this country, their abandonment represents no radical progression. Rather, the 'continuum' model, stripped of its calibrations, appears no more than a continuation, albeit a cosmeticized one, of the same linear model upon which Burt was working when he looked for his 'borderline' between the normal and the defective. The dividing line has been removed, the dimension remains.

It may well be that the Piaget-fad in English education is on the wane (Hargreaves, 1978). Certainly in developmental psychology in the United States increasing attention is being paid to 'transactionist' models, both for normal and for abnormal development (e.g., Sameroff, 1975). In the Life-Span School, the transactions of human mental development are often expressed in 'dialectical' terms (e.g., Learner and Spanier, 1978). These dialectics are largely idealistic in nature, though on both sides of the Atlantic acknowledgement is now made of the importance of L.S. Vygotskii, the major dialectical-materialist figure in developmental psychology. In this country Margaret Donaldson's work (e.g., 1978) has drawn considerably from English-language editions of Vygotskii's writings, and has evoked considerable interest among educators. There may now be a Vygotskii-fad, with aspects of Vygotskii's psychology invoked to justify certain educational practices, in the same way as Piaget's has been. Vygotskii is understood to be 'about language', and therefore his work fits well into the post-Bullock consensus. But Vygotskii was about much more: *inter alia*, his epistemology not only permits stages and qualitative distinctions, it *demands* them; in its view 'continua of need' (or of anything else) are only possible up to a certain point before being reconstituted by their own internal contradictions. As a consequence Vygotskii's developmental theory is also a stage theory (Sutton, 1980a, 1980b), and the defectology that derives from it (Sutton, 1980c) is altogether contrary in its principles from that represented in the Warnock Report. It is to be predicted that special education at its next stage of development in this country will pluck aspects from the body of Vygotskian psychology (e.g., 'language') where they suit its own immediate needs, but there will be little or no influence, either in methodology or in theory, that will flow from this developmental theory to shape general educational practice.

In other words, enormous lip-service may be paid to major psychological theories about the nature of human development. It is unlikely, however, that a theory that differs substantially from the broad consensus of our traditional modes of thinking in the state education system will be generally understood, or will have any substantial effect upon practice. Its invocation will be largely rhetorical. Of course the works of Piaget (or accounts of them) have had effects upon education and educators in this country, but any substantial changes in practice associated with them were already under way for more pressing reasons, and Piaget's ideas merely fitted in. The existence of minor reflexive responses once the process was in train do not deny this, and the unrecognized existence of these ideas (from before the Second World War), long before they fitted in with the new spirit of the time, supports the assertion. Behind the rhetoric matters will continue largely unaffected by stated theoretical positions.

What next?

Whatever the intentions of the Warnock Report, and however these intentions might be reflected in subsequent government legislation, their translation into action at local level, at least in the field of 'learning difficulties', runs the risk of dealing with possibly major criterial difficulties largely by default. The outward forms of special education may change, but as was the case following the Education Act (1944) actual practices may continue largely as before, with effective change coming in response to social and economic forces quite outside of the expectations of planners and legislators (See Wetherley, 1979; Sutton, 1981a). With respect to the relationship between educational psychology and special education for retarded children (presently the 'educationally subnormal', soon presumably the 'children with learning difficulties') two points combine to suggest that the educational psychology in terms of which the special educational needs of such children are described will continue to diverge from real psychological science.

Firstly, there are to be considered the pressing 'professional' needs of the various professions that are now entangled with special education. One important anchor of their professionalism is their claim to expert, scientifically based knowledge on professional matters. Yet despite all the trappings of training and research there has yet to emerge a tested body of knowledge that represents a science of pedagogy appropriate to the needs of retarded schoolchildren, and the general professional image does not include a scientific world view. Moreover the whole 'Multidisciplinary Movement', with its need to give mutual credence to an enormous number of professional contributions, calls for either a tacit truce between often contradictory positions, or for an overarching and universally accepted theory of pedagogy and its relationship to normal and anomalous development. To move from the former position to the latter seems impossible without acceptance that, for example, a 'psychological' view may discount a 'psychiatric' view, or that a 'pedagogic' approach may negate a 'treatment' approach. There are strong vested interests against upsetting the multidisciplinary apple-cart, shared by all the professional groups that ride upon it. To maintain the fragile structure of professionalism means that hard scientific approaches have to give way to negotiation and to the acceptance of professional myths. It is not just administrators and politicians who may experience the findings and insights of psychology and of the other social sciences as a threat, and in an area such as special education for the retarded, where 'psychology' is demanded by all the professions involved to play a legitimating role, educational psychology as a *science* occupies a very vulnerable position. An analogous situation exists in child welfare, where social workers (and *their* multidisciplinary team) have created their own psychology in whose terms they describe their work (Sutton, 1981b). In such a context, psychology as a science may in fact play a very small role indeed in generating apparently psychological, professional expertise and activity (Sutton, 1981c).

Secondly, there seems no prospect of a major shift in the ownership of psychological knowledge. The state education system maintains control over its psychologists and their psychological production by two methods (see Sutton, 1981d). At the immediate level there are the constraints of the wage relationship. The educational psychologist is employed to do a specific job, and though there is a wide tolerance in our society for quirks in professionals' behaviour, it is possible for an educational psychologist to be dismissed by a local education authority for fundamental disagreements about the nature of the work, as a recent decision by an industrial tribunal has shown. At a more basic level, however, there is the control of psychological practice provided by the general ideological climate into which the psychologist, the teacher, indeed everyone in the state education system, is socialized. Concepts about what is 'scientific', 'professional', 'ethical', 'responsible', etc. are not universal givens; they are socially defined,

defined moreover by a certain power structure that also defines what is 'unscientific', 'unprofessional', 'unethical', 'irresponsible', etc. To the degree to which practitioners internalize such concepts, so they police and control their own professional activities. In that the practitioners' very mentality is provided by a wider ideological system, then the psychology knowledge which is part of their professionalism must be critically examined in terms of its wider ideological background (see Ingleby, 1975). The urge of the Wood Report to see the dull and the deficient as a 'unit problem' was inextricably bound up, however argued psychometrically, with wider eugenic concerns. Is there an analogous connection between the recent urge to genericize all 'learning difficulties' and the trend to patholo-gize the poor (cf. Jordon, 1974)? Teachers, educational psychologists and others who utilize psychological concepts to define their professional prac-tice should have regard not just for the content of such concepts, but also for their sociology and politics. But whom would that benefit?

It does not seem unreasonable to suggest that a fundamental review of the potential contribution of educational psychology to the education of the retarded would interfere with powerful interests at all levels of the system. It would seriously question the values and practices upon which many individual teachers have based their careers; perhaps deny the need not only for special schools but also for the attractive 'community resources' that many would seek to establish; maybe even call into question fundamental social values about human equality and inequality. Given the enormous potential conflicts of interest that such a reappraisal might provoke it is perhaps unfair to expect that educational psychologists, working within the local authorities, would be able to make enormous changes to the 'educa-tional psychology' that they find all around them. They are themselves subject to powerful constraints in the workplace if they do try to swim upstream, and many of them anyway have already made a close and con-scious identification with the values of the education service. However extensive the day-to-day contribution of this group to the investigation and placement of backward pupils (there are now a thousand educational psychologists working in England and Wales), as a group they have made a strikingly minor contribution to such children's education or to the under-standings and attitudes of those who educate them – unless one counts their legitimating (and possibly socially iatrogenic) function for the system as already established.

Nevertheless, society continues to evolve, and we change with it. Special educators continue to learn educational psychology in their training courses. Increasingly this will include many new conceptualizations already worked out elsewhere; for example:

> behavioural models, which direct attention to immediate contingencies as a means to control and direct learning, rather than to events or circumstances elsewhere or long ago to explain why learning might be limited;

> the idea of a 'social-psychological practice' (McPherson and Sutton, 1981), that construes individuals' problems within the wider social and organizational context of which they are a part;

> the pedagogic psychologies (such as presented by Stones, 1970), that direct attention to the interaction of the pupils' learning with the process and content of teaching, rather than concentrating upon measuring the product of largely unstructured interaction;

> educational instructional technologies such as Distar (see Becker, 1977), that provide an enormous *demonstrable* improvement in pupils' attainments by changing what the ordinary teacher does, rather than adding new substructures and career opportunities outside of the normal education system.

In part, of course, these new approaches will be accommodated to the old system. Within the system as a whole one already finds such absurdities as children being excluded or suspended from school because of breakdowns in the social system in the classroom, and then 'treated' by behavioural methods in altogether separate special units. A more appropriately applied behavioural analysis of the problem, involving the social systems in which the child became a problem in the first place, might be much harder to arrange than the more expensive course of forming special units. The potential contribution of behaviour modification to education is all too easily distorted into a 'mindless technology' (Berger, 1979).

Changes there will certainly be in the educational psychology of our education system, though it seems unlikely that the influence of new understandings will depend primarily upon the intrinsic merit that they possess in respect to children's or society's needs. In that they threaten to oust understandings that serve important legitimating needs for powerful professional groups it seems unlikely that the effective force for change will come from within the education system. Instead, its source might be from outside, from parents or from government, in their different ways concerned with effectiveness and cost-effectiveness. Though the Education Act (1944) is often cited as a major turning-point, it has been argued here that, at least in certain aspects, our present ideas about the psychological definition of educational subnormality represent a point on a long process of evolutionary change that stretches back to Burt's early work shortly after the Great War. For much of that time, it has been suggested, psychological science has played a very small part in arriving at these 'psychological' definitions. The Warnock Report (paras. 18.17 and 18.18) has apparently anticipated no major problems in the 'translation of research into practice'; past experience suggests that, for this to be so, evolutionary change will have to give way to a revolution in the relationship between special educational practice and its avowed knowledge base in educational psychology.

References

Association de Psychologie Scientifique de la Langue Française (1956) *Le Problème des stades en Psychologie*, Presses Universitaires de France

Becker, W.C. (1977) 'Teaching reading and language to the disadvantaged: what we have learned from field research', in *Harvard Educational Review*, Volume 47, pp. 518–543

Berger, M. (1979) 'Behaviour modification in education and professional practice: the dangers of a mindless technology', in *Bulletin of the British Psychological Society*, Volume 32, pp. 418–419

Birch, H.G., S.A. Richardson, D. Baird, G. Horobin and R. Illsley (1970) *Mental Subnormality in the Community: a Clinical and Epidemiological Study*, Williams and Wilkins

Bloor, M. (1976) 'Bishop Berkeley and the adeno-tonsillectomy enigma: an exploration of variation in the social construction of medical diagnosis, in *Sociology*, Volume 10, pp. 43–62

Bower, T.G.R. (1979) *Human Development*, Freeman

Brindle, P. (1974) *The Ascertainment of Mild Subnormality in Education*, unpublished M.Ed. dissertation, University of Birmingham

British Psychological Society (1955) *Final Report of the Working Party on the WISC* (cyclostyled)

Burt, C. (1921a) *Mental and Scholastic Tests*, Staples

Burt, C. (1921b) *Report of an Investigation upon Backward Children in Birmingham*, City of Birmingham Education Committee

Chazan, M., T. Moore, P. Williams, J. Wright and M. Walker (1974) *The Practice of Educational Psychology*, Longman

Clarke, A.N., and A.D.B. Clarke (1980) 'Comments on Professor Hearn-shaw's "Balance Sheet on Burt" ', in *Supplement to the Bulletin of the British Psychological Society*, Volume 33, pp. 17–19

Donaldson, M. (1978) *Children's Minds*: Fontana/Collins

Gardner, H. (1976) *The Quest for Mind: Piaget, Levi-Straus and the Structuralist Movement*, Quartet Books

Handicapped Pupils and School Health Regulations (1945) HMSO

Hargreaves, D. (1978) 'The proper study of educational psychology', in *Journal of the Association of Educational Psychologists*, Volume 4, number 9, pp. 3–8

Hearnshaw, L.S. (1979) *Cyril Burt, Psychologist*, Hodder & Stoughton

Ingleby, D. (1975) 'The psychology of child psychology', in Richards, M.P.M., (ed) *Integration of the Child into a Social World*, Cambridge University Press

Inhelder, B. (1943) *Le diagnostic du raisonnement chez les debiles mentaux*, Delachaux et Niestlé

Jordon, B. (1974) *Poor Parents: Social Policy and the 'Cycle of Deprivation'*, Routledge & Kegan Paul

Kamin, L.J. (1974) *The Science and Politics of IQ*, Wiley

Kanner, L. (1964) *A History of the Care and Study of the Mentally Retarded*, Thomas, U.S.A.

Keir, G. (1952) 'A history of child guidance', in *British Journal of Educational Psychology*, Volume 22, pp. 12–19

Lange, C.E. and M.J. Urban (1977) 'Special bibliography: Piagetian theory and the handicapped child', in *Piagetian Theory and the Helping Professions – 6th Annual Conference*, University of Southern California, pp. 445–456

Learner, R.A. and G.B. Spanier (eds) *Child Influence on Marital and Family Interaction: a Life-Span Perspective*, Academic Press

McPherson, I. and A. Sutton (eds) (1981) *Reconstructing Psychological Practice*, Croom Helm

Mental Deficiency Committee (1929) *Report of the Mental Deficiency Committee*, HMSO

Ministry of Education (1946) *Special Educational Treatment* (Pamphlet No. 5) HMSO

Ministry of Education (1947) *Circular 146: Educationally Subnormal Children, Examination under Sections 34 and 57 of the Education Act 1944*, HMSO

Ministry of Education (1962) *Health of the School Child, 1960/61* (Report of the Chief Medical Officer), HMSO

Moore, L. (1973) *La practique des tests mentaux en psychiatrie de l'enfant* (3rd edition), Masson et Cie

National Union of Teachers (1958) *Circular E.108/1958: Day Schools for ESN Pupils* (cyclostyled)

Presland, J. (1970) 'Who should go to ESN schools?' in *Special Education*, Volume 59, pp. 11–16

Sameroff, A.J. (1975) 'Early influences on development: fact or fancy', in *Merrill-Palmer Quarterly*, Volume 21, pp. 267–285

Select Committee on Race Relations and Immigration (1974) *Report on Education*, HMSO

Stones, E. (ed) (1970) *Readings in Educational Psychology*, Methuen

Sutton, A. (1980a) 'Models and measures in developmental psychology', in *Educational Studies*, Volume 6, pp. 111–126

Sutton, A. (1980b) 'Cultural disadvantages and Vygotskii's stages of development', in *Educational Studies*, Volume 6, pp. 185–195

Sutton, A. (1980c) 'Backward children in the USSR: an unfamiliar approach to a familiar problem', in Brine, J., M. Perrie and A. Sutton (eds) *Home, School and Leisure in the Soviet Union*, Allen & Unwin, pp. 160–191

Sutton, A. (1981a) 'The powers that be' (Unit 8 of Open University Course, *Special Needs in Education*) Open University Press

Sutton, A. (1981b) 'Social services, psychology . . . and psychologists', in McPherson, I. and A. Sutton (eds), *Reconstructing Psychological Practice*, Croom Helm, pp. 145–164

Sutton, A. (1981c) 'Sorting the wheat from the chaff – the examination of expert evidence to the juvenile court', in *Reports to the Court*, Family Rights Group, pp. 21-32

Sutton, A. (1981d) 'Whose psychology? Issues in the social control of psychological practice', in McPherson, I. and A. Sutton (eds) *Reconstructing Psychological Practice*, Croom Helm, pp. 145–164

Warner, B.J. and R. Williams (1975) 'Piaget's theory and exceptional children: a bibliography, 1963–1973', in *Perceptual and Motor Skills*, Volume 41, pp. 255–261

Warnock Report (1978) *Special Needs in Education*, Cmnd. No. 7996, HMSO

Weatherley, R.A. (1979) *Reforming Special Education: Policy Implementation from State Level to Street Level*, MIT Press

Williams, P. and E. Gruber (1967) *Response to Special Schooling: an Inves-*

tigation Concerned with Children from Special Schools for the Educationally Subnormal, Longman

Wright, H. (1972) 'The interpretation of Terman-Merrill (T–M) scores for British populations', in *Occasional Papers of the Division of Educational and Child Psychology of the British Psychological Society*, number 1, pp. 29–32

Further reading

Moss, G.O. and A. Sutton (1981) 'Educational psychologists and the juvenile court', in Lloyd-Bostock, S. (ed)*Law and Psychology, September 1979*, Oxford, Centre for Socio-Legal Studies, pp.1–22

Sutton, A. (1981) 'Science in Court', in King, M. (ed) *Childhood, Welfare and Justice*, Batsford

Weatherley, R. and M. Lipsky (1977) 'Street-level bureaucrats and institutional innovation: implementing special-education reform', in *Harvard Educational Review*, Volume 47, pp. 171–197

CHAPTER 6

THE VALUE OF PARENTS TO THE ESN(S) SCHOOL: AN EXAMINATION

by *Len Barton and Susan Moody*

Two of the most important institutions in our society are the family and school. Their inter-relationship has been the topic of a great deal of research by social scientists from different disciplines; and the over-riding conclusions from such investigations confirm the significance of the home's influence in the educational experience and performance of the child.

During the past decade in particular there has been an increasing demand, by a variety of bodies both outside and within the educational system, for closer, more meaningful and effectual links between the home and school. Illustrations of these types of demands are to be found in recent government reports. For example, the Green Paper on Education in Schools, a Consultative Document, maintains that:

> Until recently many parents played only a minor part in the educational system. The Government are of the view that parents should be given much more information about the schools, and should be consulted more widely.
> (1975, p. 5)

or the Taylor Report on the role of school governors contends that:

> Both individually and collectively the parents constitute a major source of support for the school. It is not a source which has been tapped fully in the past. We believe that governing bodies should encourage the widest and deepest parental commitment to their schools.
> (1977, p. 41)

Such directives raise questions about the actual running of schools and they are also a stimulant for encouraging schools to be more open, involving a re-examination of the role, rights and responsibilities of the major parties concerned as well as the establishment of, where necessary, a more evident democratization in the decision-making procedures of schools. To this end parental involvement is justified as being intrinsically valuable and/or instrumentally necessary, a vital means of assisting teachers to be both efficient and effectual in achieving important educational goals.

In this chapter we will seek to understand, discuss and explain some of the issues involved in home-school links, as they apply to ESN(S) schools. The approach of the writers is akin to that of Berger, who believed that:

> To ask sociological questions, then presupposes that one is interested in looking some distance beyond the commonly accepted or officially defined goals of human actions. . . . It may even presuppose a measure of suspicion about the way in which human events are officially interpreted by the authorities. . . .
> (Berger, 1966, p. 41)

An important feature of our analysis will be a critical reflection of taken-for-granted assumptions and practices, including the extent to which rhetoric either mystifies or supersedes practice, and how certain features of this topic are an illustration of conflicting and contradictory ideologies and expectations in the educational system generally.

The case of ESN(S) schools

Special education has been the subject of much debate in recent years and the Warnock Report confirms the importance of the role of parents in the education of such children:

> We have insisted throughout this report that the successful education of children with special educational needs is dependent upon the full involvement of their parents; indeed, unless the parents are seen as equal partners in the educational process the purpose of our report will be frustrated.
> (Warnock, 1978, p. 150)

This is by no means a novel idea, particularly as far as mentally handicapped pupils are concerned. Parent bodies like the National Society for Mentally Handicapped Children and Adults, in conjunction with their local branches, have been endeavouring for years to obtain a better deal for these people in all spheres of life, including education.

However, by contrasting the nature and organization of ESN(S) schools with those in mainstream education, we can identify certain characteristics that possibly provide more opportunities to establish and maintain home-school relations. Firstly, the nature of the curriculum is different because these special schools do not teach formal, abstract, examinable subjects and are thus not involved in competition for qualifications. Secondly, there are smaller numbers of pupils in the school, thus potentially allowing teachers • to gain a much more intimate and comprehensive knowledge of their pupils. Lastly, pupils remain in the same school for the duration of their school experience, thus giving the teachers and parents the time to get to know each other and establish working relationships.

Prevailing practices

One of the main themes to develop in this sphere of the educational system has been that of 'Parent-Teacher Partnership'. From the professionals' viewpoint the emphasis is on engaging parents in a much more teacher-oriented role in the home situation, in order to extend the time element and manpower available to the teaching profession.

The rationale on the teacher's side is based on certain fundamental features including the belief that the particular learning difficulties of these children call for much repetition and overlearning of new skills in different situations; the content of the teaching is frequently common to both home and school, particularly with regard to basic personal and social skills; the nature of teaching methods found to be successful calls for a very consistent approach by all those in contact with the child and who are concerned with his full development; the parents are a major source of information as regards their children, and this information is invaluable if an adequate assessment of the child's abilities and needs is to be made and maintained (Moody, 1980). These types of justification form the basis of such strong beliefs as those of Mittler who maintains that:

> No matter how successfully a child is taught at school, the effort is largely wasted unless systematic steps are taken to help the child to use and apply his learning in his own home and in other real life settings in which he moves. The collaboration of parents is indispensable for this purpose.
> (Mittler, 1978, p. 248)

So parents, given the necessary advice and/or training, including support services, can become a vitally important means of extending the educational experience of these children, beyond the walls of the school.

Professional practices are treated as *non-problematic*, their work is maintained to be both good and necessary and what is required if it is to have a lasting effect in the lives of the pupils is for the teachers to gain the support of the parents who, under the guidance of the professionals' judgement, will seek to reinforce the necessary learning experiences within the home. The overall concern is to maximize opportunities for severely mentally handicapped children to progress in all aspects of their lives. The emphasis is upon a shared responsibility in which the needs of the individual child are paramount. The desired relationship between parents and teachers appears to be one requiring openness, trust and respect between the parties, through which parents may be directed into a more educative role (Butler, 1980).

The arguments presented and the desires expressed therewith for the development of parent-teacher partnership in the ESN(S) school are illustrated in practice by the growing number of 'parent participation projects'. Within this movement parent workshops constitute the commonest and most widepsread form of parent participation. Workshops consist usually of short courses for parents on the art of handling their mentally handicapped child or children. They tend to be of around eight weeks' duration on one evening per week and include talks by various professionals, followed by discussion groups and the practice of behaviour management and development skills. Homework consists of trying out the suggestions derived from the workshop session with their child, attempting a recording of behaviour and carrying out short programmes they have designed. Many of these workshops are run by bodies *independent* of schools – child guidance centres, research centres, adult education centres, technical colleges, charity organizations – and the majority have been set up for issues relating to the preschool child.

Some schools are now beginning to incorporate this method into their home-school liaison programme and have extended the workshop approach into a continuing *structured* relationship between teacher and parents of children in the class (McCall and Thacker, 1977). Here the emphasis is upon regular communication: initially face-to-face contact, but later often by the written word between teacher and parent, particularly concerning what the teacher is attempting to do with the child, and the ways in which the parents may complement this at home. Specific problems the parent might be experiencing with the child might also be dealt with in this manner. Some schools have taken the initiative of using a specific programme of development with certain groups of children which involves a specific home-teaching element. One example is The Portage Guide to

Early Education, and this method does make provision for regular communication between home and school.

The reports and research findings published on this topic suggest that parent participation projects over the last few years in ESN(S) education in England have been of the workshop or extended workshop type (Cunningham and Jeffree, 1975; Hewson, 1977). The emphasis is on the individual child, the criterion of success his or her development. However, there are some schools developing a '*multidimensional approach*' which attempts to involve the parents gradually as soon as the child enters school and to offer several areas of involvement including work with teachers on individual children's objectives, the use of school facilities purely on social grounds in the form of a family club and the development of a parent-teacher association. This approach is, at least on paper, significantly different from the parent workshop and extended workshop concept, in that it is offering a much wider basis for parent participation in schools including involvement in decision-making processes as regards the whole school and not just simply their own child. It is a much more flexible approach allowing for parents to be involved in different ways (Report of Working Party, 1980).

Impetus for parent-teacher school links has been derived from a number of sources, such as the material gathered from a whole spectrum of medical, social and educational research, from professional groups including teachers, from various directives in official government documents and from parents as individuals or through their national and local associations. An examination of the literature gives a strong *intended* message which crosses cultural, race and class boundaries, that is, parent participation or co-operation is absolutely vital and has benefits for the school, the home, the children and ultimately the community (Mittler, 1979; Chazan, 1980).

Points of contention

Despite such development, criticisms, expressions of bewilderment, frustration and anger from a number of sources are an indication that all is not what it is made out to be, or should be, and that rhetoric and good intentions are one thing, actually creating the conditions for their realization are quite another. It is quite clear that, for many, 'Often nobody asks the simple question, "What do the parents want?" ' (Spencer, 1977, p. 30). Nor is this merely a question of a few isolated incidents, but rather it is symptomatic of a much wider problem, as Mittler notes:

> . . . there are *many* schools where such a partnership has hardly begun, where parents have played *no* part in helping to assess the strengths and weaknesses of the child, far less been involved in the design and implementation of a teaching programme. There are children whose parents have *no* knowledge of the objectives set by teachers for their child, if indeed any objectives have been set at all, schools where there is *no* system of communication, such as home-school diaries, where there are *no* visits by teachers to the home and *only* yearly formal visits by parents to the school. (our emphasis)
> (Mittler, 1978, p. 245)

While home-school relations are often fraught with practical difficulties like parents having to work and not being able to get to the school, or they live too far away and have no transport or cannot afford the bus fares, or they cannot get a babysitter, these are clearly *not* the issues that have resulted in this serious indictment. The problems identified in the previous quotation are of a much deeper, fundamental sort, in which some schools and teachers are not beyond criticism.

The whole question of home-school links needs to be carefully re-examined and the taken-for-granted assumptions on which a great deal of the policies and practices are based must be critically evaluated. Analyses *must* go beyond the individual school or family and be located in the wider, but absolutely crucial, ideological, political and economic features of the social order.

Terms such as 'partnership', 'participation' and 'co-operation' are constantly being used by those who advocate the importance of home-school relations and this type of language contains assumptions about rights, respect for persons, equality and responsibility. While such language is appealing, clear definitions are notoriously difficult to find, because their meanings are ambiguous. Thus confusion arises at both an individual and group level over the nature of such practices and the extent of their effectiveness.

The frequency with which these terms are being used tends to generate a taken-for-granted attitude in which it is assumed that we all use these terms with the same basic understanding. However, upon closer reflection, a number of problems arise. Firstly, 'partnership', for example, means different things to different people. Secondly, such rhetoric does not provide adequate directions with regard to how such ideals can be implemented and maintained. Thirdly, the ideology of individualism is apparent in that issues are seen largely in terms of the individual child and his parent(s), thus minimizing collective endeavour on the part of the participants. Fourthly, we have the situation in which a single rhetoric legitimates very different kinds of institutional arrangements and practices (Taylor, 1980). Lastly, very little concern is expressed over examining the inequalities of provision and practice of home-school links, within and across different geographical areas.

The political nature of schools

One of the most serious weaknesses of much of the literature dealing with this topic is its failure to provide an analysis of these schools that seeks to identify, understand and explain the *political* nature of education. Schools are institutions and, as Edgley reminds us,

> . . . any institution is a political institution, an institution with a particular constitution or political character: for any institution needs to make and implement decisions, and it therefore requires a procedure for doing so in accordance with which it distributes relations of power, authority and responsibility among the positions that form its structure.
> (Edgley, 1980, p. 12)

According to this view questions about the nature and consequences of parent participation are political, being taken up with who gets what and why. Historically, we have no legislation or agreed social norms or rules that give clear guidance as to the nature of the 'rights' of parents, so calls for more parental involvement within the school will involve varying degrees of struggle and conflict over power-sharing. For example, Pring (1980) notes that parents have a special responsiblity for their children, therefore they have a right to have more information about what actually goes on in schools and the further right to act in the light of this knowledge. On the other hand, teachers as professionals claim the right to 'pursue their own judgement, often against that of others' because their judgement draws on their professional expertise and training. Thus, making schools more open and teachers more accountable to parents is an extremely complex and sensitive problem.

For some people parental involvement in school may seem to be potentially radical and a means to effect real changes, particularly in the democratization of the decision-making procedures. However, when we consider that there are varying possible degrees of participation, as well as to what extent parents are both able and willing to spend their energies, time and emotions in this task, coupled with the realization that the school is not situated in a vacuum but is related to and constrained by wider social and economic pressures, and reflects these in complex ways in its organization and workings in intended and unintended ways, it may well be that

> Participation within a hierarchically structured organisation, such as a school or factory, will usually mean *consultation* rather than *sharing in the making of decisions* . . .
> (Hunter, 1980, p. 226)

It is possible to argue, therefore, that the actions of parents can often be accommodated within the existing procedures and structure of the school's organization. A great deal of participation is supportive of existing policies and practices, as Salisbury maintains:

> . . . it is undertaken with the intention of helping to sustain the school (or one's own child) *rather than to change it*. From the very beginning, parent-teacher associations and their equivalents have been organised primarily to provide public support for the schools. (our emphasis)
> (Salisbury, 1980, p. 8)

Giving information to parents about school policies and practices, enabling meetings to take place between teachers and parents, are undertaken with the desire for the more favourable support of the home, and teachers expect a positive identification with the school.

Certainly this is the case so far as ESN(S) schools are concerned, the vast majority of parent participation (where it takes place), far from questioning the policies and practices of the school, has been the means of legitimating them. Parent-teacher associations have three main functions. Firstly, they provide a mutual supportive mechanism for parents to meet, share problems, gain from each other's experience or offer advice. Secondly, they provide opportunities for individual parents to meet their child's teacher and discuss factors relating to personal issues. Lastly, their major function is that of fund-raising, offering additional financial support to the school, providing equipment, vans and even buildings (Barton and Hoskins, 1978). The extent of the school's control of these associations is to be seen in that often parents have *no real say* about why or how money is spent, nor the actual use that is made of that which is purchased. In this context, participation means passively responding to the demands of the school.

The role of the head

Any adequate analysis of the school cannot fail to acknowledge the extremely powerful figure of the head. It is very important to make a distinction between the teachers and head of a school.

Heads play an absolutely crucial role in the life of a school because it is their skills, understandings and decisions that powerfully influence in a myriad of ways the organization, curriculum, teaching methods, discipline and ethos of their schools. Part of their task is to protect their vested interests and when questioned by outsiders often give the impression that their school is 'one happy family' or a 'real community'. It is difficult to discuss the position of the head in the light of issues relating to accountability, because as the recent William Tyndale affair demonstrated, although various groups make demands, the power of the head to fail to take notice or resist such pressures is extensive.

It is a salutary point that while governments make recommendations and introduce new legislation or local authorities make demands on the schools under their jurisdiction, it is the head who is able to frustrate such policies from being realized or interpret them in a manner that suits his or her own purpose in terms of the functioning of their school. This is important when we consider home-school links, for, as Taylor reminds us:

> . . . in spite of all the evidence about the value of parent-teacher co-operation and the bland endorsements of official support *it is still up to the headteacher* to decide whether or not a school has any kind of parents' organisation. (our emphasis) (Taylor, 1979, p. 74)

Thus heads using various means will influence the nature, extent and consequences of home-school relations. Indeed, initial moves are often seen to be the prerogative of the school.

Rhetoric and practice

The contributions that parents can and should be making is often ignored by those in positions of power and their participation is limited to token decisions or rubber-stamping procedures. Even the recent government White Paper on special education purports to place parents in a position in which they will be able to exercise their rights and wishes over their children's education. Yet, as Kirp maintains:

> Here the appearance vastly surpasses reality. Parents can state a preference concerning the schooling of a special child to the education authority and, should they fail there, can bring their case to the appeals committee which will review all

placement disagreements. But the parents will not be able to review all the information on which the l.e.a. bases its decision; 'It would be wrong' notes the White Paper, 'to require full disclosure to parents of the professional reports lying behind the record', thus inviting the preparation of bare-bones official records.
(Kirp, 1980, p. 4)

The very administrative machinery that the government will hope to establish will in itself frustrate the realization of the ideals it purports to be working for. That which is claimed to be established for the service of parents becomes another means of controlling them.

Various reasons can be offered as to why the potential for the real involvement of parents has not, in many cases, been fulfilled. One reason is that they have not had the necessary 'inside knowledge' about how various aspects of the system work, what their rights are, or how to go about getting their views expressed and taken seriously. In another chapter in this book, Sewell discusses the 'referral system' and the processes of interaction between the main parties involved. He seeks to identify the ways in which professional bodies deal with the parents of the children being assessed. He argues that:

> Parents who can be trusted to be 'intelligent' and 'not make a fuss' are offered 'performances' in the name of partnership. Those who are not to be trusted can often be persuaded. Those who object are subjected to visits from a succession of forceful and articulate members of the gatekeeping professions.
> (Sewell, 1981, p. 170)

The lesson to be drawn is that without such knowledge and the ability to act on the basis of it, parents are likely to be on the receiving end of both subtle and explicitly overt manipulative proceedings, experiencing frustration and even humiliation in the process. While an important distinction needs to be made between intended or unintended forms of behaviour or consequences on the part of the officials involved, the end result will still be painful for the parents.

A further reason for the prevailing situation concerns the dominant perspectives or models that have historically informed theory, policy and practice in this sphere of special education. Medical and psychological ideas, legitimated by reference to informed professional judgement, created intentionally or unintentionally a powerful message system, the theme being that all important decisions about the child's welfare should be left in the capable hands of the *experts*. They have the necessary training and experience. These developments have taken their toll on the willingness and/or ability of parents to challenge official judgements.

It cannot be assumed, therefore, that the interests of parents of children with special needs and those of the school are identical. Although both may argue that the goal of the school is to fit the child to take as responsible a role in society as possible, what the parents may feel are the actual capabilities or potential of their child, what they eventually hope he or she will achieve and the nature of the society in which the child will live, may be very different from that of the school's assessment. These differences of interpretation are often translated into conflicting expectations between home and school as to the type of teaching required and even some of the goals of the school.

The language that is used to encourage closer home-school ties is very appealing, but it tends to gloss over some crucial problems. These include the ambiguity of the directives, the relationship between these directives and other ideologies within the educational system, the problems of the inequalities of provision and opportunity, the realization that seeking to achieve these ideals involves the participants in some form of power struggle. There is no shortage of rhetoric; the major discrepancy is in the lack of conditions for ideals to be realized in practice.

Conclusion

It is necessary to make a number of important qualifications to the arguments that have been presented so far. Firstly, it would be *quite wrong* to assume that there are no schools in which imaginative, exciting and radical changes have and are taking place in the area of home-school links. There clearly are many dedicated staff and heads who are committed to this task and they are clearly an example of what can be achieved. What is needed is more of these people. Secondly, many teachers may be sympathetic to the ideas advanced so far, but they need 'more open discussion and exchange of information' with their colleagues so that the teachers as a group do support each other and share responsibility in this venture. Within the context of the cut-backs, low morale among many teachers, coupled with the institutional and political nature of school relations, it must be remembered that it may

. . . leave individual professionals who want to practise differently in a very exposed position.
(Robinson, 1978, p. 74)

This will be particularly so when those at the top of the authority structure within schools do not share their feelings, and may oppose the introduction of new ideas and practices. Thirdly, 'professional status' as far as teachers in ESN(S) schools are concerned, can be interpreted as 'more highly trained to care', and the energies and emotions that they spend on such children daily may drain them, and in these circumstances parents could be viewed as an uncontrolled force of additional worries. It may well be that the spirit is willing but the flesh is weak. Lastly, there are groups of parents who have little or no contact with the school and who, despite continued efforts on the part of the school, remain unresponsive. The school is not in a vacuum but needs to be viewed within a wider socio-economic framework, in order that we can begin to understand how social differences and divisions within the community may frustrate efforts by the school to communicate with certain parents.

Clearly there are costs to partnership for all the parties concerned, in terms of changing attitudes, organizational arrangements and practices, all of which demand effort, time, and persistence. Too much must not be expected of schools alone, and changes will be required in the wider social order, to which the struggles within schools will need to be related. It would therefore be naîve to suggest that no form of resistance or conflict will be involved because the changes required will so often, as Robinson notes:

> . . . threaten established ways of doing the job and because, generally, previous training and experience will not have provided a very adequate preparation for the different roles called for, those changes will be experienced as uncomfortable. (Robinson, 1978, pp. 73–74)

If by 'adequate preparation' is meant the extent to which parents themselves contribute to courses, or issues relating to parents are an important component of a course, then serious reconsideration needs to be given to the nature of many initial teacher education programmes. Ironically, the increased specialization and introduction of an all-degree body may exacerbate the differences between many parents and teachers as well as heads, in terms of their assumptions, knowledge and expectations, bringing further barriers to constructive relations.

Demands for a serious questioning of the assumptions and practices of home-school links in the ESN(S) sphere will not be without its critics or unsympathetic onlookers. One reason is because of the pervasive influence of the ideology of *individualism*. Hargreaves (1980) maintains that due to the 'excessively individualistic conceptions of the educational process' which he terms the 'cult of individualism', the 'social functions of education have become trivialised' (p. 187). Special education is excessively individualistic as can be seen from such working vocabulary as 'enhancing the aptitudes and abilities of the individual child', 'personal learning' and 'personal growth'. Depending on the degree of the handicap of the child, coupled with the related expectations of the parents, many parents may be content to gratefully accept any help they can get. Teachers become saints for they provide the opportunity for a hard-pressed parent to have a break from the demands of looking after their child. Or the interest in home-school relations for some parents is only considered within the context of meeting the needs of their child. The need to look beyond the individual family, their experiences and problems, thus becomes extremely difficult and a critical analysis that is directed towards the social, collective features of the school system may be interpreted as unnecessary or unhelpful. Yet it is the argument of this chapter that we need to consider the relationship between special education and the state, at both the central and local levels, and how these influence the way in which schools respond to parent participation. This includes research on the way in which schools have historically related to parents.

Another point is that the ideology of *vocationalism* is particularly pervasive in special education generally, and the sphere of ESN(S) work in particular. Teachers are members of the 'caring profession', possessing those necessary qualities of devotion, love and patience. The penetration of such powerful ideologies makes the task of critical analysis difficult, especially where the demand is for the re-examination of the rights and responsibilities of *all* the major parties involved and where necessary for changes to be introduced.

In the end the realities of participation may result in cosmetic changes that make little impact on the structural and interactional aspects of school life. It will thus be a subtle, but additional means of maintaining the status quo.

The final word is from a group of parents and it expresses their frustrations, anxieties and demands for change:

We hope that there will be some who decide that we do not invariably misinterpret the explanations we are given and that on occasion we *have* been known to think. . . . Whether or not the experts are ready to come out of their consulting rooms, committee rooms and staff rooms to communicate with us, we are publishing this book so that anyone who can recognise the reality of our position

may join us as people *sharing* a responsibility for the care, treatment and progress of all handicapped.
(Cooper and Henderson, 1973, p. 256, quoted in Robinson, 1978)

In times of austerity and cut-backs in government spending in all public sectors including education, affecting resources and the quality of the service provided, schools will become increasingly dependent upon parents for financial assistance. As parents are called upon to make more sacrifices in order to support the general running of the school system, issues about the nature of home-school relations become more pertinent, including the need for an understanding of the nature of those wider socio-economic and political features of society and how they influence the outworkings of this vitally important relationship in the life of schools.

Acknowledgements

We are grateful to Tricia Broadfoot, Martin Lawn, Sally Tomlinson and Ray Woolfe for their comments on an earlier draft of this chapter.

The views expressed in this chapter are those of the authors and do not represent the position of their respective institutions.

References

Barton, L. and K. Hoskins (1978) 'The parent/teacher association – an instrument of change?' in *Parents' Voice*, Volume 28, number 4, pp. 21–22

Berger, P. (1966) *Invitation to Sociology: A Humanistic Perspective*, Penguin

Butler, A. (1980) 'Parents as partners', *Parents' Voice*, Volume 30, number 1, pp. 14–15

Chazan, M., A.F. Laing, M. Bailey and B. Jones (1980) *Some of Our Children*, Open Books

Cooper, L. and R. Henderson (eds) (1973) *Something Wrong?*, Arrow

Cunningham, C.C. and D.M. Jeffree (1975) 'The organisation and structure of workshops for parents of mentally handicapped children', *Bulletin British Psychological Society*, 28, pp. 405–411.

Edgley, R. (1980) 'Education, work and politics', in *Journal of Philosophy*, Volume 14, number 1, pp. 3–16

Hargreaves, D. (1980) 'A sociological critique of individualism in education', in *British Journal of Educational Studies*, Volume 28, number 3, pp. 187–198

Hewson, S. (1977) 'School Based Parents' workshops – do they work?' paper given to annual conference of the British Psychological Society

Hunter, C. (1980) 'The politics of participation – with specific reference to teacher-pupil relationships', in Wood, P. (ed) *Teacher Strategies*, Croom Helm

Kirp, D. (1980) 'Opening the door to the gilded cage', in *Times Educational Supplement*, 19 September 1980, p. 4

McCall, C. and J. Thacker (1977) 'A parent workshop in the school', in *Special Education Forward Trends*, Volume 4, number 4, pp. 20–22

Mittler, P. (1978) 'Choices in partnership', in *Lebenshilfe fur Behinderte* (ed) The World Congress of the ILSMH, on Medical Handicap, ILSMH, pp. 242–251

Mittler, P. (1979) 'Patterns of partnership between parents and professionals', *Parents' Voice*, Volume 29, number 2

Mittler, P. (1979) 'Learning together', *Parents' Voice*, Volume 29, number 2, pp. 14–15

Moody, S. (1980) 'Teacher and parent: the new partnership in special education', unpublished dissertation submitted as part of a B.Ed. (Hons) degree, Westhill College, Birmingham

Pring, R. (1980) 'Confidentiality and the right to know', paper given at B.E.R.A. Conference at Cardiff, unpublished

Report of the working party on the future of special education in Birmingham, 1980

Robinson, T. (1978) *In Worlds Apart*, Bedford Square Press

Salisbury, R. (1980) *Citizen Participation in the Public Schools*, Lexington Books

Sewell, G. (1981) 'The microsociology of segregation', published in this volume

Spencer, D. (1977) 'What do the parents want?' in *Apex*, Volume 4, number 4. p. 30

Taylor, F. (1979) 'What to do when a head doesn't want a P.T.A.' in *Where*, 146, pp. 73–76

Taylor, T. (1977) *A New Partnership for our Schools*, HMSO

Taylor, W. (1980) 'Family, school and society', in Craft, M., J. Raynor and L. Cohen (eds), *Linking Home and School*, 3rd edition, Harper & Row

Warnock, M. (1978) *Report of the Committee of Enquiry into Education of Handicapped Children and Young People*, Cmnd 7212, HMSO

Further reading

David, M.E. (1980) *The State, the Family and Education*, Routledge & Kegan Paul

Hannam, C. (1980) *Parents and Mentally Handicapped Children*, Penguin

King's Fund Centre (1976) 'Collaboration between parents and professionals', *Mental Handicap Papers*, number 9

McCormack, M. (1978) *A Mentally Handicapped Child in the Family*, Constable

PART TWO

EMPIRICAL STUDIES

INTRODUCTION

Alternative perspectives on special education are not solely the product of theoretical study and speculation. The studies in this section of the book demonstrate that there already is a tradition of empirical research and they examine some of the questions raised in the introduction to this book.

The first three chapters report on original research into the process of labelling and categorization. Sewell, investigating why some children come to be categorized out of and excluded from ordinary schools, examines the powers and preoccupation of heads, teachers, psychologists and parents, and notes that the nature and outcome of the assessment process could be different. Labels are not objective statements indicating factors located within the child, but may relate more to the belief and needs of the professionals involved. Woolfe, in research into the decision-making process in local education authorities, examines the way in which maladjustment has come to be regarded as a physical condition to be 'treated', whereas the labelling of children as maladjusted may have more to do with the needs of organizations and professionals to maintain their own viability. Tomlinson examines the process by which some children come to be defined as mildly educationally subnormal and points out that the category ESN(M) is a non-normative category and that there is disagreement about its definition. However, ESN(M) children are seen to be a largely powerless group in society and it is suggested that the category may function more as a solution to problems of social order than as answering the needs of individual children.

The last two chapters in this section report on research into two major problems which are crucial in current debates on special education. How will schools cope with directives to 'integrate' and how, in a situation of high youth unemployment, do handicapped pupils find employment in a society which is still work-orientated? Jones reports on the development, in our secondary schools, of a resource room and resource programme, to help integrate handicapped children into the school, and notes the problems that arise for teachers and pupils. Atkinson et al. report on the work of an industrial training unit in a college of further education, set up to prepare ESN(M) young people for the world of work. Their research found that as much effort was devoted to producing 'good' workers with the 'right' attitudes as to teaching specific work skills. The research suggests that there might be a relationship between the treatment of the 'mildly handicapped' and the production of a docile, productive workforce.

These studies do demonstrate that rhetoric and reality or practices within special education are often quite different things. To examine who actually defines handicap as need, how professionals really work, how resources are distributed and how the handicapped are actually treated within various settings does mean going beyond complacent rhetoric that says it is 'all for the good' of those with 'special needs'. Empirical research vividly highlights, as C. Wright Mills maintained, that private troubles and public issues are interwoven in the complex web of human experience.

CHAPTER 7

THE MICRO-SOCIOLOGY OF SEGREGATION: CASE STUDIES IN THE EXCLUSION OF CHILDREN WITH SPECIAL NEEDS FROM ORDINARY SCHOOLS

by Geof Sewell

For micro-sociologists, the labelling of deviants cannot be clearly understood except with reference to the social context in which the act of labelling takes place. The emphasis is not so much on the sociological concomitants of those defined as deviant as on the social process through which definitions are constructed. As a seminal figure in the generation of labelling theory, John Kitsuse summarized the approach in these terms:

> I propose to shift the focus of theory and research from the forms of deviant behaviour to the processes by which persons come to be defined as deviant by others. Such a shift requires that the Sociologist view as problematic what he generally assumes as given – namely that certain forms of behaviour are per se deviant and are so defined by the conventional or conforming members of the group.
> (Kitsuse, 1962, pp. 87–88)

The 'facts' of deviance, how it was caused, the effects it had and how it could be treated are of secondary importance to the micro-sociologist. Of greater concern is the way such attitudes came to be conceived as they did. Attitudes towards the 'abnormal' differ between social contexts. In her study of young adults released from mental subnormality hospitals in California, Mercer (1965) found considerable variation in parents' willingness to accept their children into the home again. In a later study (Mercer, 1973), she found that referral rates for psychological examination varied fivefold between schools.

The attitudes of the labellers and the role of supposedly irrelevant contingencies have come under closer critical scrutiny. Those who deal with deviants in a routine way – policemen, magistrates, psychologists and so forth – are thought to develop their own preferred ways of working and 'commonsense' stereotyping. This produces its own ideology, a mental set appropriate for performing the role. This shared approach will determine the kinds of people perceived and treated as deviant.

The effect of labelling on the deviant's sense of identity has also become a source of greater concern. The act of being perceived to be abnormal may well bring about changes in the way the individual conceives of himself. In a study of partially sighted adults entering rehabilitation agencies in the United States, Scott (1969) found that the solicitous attitudes of the staff made life more difficult for their clients. They were treated as if they were blind and encouraged to develop more dependent relationships.

> Strong pressures are often exerted upon them to begin to think of themselves as blind. These pressures sometimes take the form of admonitions to 'face the facts'. More often, however, they are insidious, resulting subtly from the reactions of medical and welfare specialists, friends, family members and even the impaired person himself to the new label that has been applied to him.
> (Scott, 1969, p. 71)

In this way, the attitudes of the individual may become more handicapping than the original disability.

Recent evaluative studies in the mainstreaming of mentally retarded pupils have emphasized these reflexive aspects of special educational needs (Jones et al., 1977; Gottlieb, 1980). The teacher and the social context he creates are seen as crucial to the adjustment and achievements of the child. The Warnock Report (HMSO, 1978) acknowledges that the knowledge and interpersonal skills of the teacher play an important part in the development of a child with special needs. In examining the assessment procedure, they recommend that the relationship of the child and teacher should be investigated in certain circumstances. Yet the main tenor of their recommendations is that the needs of the child should be of prime consideration.

According to my research, classroom observation by psychologists is almost non-existent, especially with older pupils.

Neither profession is enthusiastic about the idea. Many psychologists operate what they refer to as a 'Fire Brigade' service, attending to crises and giving objective tests. They may recently have been under pressure to spend more time liaising with headteachers, and giving them support on a preventative basis. But they find teachers suspicious and entry into the classroom difficult.

Though a few teachers expect psychologists to give an objective view and so indirectly help the child, most want their aid in making the child more manageable. They think of psychologists as secretive and are dismissive of their reports. They dislike the prospect of being observed dealing with difficult children. There is a widespread feeling that 'problem children', children who are 'really abnormal', 'really thick' and so on, should not be the concern of the ordinary teacher. They take up too much time, and the teachers argue that they were never trained to work with them. It thus seems 'unfair' that their competence in this area should be assessed. They would not want to utilize the period of ascertainment to re-evaluate their own skills and attitudes. The prime object of referral is getting rid of a child who does not fit into the working routines of the school or who otherwise threatens its smooth running. They know little of the methods or populations of the schools to which the children are sent. Referral is 'an act of blind faith' so far as the future of the child is concerned, 'another weapon in the armoury' for the schools. From this perspective, psychologists, doctors, social workers and 'the man from county hall' are perceived as a series of 'blocks' on justified teacher initiatives. The last thing many of them would want is that these outsiders should actively investigate their classroom behaviour.

As a result, many important details of teacher-pupil relations are withheld from the official assessment. This may be because the teacher is genuinely unaware of the social context he is creating. There may be a gulf between what he intends to happen and the effect he is actually having on a class and the teacher might never realize. It could also be that in writing a report that concentrates on the needs of the child, the teacher is simply playing language games with the psychologist. Unless the psychologist knows what the classroom reality of the child is like, he has little way of checking. For their part, the heads would like to retain all possible freedom of manoeuvre in their dealings with troublesome children. And psychologists who have built up 'good relations' with the staff may find themselves implicated in the teachers' role as agents of social control. In order to preserve their own power as legitimators of definitions, psychologists might want to reduce areas of ambiguity, rather than widen them through independent observation.

In cases where teachers and psychologists concur in wanting a child to be transferred to a special school but the parents object, there is considerable variation in the parents' ability to withstand official pressures. The more articulate probably have a greater advantage, and the psychologists might even bring them into some of the decision-making procedures. For others, there is hardly even an attempt to treat them as the 'partners' that Warnock recommended. This suggests further inconsistencies in the processing of these children.

Teachers, headteachers, psychologists and parents act as an 'audience' to the labelling of the child. They are rarely passive or impartial and they all play a part in the way the child learns about his identity. In this sense, labels like 'partially sighted', 'maladjusted' and so on cannot be considered objective statements, indicating some sort of unitary phenomenon, to be located within the child. They are aspects of the social groups that provide them. These four case studies examine the importance of the audience when appropriate schooling for children with special needs is discussed. Two show instances of where children were transferred to special schools, one where there was a positive effort to 'integrate' and another where a move to segregate was allowed to lapse. Between them, they illustrate the power and preoccupations of teacher, headteacher, psychologist and parent. And they all demonstrate that the outcome of such processes would have been difficult, if not impossible, to predict, if only because of the reflexive aspects of special educational needs.

First case study: Philip

This first case study would seem to illustrate the distinction drawn by some writers (e.g., Meighan, 1981) that teachers are more likely to tolerate sensory impairment than deviant behaviour or low attainment. This would appear to be somewhat of an oversimplification. There are wide variations of response to the whole range of special educational needs. As one partially sighted adult remarked, 'Teachers like to think they are bothered. . . . Except for one or two they are not really bothered.' An assistant education officer would seem to have corroborated this when he suggested that many teachers felt untrained and so unable to help those with severe sight problems. Yet in most cases, he found it possible to talk them into making an attempt. The form that teacher response takes would seem to be crucial to effective integration, yet so far there have been few attempts to chart the effects of teacher-pupil interaction in the classroom on pupil handicap.

Philip was an able nine-year-old who suffered from congenital cataracts. He had had eight operations on each eye and though sight in one was sufficient for him to read ink print, an infection in the other had caused complete impairment. He was resilient and outgoing. His parents had bought him his own child-sized motorbike and they were insistent that he should stay at the local junior school. The assistant education officer responsible for special education concurred. There were no units or residential schools in the county and the cost of out-of-county provision had risen sharply. Following Warnock, he had made his own survey of schooling for the 'severely partially sighted' and had concluded that all children who could read ink print and who were neither exceptionally able nor ESN should be integrated. This would benefit the children socially and, even in cases where expensive electronic aids and peripatetic teachers were required, it would save the county a considerable amount of money. The numbers of visually impaired children would be small enough to permit the assistant education officer to monitor each case individually.

In the event, Philip's teacher had been lent the electronic aid, but while his classroom was being rebuilt, the class was temporarily rehoused in the gym, and the aid was in its original cardboard box. There were no plugs near the working area and Philip's teacher, Mr. Black, assured me that Philip had not wanted to use it after the first month. The teacher had not heard of any teacher for the partially sighted and he had never made use of the peripatetic teacher in remedial reading for Philip. This teacher called at the school for half an hour, once a week, but the service was due to be withdrawn altogether at the end of the year, due to 'cut-backs'. Mr. Black thought that Philip was 'very bright', but he did not know about county policy for able partially sighted children and had never requested an intelligence test. It would have appeared that there had been a culpable failure of communications and that resources were not being used as they had been intended. But this draws attention to the social context of the classroom and the importance of the teacher.

Mr. Black was a large confident man who had entered teaching in middle life. He had a booming voice and his presence dominated the school hall. He had an open classroom and allowed the children to wander round, even when addressing them as a group. The class worked to an integrated day and they had individual programmes. It was rare for neighbours or members of the same small group to be using the same book at any one time. Yet there were definite limits to pupil freedom. The class was divided into four mixed-ability groups – green, yellow, pink and blue – which each worked on a subject for a thirty-minute block of time. Blue would be on arithmetic assignments, while pink used their writing workbooks and so forth. The programme each child followed was prepared in advance, so when Philip had finished exercise 10, he would be directed to exercise 12. Reading was managed by a class library arranged according to another colour scheme. White stickers corresponded to a reading age between seven and eight, red stickers between eight and nine. The book that Philip had chosen to read was too difficult for him technically, but it was about the Wright brothers, and Mr. Black had let him attempt it because he knew of Philip's interest in machines.

All the children in the class had their own folders. Inside were duplicated sheets with a block of number squares. Philip would normally be on 'white' books and when he started the book he turned to the 'white' page and put a line round the number of the book. When he had finished it, he put a line through the number. In this way, books could be chosen by the children according to their interests and yet within their reading ability. With reading ages tested termly and each child listened to once a week or more, Mr. Black kept a firm check on progress. The movement round the classroom was far from random. It had developed a pattern or routine which would incorporate exceptional needs.

This was also true of the kind of group activity, referred to by most teachers as 'chalk and talk'. On discovering the extent of Philip's difficulties, Mr. Black had abandoned the use of a blackboard. He had had an overhead projector installed in his room and, while the rest of the children sat in front of the screen, Philip stood by the projector and watched Mr. Black as he wrote on the celluloid. If there were notes to be copied, Philip was free to move to a different table, so he could sit next to someone whose writing he could read. As Mr. Black said, 'Philip arrived in this class a handicapped child, but now he's the same as all the rest, except for his sight.'

Philip had in fact arrived with no reading abilities at all and Mr. Black had protested to his headteacher about having to teach him. He described himself as a 'bolshie character' and he persuaded the head to contact county hall. The response had been immediate and encouraging. A letter was sent from the assistant education officer, promising an electronic aid and his continued support, if the school attempted to 'integrate' Philip. As it happened, Mr. Black had just started an Open University reading course and he started an individual course of reading. With the parents' blessing, he kept Philip behind after school for ten minutes every night for a year and a half, and his reading was now at about age eight. He had been a good student, who picked up ideas quickly, and when a book interested him he could manage something harder.

The relationship had been far from simple, even so, especially at the beginning. As by chance again though, Mr. Black's previous career had been as a social worker. He had worked with handicapped people 'for twenty years' and if ever Philip threw a tantrum or said he could not do a piece of work 'because he couldn't see', Mr. Black refused to give way. At times, there had been 'bloody confrontations' and Mr. Black had often threatened Philip with a smack if he wanted to give up, but the relationship had never been put in serious jeopardy.

The electronic aid – a closed circuit TV scanner which could magnify print and convert it from black on white to white on black – did not arrive for a whole year. In that time, the foundations had been laid. But when it did arrive Philip had used it for every possible kind of assignment and the progress, in terms of his improved reading age and his confidence, was remarkable. After a month, Philip realized how far he had come and how much more he could do without it. He told Mr. Black that he now felt it 'showed him up' among the other children. So it was put back in its box and had stayed there. Philip knew he could get it out again whenever he wanted, but he felt some stigma attached to its use and wanted to be independent of it. Mr. Black had read Goffman's *Stigma* (1968) and knew enough about 'the moral career' and handicapped adults to encourage this step.

Mr. Black and the head were aware of the progress Philip had made and of the responsibility Mr. Black had had for this. Yet in focusing on Philip's reading age, his visual defects, his strengths of character and so forth, they had not realized the effect of the classroom context. Even within the same school, there was not another teacher who had taken a specialized course in reading or who had extensive experience of handicap. In a different school there would not have been a head who had organized a reading experience scheme or an individualized maths and writing structure. This gave the children permission to show their individual differences and preferences without stigma. Philip's two previous teachers had not realized that the corollary of such freedom was that a teacher should check up on children and do something for them on an individualized basis if they were failing. Mr. Black was a teacher who could permit 'irregularities' like children moving round the classroom 'if they couldn't see' and who would also impose definite boundaries in terms of time, space and academic standards, where these were appropriate.

Philip had been a 'good pupil' and in concentrating on the child's capabilities Mr. Black and the head felt quite confident that, provided his sight did not deteriorate further, he would continue to do as well. Yet just as Philip's previous teachers had failed to provide Philip with a satisfactory education, it was possible that his next ones might feel insufficiently trained or confident to help. Peripatetic remedial help was being withdrawn from the school and a comprehensive school might not have staff capable of stimulating an able child with particular learning difficulties.

Mr. Black said, 'If Philip had been a dimbo, I would never have tried. It would not have been worth the effort.' In the class he was about to take over next year, there was a child with learning and behavioural difficulties. Previously, this child had been having daily support from a part-time teacher and she could have looked forward to peripatetic help in the junior department. But because of the 'cut-backs' such auxiliary help was being withdrawn. The head had therefore referred the child for psychological assessment, with Mr. Black's approval. The psychologist had come to the school, met the parents and assessed the child, and the child was now to be sent to an ESN(M) school in a city almost twenty miles away. She had not spoken to Mr. Black or observed the kind of classroom he might have been able to construct for this retarded child. Thus a teacher with particular interests, attitudes and capabilities had been able to create a classroom setting which had provided one child with a genuine experience of 'normalization'. Under pressure from wider political and financial changes, he had been a party to the segregation of another. Boundaries between the normal and the abnormal had been redrawn at a local level and in neither case had there been a critical examination of how much the teacher could benefit the child.

Second case study: Gillian

In formal administrative terms, the power of the head to remove children with special needs is hedged about with a number of restrictions. It is no longer legal for a child to be expelled. The head may suspend and may set no time limit to his return. But he is normally required to advise parents of their power of appeal to the governors or managers. He himself must inform the board and have their support. On the board, there will probably be a representative from county hall. If a child is suspended *sine die*, it becomes the LEA's responsibility to find suitable provision. It is also the LEA's responsibility to provide special education and their legal terms of reference have always been very broad. If the administrators or psychologists feel that the reason for a suspension reflected inadequacies in the school, it is possible for them to call for an inspection. This is rarely done, however.

Recently, it has become more common for psychologists to discuss children who have special needs before the formal referral process is broached. This is one of the main recommendations of Warnock. In cases where the head presses for a child to be removed, it is quite possible for psychologists to block or delay this. They may suggest alternative strategies and say they will follow the case up in six months' time. This makes it more difficult for the head to press for suspension as he has still not exhausted all the other possibilities. But it may commit the psychologist to more definitive action once six months has passed. This ensures that the exclusion of these children is a time-consuming and an apparently well thought out process.

In practical terms, however, the head is left with considerable latitude. He makes the formal referral. He writes or at least countersigns the school's referral sheet, the SE.1. And there is much he can do in a covert way to increase the pressure on the child and the school's psychological services. If his staff are under pressure, and he himself finds that his own sense of control is threatened, there is a great deal he can do to precipitate a crisis. How crucial his role can be is illustrated in the second case study.

Gillian presented as a shy girl of average ability when she arrived in the second year of a comprehensive. Two weeks after the start of the third year, her mother informed the school that she had spent the weekend in hospital after taking an overdose. Although the girl was discharged with no follow-up from the hospital, the school counsellor, educational psychologist, family therapy unit, two social workers and her doctor were subsequently involved with Gillian and her family. It appeared to the head that as soon as significant progress was made with any agency, her mother withdrew Gillian and applied to another. Halfway through the third year, her concentration and behaviour began to deteriorate in school. She began to throw tantrums. The first of these took place when her class was taken by a student teacher. The whole group had got out of hand, and in these circumstances, the behaviour of individual children normally would have been 'explained' in terms of the teacher's inexperience. Gillian was too 'visible' for this to happen. She was sent to the head following such misbehaviour and while most children could be induced to accept responsibility for their actions or at least cry, Gillian disconcerted the head by 'looking blank and saying nothing'. The head was too sophisticated to pass judgement on this response and her journey from counsellor to psychologist to family therapy. But he did feel, 'You just can't get through to her. I get children in here who've been up before the courts, and they all give in. But she just looks straight through you.'

By the start of the fourth year, a rather bulky file had begun to accumulate in the head's office. Among the information it contained was a psychologist's assessment. This stated that she was a child of above-average ability with a Weschler Intelligence Scale for Children score of 135. Yet she was put in the lowest maths set alongside children who had difficulties with subtraction and multiplication. The reason for this was of course strategic. She had missed a lot of school and was disruptive, so she was not considered for the upper sets. The teachers in the other low-ability sets could not manage her. The teacher of the bottom set had a small group and a reputation for being experienced and sympathetic. In his relationship with Gillian, he proved also to be obstinate. For a term everything went well, with Gillian doing the same simple sums the rest of the class did. Then an argument blew up about some writing on the desk. Writing on desks was endemic in the school. Elvis had just died and his name had appeared in the violet ink that Gillian used. Gillian refused to admit she had done this and refused to rub the words off the desk. For a week the argument persisted. Then Gillian ran out of the lesson. She was sent to the head and he too was unable to get a 'reasonable' answer out of her. He reminded her of how she had had a lot of problems at the school in the past and that she could always rely on him. But if she ran out of lessons again she would have to be expelled. She was excused the maths teacher's lessons for a week. At the end of that period, the same argument blew up with the same teacher and he insisted she clean the handwriting off the table. She refused and she was sent to stand outside the head's office. Rather than face the consequences, she truanted and stayed out all night. She was expelled. She was taken into care and sent to a social services assessment centre. She ran away several times and stayed out overnight. While she had been at the comprehensive the psychologist had explicitly stated she was not maladjusted. After her stay at the assessment centre, it was decided she was. She stayed in a maladjusted school for a term and they found her too difficult to cope with. So she ended her schooling in a community home.

If Gillian's mother had not seen fit to move her from one agency to another, she might have had some chance of appearing 'normal' to the head. As it was, misdemeanours for which other children would have been given a telling off or a detention were magnified out of all proportion. And at the time of the handwriting incident, Gillian's mother had at last exhausted all outside help. Her mother had previously informed the head that Gillian was 'epileptic' or 'schizophrenic'. There was now no one with whom the head could share responsibility. Unable to develop a productive relationship, he had retreated to making threats. And when she stayed out all night, the head felt he had thereby been relieved of all responsibility. He could carry out his threat with impunity.

The staff only got to hear about the suspension indirectly. The head was not alone in not being able to 'get through to her', but several staff had in fact been able to form quite strong relationships with her. Yet it would have been unthinkable for them to have openly questioned his decision. Their authority was implicated in the struggle. The governors could not have objected. Gillian had had a history of unsuccessful psychiatric treatment and her tantrums and suicide attempt made her appear plainly disturbed. The psychologist would not have heard about the behaviour of the head or the maths teacher except from Gillian, and few psychologists seem to take the child's view of such matters seriously. Even if the psychologist had objected, there was little she could do. The child might have been subject to an unreasonable degree of pressure, but by running away, she had put herself in the wrong. Her exclusion was a *fait accompli*, and it was abetted by the swift action of the education welfare officer and social worker in placing her on a care order. An inspection would have revealed little wrong in the school's general organization. When social organizations draw the line between normal and abnormal behaviour, they often do so for strategic reasons. These may include the peace of mind of those who lead those organizations. The head may have felt himself to be powerless in this situation but in reality he had an unreasonable amount of power. And the outcome for Gillian was harmful.

Third case study: Simon

Aaron Cicourel (1974) refers to the group of professions that control access to deviant identities as 'gatekeepers'. He characterizes them as constituting a special mutually dependent relationship with deviants. If no one was defined as a criminal, there would be no policemen. If no one was defined as ESN, there would be no need for psychologists. This sounds a superficial argument, for if there were no criminal codes or policemen, all stable social groups would probably have to invent some other way of labelling behaviour it considered anti-social. Yet the force of Cicourel's argument is that the approach of each gatekeeping group conditions the kind of deviance they typically perceive as such. And it also influences the way official records are kept. With police and registrars these are there merely for the official's protection, and where details of a case have no bearing on this they are often neglected.

In the case of children being 'processed' through the special education assessment procedure, the appearance of a proper examination into the child's needs may be more important than a thorough investigation into practical outcomes. The motives of teacher, head and psychologist in pursuing a referral could then legitimately seem irrelevant. Recently the twists and turns in public policy about special schools have put the psychologists into an overtly political position. From having to keep children on long waiting lists, they have had to lead public relations exercises in persuading heads and teachers to keep more children with special needs. Then as the cut-backs have threatened remedial teaching and the fall in the birth rate has menaced the infants department of special schools, they have had to win back support for them.

Few psychologists would seem to enjoy an explicitly political position and their power has more often been exercised through their role as experts in labelling. Warnock encouraged them to reject the idea that children could be categorized according to handicap, but those few who have tried this have found that it diminishes their power. In a fraught case conference the ability to stereotype this child as 'ESN(M)', that child as 'not maladjusted' is a very useful weapon. And it reflects well on the profession. Yet it does hide the fact that psychologists can and do disagree about the criteria on which they take their decisions. Some place a great deal of faith in IQ scores, others very little. Some look for underlying pathology, others for measurable behaviour. Yet while ideological differences within the profession are well know, this is rarely considered in specific assessment decisions. For the teachers and heads, beset by the ambiguities involved in relationships with exceptional children, the expert judgement of the psychologist comes as a release. Whether or not it accurately predicts the best outcome for the child as much as it helps the teaching staff is open to doubt.

Simon certainly appeared to have benefited from the exercise of this sort of power by the psychologist. He entered the comprehensive with no score on the NFER Group Intelligence Test C.D. (NFER, 1977) and a reading age of 6.7. The year tutor and headteacher had an unusually advanced understanding of group-test reliability and of the conditions that obtain for some backward readers in some primary schools. Like most of his peers, Simon reacted positively to the new range of subjects offered, and it was not until the second term that he began to stand out. He had some low-effort grades and was withdrawn for a weekly session with the counsellor. The home was visited, parents informed that Simon might see a psychologist and they were asked if they would help with homework and reading. Simon was tested and the psychologist told the head at a liaison meeting that he was 'a typical ESN(M) pupil'. Simon went to a special school for two years where he became 'much more confident'. He then returned to the comprehensive and is at present preparing to take CSEs. During this time, the head of the special school visited the comprehensive twice and the head of the comprehensive spent a morning at the special school.

This account would correspond with much that is in the written records of Simon's case and it represents a heartening account of a liaison system that is sensitive to changing needs. Yet there are aspects of the case which appear on no records, which show how much of the outcome rested on hidden contingencies. Firstly, Simon had had a very unpleasant time in the last year of his junior school and this seems to have conditioned the view Simon's parents took of his identity. His teacher made the children feel:

> if you were in this teacher's good books, that was fine; but if you weren't, he didn't want to know.
> (Parent)

Simon was kept on the same reading primer all year. When he told his mother, it was not until a few days before the end-of-year parents' evening:

> So I went down when Simon was moving up to the senior school. And I asked him why Simon had been kept on the same book all year and he could give me no answer. He said, 'I've done my best. Simon's either downright lazy or stupid.' I was very upset.

The mother was obviously aware of the possibility that this teacher's attitudes had handicapped her son. She decided not to complain, but the words had made a deep impression on her. When she was told about the referral, she was shocked, but she did not make any difficulties:

> I honestly thought this teacher from the Junior School was right all along. There was back-up there.

Even when the doctor told her there was little medical reason for Simon's 'abnormality', she still did not protest:

> The doctor couldn't see any reason why Simon was like this. He thought it was lack of confidence, because he was quite a healthy child and when he was speaking to him, he didn't get the impression there was anything wrong, you know, anything lacking. I got the impression that the psychologist and doctor were there to help him. It was too much for him at school.

The official records would not show that there was disagreement among the teachers as well. Some saw him as 'definitely unhappy', a boy with 'tremendous problems', who did not have the 'personal resources' to overcome them. Others had quite a different relationship, but because of the political structure of the school, their comments were not invited:

> My particular involvement was in terms of a subject. The power rests with the Head and the Pastoral Team and the S.P.S. I expressed reservations but they weren't taken note of.
> (Teacher)

After a few weeks' counselling, Simon's efforts grades improved and his reading age rose one and a half years to 8.3 (Schonell). The headteacher was informed and he began to think that though Simon was a shy lad, without many friends, his problem seemed to have been a temporary one, caused by changing schools. This explanation might have satisfied another psychologist who had less faith in IQ scores and different political pressures on her. But these aspects of the psychologist's role were hidden from the other actors. This case coincided with the publication of Section 10 of the 1976 Education Act and the area education offices, schools' psychological services and special school heads had good reason to fear that the Education Committee might take immediate action to cut special education funding. The psychologist informed the counsellor, with whom there was a very good relationship, that it was imperative to show long waiting lists. When Simon was discovered to be having extreme difficulties, the counsellor suggested referral. So, because of decisions taken at county hall and Westminster and the school's good liaison with SPS a child who, in another 'less caring' school, might have been left to 'sink or swim' was referred and quickly seen.

When, a few weeks later, the head suggested that Simon stay on at the comprehensive, the psychologist had already tested him and arranged a visit to the special school. She did not dispute the head's definition directly but she openly categorized Simon as 'a typical ESN(M) child'.

In point of fact, this projection turned out to have been misleading, but not for any reason that a formal examination could have predicted. Simon was among the top three or four children in his class. He had always objected to the idea of going to a school for 'dopes' and though he allowed his mother to over-ride his judgement, he worked hard to 'neutralize' the label (Sykes and Matza, 1957). It could be argued the psychologist's certainty about Simon's abnormality acted with the teachers' needs to have their own ambiguities about Simon's identity resolved, and that this coincidence of personal and political needs played a stronger part in the referral decision than any consideration of Simon's needs. Even had these needs been discovered, any predication would have been unable to cope with the reflexive aspect of special needs. Luckily the episode turned out well and Simon was able to 'neutralize' his deviant identity. Yet if he had reacted to the placement with despair, as so many children do (Younghusband et al., 1970), there would probably have been little question of his return.

Fourth case study: Adrian

The Warnock Report explicitly invokes the concept of 'Parents as Partners' and it would seem that psychologists spend more time with parents than they used to. Ten years ago, it was not unknown for parents to be told to attend a meeting at the school, whose purpose they did not understand, to be interviewed by a panel and informed that attendance by their child at a special school might only be for a year, while in fact such temporary stays were quite rare. Nowadays, parents have to grant their permission before psychologists examine a child and they are often told that notes of this meeting will be taken and a further case conference held. In some instances, parents are shown the SE4 form, though I have never met anyone to whom this has happened. In others, parents are invited to attend the case conference. These are not always all they appear, though. The issues may already have been decided at an earlier meeting by the professionals, and all the parents see is a 'performance'.

If parents reject the first suggestion about an examination, further pressure may be put on the parents by others, including the education welfare officer, and suspension might be threatened. If the parents agree to examination and reject its findings, similar pressures may be brought to bear. In this case it takes determination and an inside knowledge of the rules for parents to carry on their fight. This might not be too difficult for a doctor or another articulate member of the dominant social groups, as this head illustrates:

> I must say he was a very lovable little lad, but his learning was very, very poor and the whole reflection was bad. The parents went to their own child psychologist, privately. They spent quite a considerable amount of money. He said the boy was university material. They were a little dissatisfied and they moved house. Now he's at a private school.

Without these advantages, the parents' power to pursue definitions of their child's normality in opposition to the school and its gatekeepers might be considerably more circumscribed, but it still exists, as this last case study illustrates.

Even before Adrian left his primary school, the comprehensive had been notified that he was an immature, slow-learning pupil, who had been disruptive in his last year. He failed to score on the NFER Group Verbal Reading Quotient and his reading age was more than four years lower than his chronological age. Both his parents had been at special school and, as one had risen to the board of his firm by studying hard at night school after he had left, they both felt suspicious of assessment procedures.

Adrian broke his arm in his first term at the comprehensive. This made it difficult for teachers to keep him occupied and this factor often makes it easy for a pupil to drift into deviance (Sharp and Green, 1975). He could not read independently, write or draw and he had already learned how to disrupt lessons. When challenged about his misbehaviour, he reacted with a series of temper tantrums. Misbehaviour by Adrian and his friends in the lesson of one notably incompetent teacher, culminated in song books being thrown about the room. It was decided that Adrian probably 'needed' a less demanding environment with a less complex timetable, fewer staff and a smaller pupil-teacher ratio. This was agreed at an informal level with the psychologist, who suggested either an ESN(M) school or the local unit for disruptive pupils, whichever proved the more suitable after a full examination.

Adrian's behaviour did not improve after this decision had been taken and a teacher visited the home to ask the parents' permission for a full examination. Mrs. Smith said she did not like the idea of him going to a special school because she had not been happy at hers, but if this was for the best, she would agree. A letter was then sent asking her to meet the psychologist with Adrian at a certain time. Mrs. Smith did not reply and she did not come. Another teacher visited, on the assumption that Mrs. Smith might not be able to read. Mrs. Smith said she would help Adrian with his homework and tell him to mend his behaviour, and that she would definitely attend the next meeting. Meanwhile his behaviour grew even worse and this time the deputy head was subjected to a tantrum. Mrs. Smith did not attend the next meeting. The education welfare officer visited, pointed out the seriousness of the position and got her to sign a written document giving her permission for Adrian to go to the disruptive unit. This would not have required the full special education assessment procedure. The head of the unit stipulated that all the parents visit the unit before their child would be accepted, and Mrs. Smith failed to keep the appointment made for her. Adrian kept coming to the comprehensive. But from that time, there was a slight improvement in Adrian's behaviour. The arm came out of plaster and he started to join in the 'normal' class activities. He began to wear school uniform. And his tantrums declined. He settled to work and the referral was allowed to lapse.

Two years later, Adrian was described by one of his teachers as, 'One of the lads. There's no difference between him and the others.' His reading age had improved considerably and though much of his work was probably beyond him, this did not make him unusual. He was, at least in some minimal sense, 'coping'. His parents never explicitly resisted the referral. But as so much of the procedure rests on active consent, if not sincere co-operation, the parents could enforce their view of Adrian's normality simply by stonewalling.

Conclusion

When teachers and heads initiate referrals, it may be for a number of different reasons. They might perceive a child to be plainly unhappy or obviously 'abnormal'. They may think there is strong medical evidence that there is 'something wrong', and feel unable to help. They might feel that the child is a menace to the stability of the social system for which they are responsible. Micro-sociology emphasizes the diversity of audience responses. Structural explanations which show segregation as a form of class or ethnic repression might have a general validity, but they do not do justice to the full complexity of individual cases. Direct observation of the role of the audience would suggest that even if there were no consistent prejudice at work, heads and teachers can hardly be trusted to be impartial. The SE procedure rests on written evidence from the professionals alone. It focuses on the needs of the child and it allows the needs of the heads, teachers and psychologists to remain hidden.

The head will almost inevitably have other organizational interests to be considered. Erikson (1964) draws attention to the possibility that, when labels are being considered, the social system is in effect determining the precise form of its boundaries. There are limits to acceptable pupil behaviour and teacher responsibility and labelling re-establishes the lines these will take. As the highest authority in a particular social system, this is a moment of great political importance for the headteacher, and through his decisions he indicates his own policy and his support for his staff.

Psychologists do not make routine investigations of teacher behaviour. They do not examine the way everyday working conditions and discipline are structured in the classroom. Instead they liaise with the teachers, and through their objective tests and written evidence they legitimate the idea that the child is and should be the first consideration. How accurate their predictions are is open to doubt. It seems strange that the justification for segregating pupils is that this is to satisfy special needs, when so many comparative studies of children with special needs in ordinary and special schools have been so lukewarm about the value of special schools (Goldstein, Moss and Jordon, 1965; Jamieson, Parlett and Pocklington, 1977, etc.).

Parents who can be trusted to be 'intelligent' and 'not make a fuss' are offered 'performances' in the name of partnership. Those who are not to be trusted can often be persuaded. Those who object are subjected to visits from a succession of forceful and articulate members of the gatekeeping professions. Even so, it is still possible for those who possess inside knowledge to resist.

In these circumstances, the suggestion of the Warnock Committee that headteachers and psychologists are suitable candidates for the role of 'Named Persons' to parents of school-aged children seems either naîve or conspiratorial. The supposedly hypocritical Victorians at least recognized that teachers might show bias in getting rid of their slow children. The Report of the Department Committee on Defective and Epileptic Children (HMSO, 1898) recommended that a medical certificate be the *sine qua non* of segregated schooling, so that medical officers could provide some sort of check on teachers' powers. Doctors would seem to play a much less significant part in the transfer of school-age children and, where matters of educational need are supposed to be considered, this sounds only reasonable. But psychologists, who are being encouraged to disregard categories of handicap and who may feel unease about the iatrogenic aspects of concepts like IQ and maladjustment, hardly seem in a strong enough position to defend the children's interests against those of its school.

In the last ten years, various alternatives to the concept of 'Named Persons' have been suggested. Instead of the professionals choosing among themselves, Dr. John Cash and 'Miff' wanted the parents to have someone they felt they could trust (Face to Face Conference, Warwick University, 1980). Wolf Wolfensberger initiated the idea of 'citizen advocates', who could befriend an individual who was mentally handicapped and also help them fight for their civil and welfare rights, should the need arise (Gottlieb,

1980). Szasz (1970) argued that placement in mental hospitals and special schools was often a cynical exercise in dumping unwanted people. He suggested that decisions should be made by a tribunal, with a 'prosecuting psychiatrist' who would argue on behalf of the state or an official institution and a 'defense psychiatrist' who would be paid to secure the least onerous 'result' for his client. And one Midlands psychiatrist has dismantled his local child guidance service, making a clear division between child psychiatry and educational psychology. He has also closed a local psychiatric unit and made allowance for children between the ages of twelve and sixteen to refer themselves, providing their doctor agrees to this (McTurk, private communication, 1980).

All these schemes suffer the same disadvantage: they depend on the goodwill of people who may not be directly affected by the outcome. Many of the parents and children might never get to hear of their rights unless this were made mandatory. Parents should be informed of the date and place of the case conference and invited to bring along a friend or advocate, who would be allowed to ask questions on their behalf. This friend or advocate should also be allowed access to written evidence like the SE4 and previous school reports, and also bring along 'witnesses' of his own.

It was not the intention of this chapter to suggest that segregation from mainstream education is always wrong for the child. It may be the lesser of two evils. And it might provide the child with access to educational experiences and relationships that really are special. Yet it seems a point neglected by psychological approaches to assessment procedure that such is the diversity of reactions to 'deviant' pupils that selection for special schools and the outcome of a special education can be quite arbitrary. The professionals have an almost complete monopoly on the linguistic and symbolic power. They could act in good faith and still harm the child. They could act in defense of their own interests and neither parents nor children need ever know. The use of advocates will not affect the underlying disability. But it would enable someone with a private concern for the well-being of an individual child to investigate the personal bias and the public needs of the rest of the audience. If handicap and deviance relate as much to the micro context of the school and the family as they do to the child, this would at least make the procedures for excluding children with special needs from ordinary schools less haphazard and less hypocritical.

Note

This article is based on research undertaken in and around a Midlands market town for the M.Ed. dissertation: *Transfer to Special Schools – a Sociological Critique* (Birmingham University, 1981, unpublished). This involved a participant observation study of more than 20 children, whose special educational needs were discussed over a two-year period in liaison between teachers, headteachers, psychologists and social workers. In order to further elucidate variations in audience response, an open-ended questionnaire survey of 149 teachers, 6 psychologists and 20 doctors and semi-structured interviews of 17 teachers, 6 psychologists, 6 doctors and 6 pupils or ex-pupils of special schools were also carried out.

References

Cicourel, A.V. (1974) 'Police practices and official records', in Turner, R. *Ethnomethodology*

Erikson, K.T. (1964) 'Notes on the study of deviance', in Becker, H.S. *The Other Side: Perspectives on Deviance*, New York: The Free Press

Goffman, E. (1968) *Stigma*, Penguin

Goldstein, H., J.W. Moss and L.J. Jordon (1965) *Efficacy of Special Class Training in the Development of Mentally Retarded Children*, University of Illinois Press

Gottlieb, J. (1980) *Educating Mentally Retarded Persons in the Mainstream*, Baltimore: University Park Press

HMSO (1898) *Report of the Department Committee on Defective and Epileptic Children*

HMSO (1978) *Special Educational Needs*, Committee of Enquiry: Chairman: Mrs. H.M. Warnock

Jamieson, M., M.R. Parlett and K. Pocklington (1977) *Towards Integration*, NFER

Jones, R.L., J. Gottlieb, S. Gaskin and R.K. Yoshida (1977) 'Evaluating mainstreaming programmes: models, caveats, considerations, guidelines', *Exceptional Children*, Volume 44, pp. 588–604

Kitsuse, J.I. (1962) 'Societal reaction to deviant behaviour', reprinted in Becker, H.S. (1964) *The Other Side: Perspectives on Deviance*, New York: The Free Press

McTurk, P. private communication, 1980

Meighan, R. (1981) (ed) *A Sociology of Educating*, Holt Saunders

Mercer, J.R. (1965) 'Career patterns of persons labelled as mentally retarded', reprinted in Rubington, E. and M.S. Weinburg (1977) *Deviance: the Interactionist Perspective*, 2nd edition, Macmillan

Mercer, J.R. (1973) *Labelling the Mentally Retarded*, University of California Press

Scott, R.A. (1969) *The Making of Blind Men*, Russell Sage Foundation

Sharp, R. and A. Green (1975) *Education and Social Control*, Routledge & Kegan Paul

Sykes, G.M. and D. Matza (1957) 'Techniques of neutralization: a theory of delinquency', *American Sociological Review*, Volume 22, pp. 667–670

Szasz, T.S. (1970) *Ideology and Insanity*, Calder and Boyars

Younghusband, E. (1970) *Living with Handicap*, National Child Bureau

Further reading

Becker, H.S. (1964) *The Other Side: Perspectives in Deviance*, New York: The Free Press

Berger, P. and T. Luckman (1967) *The Social Construction of Reality*, Allen Lane

Bernstein, I.L., W.R. Kelly and P.A. Doyle (1977) 'Societal reactions to deviants', *American Sociological Review*, Volume 42, pp. 743–755

Bittner, E. (1967) 'The police on skid row: a study of peace keeping', *American Sociological Review*, Volume 32, pp. 699–715

Brophy, J.E. and T.L. Good (1974) Student-teacher relationships, Holt

Davitz, J, L. Davitz and I. Lorge (1964) 'Terminology and concepts in mental retardation', Teachers College, Columbia University, New York

Egerton, R. (1967) *The Cloak of Competence*, University of California Press

Foster, G.G., J. Ysseldyke and J.H. Reese (1975) 'I wouldn't have seen it, if I hadn't believed it', *Exceptional Children*, Volume 41, pp. 469–473

Garfinkel, H. (1956) 'Conditions of successful degradation ceremonies', *American Journal of Sociology*, Volume 61, pp. 420–424

Halliwell, M.D. and B. Spain (1977) 'Spina bifida children in ordinary schools', *Child Care Health and Development*, Volume 3, pp. 389–406

HMSO (1971) DES Survey 15, *Slow Learners in Secondary Schools*

Hewitt, J.P. (1979) *Self and Society*, Allyn and Bacon

Junkala, J. (1977) 'Teachers' assessments and team decisions', *Exceptional Children*, Volume 44, pp. 31–32

Lemert, E.M. (1967) *Human Deviance, Social Problems and Social Control*, Prentice Hall

Lofland, J. (1969) *Deviance and Identity*, Prentice Hall

Matza, D. (1969) *Becoming Deviant*, Prentice Hall

Nash, R. (1973) *Classrooms Observed*, Routledge & Kegan Paul

Rock and McIntosh (1974) *Deviance and Social Control*, Tavistock

Roberts, B. (1977) 'Treating children in secondary schooling', *Educational Review*, Volume 29, pp. 204–212

Rubington, E. and M.A. Weinburg (1973) *Deviance – the Interactionist Perspective*, 2nd edition, Macmillan

Salvia, J., G. Clark and J. Yssledyke (1973) 'Teacher retention of stereotypes of exceptionality', *Exceptional Children*, Volume 40, pp. 651–652

Salvia, J. and M. Ysseldyke (1978) *Assessment in Special and Remedial Education*, Houghton Mifflin

Schur, E.M. (1971) *Labelling Deviant Behaviour*, Harper & Row

Thomas (1978) *The Social Psychology of Childhood Disability*, Cambridge University Press

Tomlinson, S. (1979) 'Decision making in special education (E.S.N.(M)) with some reference to the children of immigrant parentage', Ph.D. thesis, Warwick University

CHAPTER 8

MALADJUSTMENT IN THE CONTEXT OF LOCAL AUTHORITY DECISION MAKING

by Ray Woolfe

Introduction

The philosophy underlying the research reported in this chapter is that the way in which we perceive the social world is dependent upon the conceptual structure we employ.[1] It is contended that this statement is relevant in understanding the nature of maladjustment and the problem of the maladjusted child and that, if one breaks away from the traditional approach to this subject, a number of valuable insights emerge.

In practice, the paradigm which has dominated thinking in the field of maladjustment has been that employed by doctors and psychologists. It has derived from the positivistic philosophy of medicine and psychology and the experimental research design with which this is related. The model which has resulted has rendered maladjustment as equivalent to an individual illness or pathological condition which has specific symptoms and recognized forms of treatment.

The weakness of this approach, however, is that it assumes maladjustment can be identified and treated with the same degree of precision as a physical condition. It is argued here that this is not possible because the definition of maladjustment on which it is based takes little or no account of the social context in which a child comes to be labelled maladjusted. This milieu includes the attitudes of professionals working in the field, the way in which individual departments of a local authority relate to each other and the type of facilities which are available to help children. These factors interact to influence the crucial issue as to who is labelled maladjusted and what form of treatment is offered to that person.

If we accept this form of analysis of maladjustment, then attention is shifted away from questions of individual pathology onto the processes by which the label comes to be attached. It is argued that a pattern can be observed which transcends individual needs and can be seen to be rooted in the need of the organization and the professionals who work within it to maintain their own methods of operation and autonomy. The career of the pupil ascertained as maladjusted, and the steps through which he goes before he or she is labelled, have a logic when perceived through this conceptual paradigm that does not exist if the system of schools, clinics and other forms of treatment is seen simply as some kind of rational attempt to deal with the needs of a specific individual. We need not deny that some pupils are emotionally disturbed and need special help to argue that maladjustment is best understood as a social process rather than as an individual pathology.

The research

The research is essentially a case study of one local authority, though there is no reason to believe that its findings cannot be regarded as of more general validity. Its origins lie in the simple fact that many more children are declared to be in need of treatment at schools for the maladjusted than can be accommodated in such institutions. Thus many never receive this treatment. The initial objective had been to compare a group who had been to special schools with one which had not. It was hoped that this would reveal the key factors influencing selection for special-school education. In addition by looking at progress made after leaving school, these developments could, then, be examined in the light of educational, social and medical history.

This early plan was modified as doubt emerged about the validity of dealing with the field of maladjustment and special schools relying solely on the experimental paradigm outlined above. To perceive the problem as initially posed, in terms of a comparison between two discrete groups, children who go and children who do not go to special schools, is to simplify it so much that there is a danger of it ceasing to be meaningful. For example, pupils do not normally attend a special school for the maladjusted for virtually a whole school career from six to sixteen. A child may go at any age for a year or two or even longer, but almost all who spend some time at a special school also spend an even longer amount of time in an ordinary school. The result is that we do not have two discrete groups, but a whole variety of permutations of educational, social and medical influences which impinge upon the child. The pattern is even more complex if we bear in mind the fact that many children who are ascertained as maladjusted spend some time in what used to be callèd approved schools (now community homes) or else local authority children's homes.

The outcome is that the research came more and more to concentrate upon revealing the processes and procedures surrounding the way in which a child comes to be labelled as maladjusted and, therefore, handicapped. What emerges is that in explaining why a particular child is sent to special school while another is not, one must examine not only the needs of the individual child, but also the way in which these interact with the whole welfare superstructure designed to cope with his or her needs. While the formal system may claim to operate according to a rhetoric of meeting individual needs, the reality of the situation is that the need of the organization to maintain itself and the needs of professionals within the organization to maintain viability for their own roles are also important factors in determining the nature of events.

The research was carried out while the author was employed on the administrative staff of an English county local education authority and the nature of the researcher's role had a number of implications. It made possible access to the files of the authority and of its schools, which would not normally have been made available to the research worker. It also gave him easy access to many of the people involved in the decision-making processes in the field of special education. Indeed he was present as an observer at a number of meetings at which formal decisions were taken, although he himself was not involved in or party to the making of those decisions. This intimacy with the workings of the organization made feasible the type of research reported here. It made it possible to examine the processes through which children came to be labelled maladjusted and it facilitated an exploration of the complex interaction between pedagogic, administrative and professional factors as variables in this particular area of educational decision making.

The nature of maladjustment

Maladjustment has always been an elusive condition to define, identify and measure. The term was given official recognition and legal status by the 1944 Education Act, when it was first included as a category of educational handicap. The then Ministry of Education (1946, p. 7) defined maladjusted pupils as pupils who show evidence of emotional instability or psychological disturbance and require special educational treatment in order to effect their personal, social or educational readjustment.

However, this definition is legalistic as well as containing a number of weaknesses. In particular the explanatory concepts of emotional instability and psychological disturbance are themselves problematic and therefore in need of explanation. However, as another Ministry of Education document, the Underwood Report (Ministry of Education, 1955, para. 86) points out, the definition is deliberately not expressed in exact clinical terms. It merely suggests the limits within which maladjustment may be found and attempts to provide a legal cover for those whose task it is to decide on which children shall receive special educational provision. Chazan (1963, p. 30), reviewing postwar theory and practice, points out that

provided it is used not as a medical entity but as an umbrella term which is administratively convenient, there seems little reason for changing a term which now covers such a wide variety of psychological conditions.

This view, however, has by no means been universally shared. For example, Younghusband et al. (1970) accept that the 1945 Handicapped Pupils and School Health Service Regulations represent a major advance in the labelling and categorization of handicapped children in that they move away from identification by defect towards identification by need for special educational treatment. They consider, however, that this development should be continued so as to reflect current knowledge by replacing the category maladjusted with the new categories of 'emotional handicap' and 'severe personality disorder' (p. 207). In complete contrast, another advocate of change, Whitmore (1975, p. 55) stresses the problems and anomalies raised by linking maladjustment 'too closely and too narrowly to mental ill health'. He prefers to talk about 'behaviour problems' rather than unsatisfactory personal relationships or emotional development which is the vocabulary employed by Younghusband et al. Significantly no critique of the present system of labelling challenges the theoretical structure which supports it. So, for example, Whitmore uses the traditional language of psychiatric theory with its medical model of individual pathology and illness (conduct and anxiety disorders, for example) in order to support his views. There would appear to be a contradiction between, on the one hand, rejecting a model of the behaviourally disturbed as mentally ill while, on the other hand, employing a psychiatric vocabulary of motive (Mills, 1940) to support the contention that such a category does exist and is meaningful.

This point reminds us of the powerful role played by psychiatry and psychiatrists in developing the model of maladjustment which is employed in such a taken-for-granted way by practitioners in the field. The fact is that the professional plays a crucial role in defining reality for the client. As Szasz (1974, p. 14) puts it,

> the question, what *is* mental illness? is shown to be inextricably tied to the question, what do psychiatrists *do*?

The idea of the client being ill or having a type of disease, according to Szasz, is one which is highly dependent on the professional ideology of the psychiatrist, which in turn is rooted in the philosophical tradition of positivism and the occupational framework of medicine. Hence there arises a vocabulary of illness, disease, symptoms, treatment, cause, effect and so on.

> The psychoanalytic theory of man was fashioned after the causal-deterministic model of classical physics

says Szasz (1972, p. 21) and he questions the relevance of this model to the analysis and treatment of the mind. Berger (1965) has indicated the way in which the philosophy and methods of psychoanalysis have permeated medical and educational thinking in the USA and become part of our taken-for-granted world. Concepts such as sublimation, the unconscious or the libido have become part of the fund of commonsense everyday knowledge, one aspect of the vocabularies of motive we employ without questioning in explaining and making sense of the world in which we live. It follows that the measurement and assessment techniques and the treatment used in the field of maladjustment are ideologically rooted in the culture of the professionals involved, particularly the psychiatrists. To paraphrase Szasz, one could say that the question, what is maladjustment?, can be shown to be inextricably tied to the question, what do professionals, particularly psychiatrists, do?

In consequence, it is important to examine methods of assessment and classification which are currently being employed. It is useful as we do this to remember that those who would seek to measure maladjustment are faced with two problems. The first is that to measure something accurately it is necessary to have an accurate instrument or tool (a reliability problem) and the second is to be sure that one is in fact measuring what one purports to be measuring (a validity problem). What we in fact find is that just as maladjustment is such an elusive concept to define theoretically, in a similar way serious reservations can be raised against most of the attempts to identify, classify and measure it in operational terms. More specifically, we can raise the question, what happens when a local authority attempts to deal with what it perceives as the problem of maladjustment? In particular we can focus attention upon the question of how the local educational authority in question made manageable and coped with what on the surface appeared to be a highly intractable problem: too many pupils chasing too few special school places.

The process of ascertainment

To do this, it is helpful to introduce the concept of ascertainment. Section 34 of the 1944 Education Act states that it shall be the duty of every LEA to ascertain or discover which children in their area need special educational treatment. The term was, however, often used in the local authority in question as though it were synonymous with certify. Thus, children were sometimes informally described as originally ascertained and eventually 'de-ascertained'. However, in theory the meaning of ascertainment is that the child has been found to be maladjusted and is, therefore, in need of help. In an ideal world one could presume that the number of children ascertained as maladjusted represented the entire cohort of maladjusted children. But in the real world, a local authority creates difficulties for itself if it discovers children for whom help is needed but for whom no appropriate provision is available.

This problem becomes acute, if, as in our particular local authority, the two procedures of ascertainment and placement are the responsibility of different departments. Thus we have a situation in which a health department had been active over many years in screening children for indications of handicap. This had unearthed a substantial reservoir of unmet need. The only way in which the placement agency, which in effect was the educational department, could cope with this situation was to question the validity of the procedures used by the assessing agency. This was done by interpreting ascertainment in a narrowly legalistic manner. It would not readily accept that a child was maladjusted and in need of special educational provision unless he had gone through an elaborate, formal and semi-legal process of ascertainment involving the completion of documents such as form 2HP. This procedure has, according to Younghusband et al. (1970, p. 139), 'widely fallen into disuse', but this statement would not be accurate if applied in this case. It can also be questioned whether the LEA followed the spirit of the Ministry of Education's circular on the subject, to make the administrative arrangements as informal as possible (Ministry of Education, 1961).

What is being argued, therefore, is that the subject of ascertainment and categorization involves more dimensions than the medical-scientific paradigm would suggest. To understand the overall picture, we have to look at a complex inter-relationship of many factors such as the educational facilities available in an area, the knowledge of teachers, the kind of medical and health services which exist and the policy of educational administrators. If one unravels this network, we find in existence a whole series of professional and occupational conflicts of attitudes, values, expectations and constraints. It is through an examination of these that one begins to understand how the practices involved with maladjustment deviate from traditional theoretical accounts of the handicap.

Let us start at the chronological end of the process by giving an example of how an apparently insignificant procedure can assume major importance. Consider the final stages of the ascertainment process as developed in this local authority. The practice was that the medical officer of health wrote to the chief education officer to recommend a child for special educational treatment as maladjusted.[2] The name should then have been submitted on a schedule to the special services sub-committee of the education committee for its approval. This should have been a formality as the recommendation was normally the end of a long process of interdisciplinary co-operation and effort to help a child. But what if the professional administrators in the education department were presented with a situation in which they knew that no suitable educational placement was available? One answer to the problem of fitting the quart of need into the pint pot of places available was to prevent the names presented by the health department from reaching the education committee involved. This was done in two ways. Neither of these practices received publicity. The first was to classify some of the names submitted by the health department as not in any urgent need of special school placement. Thus there existed an unofficial internal document, a form of supplementary register. The legitimation for its existence was that psychiatrists and other health department officials were extravagant in their claims and that the officials in the education department had to represent the reality principle. Once graded in this way, such pupils had a considerably reduced chance of a special school placement. The second practice was to defer placing names before the committee. In one year (year A), for example, twenty children had been recommended by the medical officer of health for special placement, yet, although the committee concerned sat every month except August, not one name was placed in front of it until its October meeting. During the whole of that year, 34 pupils were recommended in the officially prescribed manner, but by March of the following year (year B) only 10 names had been presented to the committee. Of these 10 (whom it should be remembered were the most rapidly dealt with), a gap of at least seven months had elapsed in the case of 4 and a gap of at least three months in all but 1 case. By March of year B, of the other less favoured 24 pupils, 17 had been recommended for at least six months and 5 for at least eleven months. It should be remembered that the gap being talked about was not that between recommendation and the offer of special placement, but between the former and presentation before committee – the statutory prerequisite before placement could be attempted.[3]

Between January of year A and February of year B the committee in question sat thirteen times. Up to October of year A, only 2 names were submitted to it. Twelve names were then presented in October and another 14 in November. The great majority of these persons were recommended for placement during or before year A. We may presume, therefore, that the majority of year B recommendations were not submitted until late in year C. A side-effect of this and the previous practice was that statistics declared annually by the LEA to the DES were not entirely accurate, for they excluded from the list of ascertained pupils first those on the supplementary register and secondly those not yet presented before committee. In other words, ascertainment was defined in precisely that narrowly legal sense which central government documents had attempted to discourage.

The limitations of this data as hard research evidence must be acknowledged. It cannot be supported by reference to publicly available documents. In addition the interpretation presented here can be challenged. For instance, it could be argued that the optimum time to bring a name before committee was at the point negotiations for special school placement appeared to be reaching fruition. However, the response would be to argue that at the very least the observations made demonstrate the enormous power possessed by an administration to frustrate or for that matter to further the implementation of educational decisions taken by practitioners in the field of education, social work and medicine. In addition, at a purely pragmatic level, there is no doubt that a large waiting list exists nationally for special school placements and in the light of this it would be surprising if local authorities did not take adaptive strategies to deal with this contingency.

Supply and demand

Having gained an insight into the mechanics of decision making, we can now move from the end of the process to the beginning in order to fully articulate the factors which influenced the number of pupils ascertained as maladjusted. In practice, two variables were of prime importance. The first was the provision of special educational facilities, the second was the provision of psychiatric, psychological and child guidance services. The influence of the former is a well-recognized fact. As Younghusband et al. (1970, p. 202) put it,

> whether children are ascertained as . . . maladjusted is also influenced by the availability of special school places.

In other words the consequences of an increase in supply is a stimulation of demand. Conversely, if the supply of places is for any reason depressed demand is reduced accordingly.

It does not call for a great deal of imagination to see how this law of supply and demand operated. Unless a psychiatrist was deliberately putting pressure on his own school medical officer or the education department, there was little purpose in recommending special-school educational provision for a particular child when it was well known that none was available or was likely to become available in the near future. It was known that the more conservative was the policy of recommendation, the more likely were other decision-makers to take notice when a child's name *was* put forward. Thus, only the major priority case was ascertained; many other children who attended child guidance clinics, and might well have benefited from some form of special school provision, never emerged as cases of need. This was unfortunate from the point of view of other people who dealt with the child, for whom knowledge that his difficulties were serious enough to be formally recognized might have been a useful piece of information and possibly a motivating factor.

One consequence of a state of affairs where too many people are chasing too few resources is that a service tends to become crisis-oriented rather than preventive in orientation. Thus it was a well-accepted belief in this local authority that the surest way for a child to get into a special school for the maladjusted was for him or her to become an habitual school absentee. To the education department, constrained by its statutory requirement to educate all children up to school-leaving age, the chronic truant became a prime case of need. The clinic, however, may have had a quite different perspective on the problem. To them this behaviour was perhaps an expression of only mild or temporary disturbance and not regarded as a high priority. But the facts of life were that the education department provided the places and, given this state of affairs, no psychiatrist could sensibly do otherwise than cut his suit according to the cloth available. So the child who was recommended was not so much the one with the greatest need as the one whose type of case it was known from past precedent the education department would treat most sympathetically. The outcome was that the power in determining issues such as who was maladjusted and who needed special education was in a subtle way shifted imperceptibly away from the practitioner working in the field to the professional administrators employed in theory to implement their decisions. The roles of demand and supply became reversed. The latter became promoted to an independent defining force, the former was relegated to a state of dependence – and they remained in a state of dynamic equilibrium. The moral is that if an LEA makes little or no provision for the maladjusted, recommendations for special education represent an academic indulgence. The inherent danger is that, if the situation persists over a long period, it becomes taken for granted and accepted that professional expertise is subordinated to administrative requirements. Put in another way, it can be said that in such a situation the actuarial exercise of balancing the books becomes the most important organizational goal.

The second major factor noted above is the provision of school psychological services and child guidance facilities and personnel. This too is referred to by Younghusband et al. (1970, p. 203). They point out that the considerable variations in ascertainment which exist between regions are

> no doubt related to the distribution of child guidance staff for ascertainment work, as well as to the availability of special schooling for the maladjusted.

They add that

> it is a common experience that establishing any kind of special school facility results in the discovery of more children needing it than was estimated originally. Needs can in fact easily be concealed either by failure to ascertain because there is no suitable provision, or because some placement, though not altogether suitable, is made.

Overall, the general shortage of psychologists, psychiatrists and child guidance facilities generally produces its own consequences. It means that teachers eventually come to recognize the difficulty in securing help of this kind for the child. Problems are often immediate and urgent and a six months' waiting list offers little prospect of help in the short term. Thus, once again, the person in the position to indicate that a child needs help may hold back because it is known that a recommendation will, in effect, not be acted upon. Even if clinical services are available, overworked staff are not always able to give individual children and families the degree of help they need. This too becomes known to teachers and it remains a factor in future decision making over referrals. So yet again, the demand or need emerges as subordinate to the supply, with the net effect that the stream of maladjusted children who would come forward to clinics if services were readily available is reduced to the number with which the clinics are able to cope. The fault, if there is a fault, lies not with those who refer or fail to refer the child, or those who provide the eventual service, but in the sheer lack of provision of suitable facilities.

Policy as a function of provision

The thrust of the argument has been that the practice of ascertainment is heavily dependent upon the type of resources which are available in meeting needs. So far the discussion has centred around the fact that these resources are quantifiably limited, but there is a complicating factor which should be introduced concerning type of provision. As Gulliford (1971, p. 8) points out, there are at least thirteen different ways of providing for handicapped children. In the case of this authority however, the only provision made for maladjusted pupils was either full-time residential special school or residential hostel with the child attending a local ordinary school. The absence of day schools or classes meant that ascertainment policy was heavily oriented towards those children for whom residential treatment away from home was thought to be desirable. Let us consider the implications of this state of affairs and the latter statement in particular.

While the authority had eight so-called day 'remedial centres', many of whose clients were children with specific learning difficulties or problems of incipient maladjustment, they were not intended as nor did they primarily function as institutions for the maladjusted. To all intents and purposes the authority could be said to be completely lacking in day provision for the maladjusted. Even when, as sometimes happened under pooling arrangements, pupils were sent to schools located in other authorities, these were invariably residential institutions. A number of child guidance clinics had attempted to go some way towards meeting this deficiency by providing their own teaching facilities but this could only go a small way towards bridging the gap. This created another problem: the last thing which some children who displayed symptoms of maladjustment needed was removal from the home environment. On the contrary, what was required for them was support and therapy for the whole family unit combined with sympathetic and knowledgeable educational treatment for the child. Unfortunately, as day provision was not readily available, the psychiatrist was placed on the horns of a dilemma. Either the child was recommended for residential treatment which was known to be a second-best course of action or he continued with treatment confined to the child guidance clinic but without the stimulus which special education could provide. So far as ascertainment policy was concerned, this meant that it was best described as providing a statement about the subgroup of maladjusted children who were felt to be capable of benefiting from a residential education rather than as a statement about the total cohort of maladjusted children. In other words ascertainment assumes different meanings in different contexts. In this local authority it became inevitably tied to a wholly residential provision, but this is an artefact resulting from organizational imperatives and it need not necessarily be like this. Earlier evidence from Roe (1965) suggests that the greater variety of provision in the ILEA allowed a greater degree of sophistication in placement and that this in turn implied a rather different type of policy over ascertainment.

The 'needs' of the organization

What emerges is that it is imperative to examine the processes which go on as a local authority attempts to deal with its statutory responsibilities to one group of educationally handicapped children. The suggestion has been made that the practices which emerge reflect not just the needs of the individual children, but also the need of the organization to preserve itself, which necessitates a coming to terms with the reality of the situation by all personnel involved in the social system concerned with helping the maladjusted child. Thus the answer to questions such as why some children receive help and others with apparently greater need do not or which kinds of cases receive help lies at least partly in an examination of the structure created to deal with the problem. In particular one must look at the social roles and the organizational constraints imposed upon actors who participate in this decision-making process. While this research is unusual in that it examines the context of the treatment of maladjustment by a British local education authority, there is no reason to believe that the above comment is in any way out of line with research carried out generally on complex organizations and their treatment of clients. Indeed one can best put this research in perspective by making a comment from a recent American project on the classification of handicapped children (Hobbs, 1975, p. 124).

> Institutions, like other purposive organizations, generate their own inexorable imperatives out of two determinants: the need to accomplish a recognized mission and the need to preserve and enhance the institution itself as it is perceived by all who are associated with it.

Thus a local authority not only has to deal with the problem of maladjustment, but must ensure that in doing so it maintains the stability and continuity of its own operations.

These processes are not academic. They have implications for many units and individuals, particularly the ordinary schools and maladjusted pupils. If ascertainment policies reflect the needs of the organization rather than those of the client we should be able to identify the effect of this administratively oriented definition of maladjustment in the actions of teachers and in the careers of maladjusted pupils. This will further help us to articulate the model of maladjustment which has been developed. For reasons of space, it is intended here to concentrate on the former aspect: the actions of teachers. Readers who wish to explore further the processes through which individual pupils went in order to become labelled maladjusted and reach a special school are advised to read the more detailed report of this research (Woolfe, 1977).

We have already noted the way in which the manoeuvrings of the education and health departments reflect the practical problems which exist in dealing with the need to provide an adequate special education. But of course the adaptive tactics described have a 'knock-on' or ripple effect right down the line of responsibility into the schools. It is instructive, therefore, to focus on the highly complex institutional structure laid down by the LEA as guidance for its ordinary schools and teachers when they wished to seek help for children who displayed an apparent degree of handicap. Having done this we can make an estimate of how far this structure could be regarded as a help to the teacher in the ordinary school. We shall look in detail at the formal procedure laid down when a school wished to seek help with a child. The high degree of formality should be noted.

The first step was for the headteacher to fill in a specific form. This was submitted to the divisional education officer, who then submitted it to his medical counterpart (the divisional medical officer). The latter would then, in the words of the official authority handbook,

> send an acknowledgement to the Head, pointing out that a period of time may elapse before an examination can be carried out (in some areas it is only possible for the Medical Officer to carry out these somewhat lengthy ascertainment examinations, involving intelligence testing, during school holidays).

This was just the beginning of the process. After the examination, the doctor would complete his assessment and recommendations and submit them to the divisional medical officer who passed them to the chief medical officer who sent them to the chief education officer for consideration of the action to be taken on the child's behalf. When submitting his recommendation

> the Medical Officer will send a personal note to the Head giving briefly the result of the examination and recommendations which have been made.

It is ironic that the person who requested advice is given the shortest report and, if the head was ever pessimistic about the result of his completion of the original form, the document reinforces it by concluding that

> it is important, however, that Heads should understand that this will be a recommendation from the Medical Officer which will be considered along with their own report, and it may not always be possible for the recommendation to be carried out.

One may be forgiven for thinking that this machinery looks clumsy and ill equipped to provide urgent advice to the teacher and immediate help to the pupil in need. Yet the fact is that this represented a considerable advance in communication over a previous situation, where direct links between the headteacher and the divisional medical officer were discouraged by divisional education officers on the grounds that they were inimical to efficient administration. In fairness, however, one should mention that many of the reports submitted to schools by doctors were written in some detail, and doctors were encouraged to visit the schools to discuss individual cases. However, one should also add that this innovation met with some resistance from educators on the grounds that doctors should not be allowed to interfere in what were claimed to be purely educational matters.

It would be wholly inaccurate and misleading to suggest that any person or persons sat down and deliberately wrote a memorandum designed to obstruct and delay the provision of help and advice to children and schools. But the formality of these rules and regulations symbolized the philosophies, ethos, values and goals of the organization to which they referred. While every system of administration must be based on a set of rules, a danger arises at the point when these become ritualized as ends in themselves instead of means to ends. The suggestion is, therefore, that the structure was inclined to be ponderous. What the teacher completing his form wanted was quick, informal guidance and information, followed where necessary by formal and decisive action. But instead of a straightforward process of communication in which the concerned parties discussed the child's needs and sought solutions, teachers in the authority found that they were activating a bureaucratic procedure, whose main objective would ostensibly appear, by its own admission, to inform them, as late and in as few words as possible, exactly what limited chance of help they had.

In practice, teachers grumbled about two things: first, that they sometimes did not receive the result of the divisional medical officer's recommendations and, second, that if they did receive the result, it was of little or no immediate help to them. The first point was easily remediable but the second was the more important of the two. If the health department recommended a special school for the child, the teacher knew that the child had a limited chance of placement and that even if this happened it might take some considerable time. Thus, the school was in many cases left with a problem until such time as the child went to special school. In other cases it knew that it had no hope of relief whatsoever. In addition, some children, not sufficiently handicapped to be classified in this way, might be recommended for special attention within the ordinary school system. But what did 'special education' mean if no help or advice was given to the school? In almost all cases, therefore, the recommendation stopped at the point where the teacher wanted it to begin. What it said was that the child needed special help either in the ordinary or in the special school. But the teacher knew that already, that was why advice had been sought. What was wanted was information about how to help the child.

It could be argued that there is nothing here which could not have been solved by better interdepartmental communication and attitudes. This view possesses some degree of plausibility, but is at best a partial answer. Professional relationships are mediated through a social and organizational structure. The teacher/educational welfare officer relationship for example would have been very different from what was if each time the head wanted an 'expert' opinion he had had to make a formal request on an official form. In addition, of course, a two-way flow of communication is facilitated by a flexible structure. Thus, the educational welfare officer might be in a position not just to respond to a request for help, but also to take the initiative and to advise the head when special care was needed in particular cases of which the latter might not otherwise be aware. Even so, despite this informality, educational welfare officers still complained, and often with some justification, that teachers were tardy in referring cases to them. It is not surprising that the delay was much worse when the referral had to be mediated through the official ritual of form completion.

As a generalization or working hypothesis one might argue that the more formal the procedures which had to be undergone to get a child investigated, the less willing was a school to get involved. It may well be that schools laid down for themselves some kind of self-regulating norm about the number of pupils they could refer in a period of time and the amount of help they could reasonably ask for. The absence of a school's psychological service exacerbated the problems. As things stood the education department had only one psychologist on its staff; all other psychologists were employees of the health department and attached to clinics. The situation where a headteacher in need of help could pick up a telephone and ask, at short notice, for help and advice was not common. In addition, in the highly formal situation which existed, teachers may have felt sensitive about calling in outside help in that this could be interpreted as a reflection upon their own competence and admission of their own failure.

Conclusion

Accepted methods of identifying and measuring maladjustment should not be regarded as self-evidently correct by virtue of the fact that they are products of accepted professional expertise. Rather, the suggestion is that we can best understand the nature of maladjustment if we look at the phenomenon in a social context and understand the meaning of terms used to the professionals who employ them. This context can be perceived as an arena in which, at one and the same time, actors seek both to understand the world and to make their role in it more manageable. The institutional structure which has emerged to deal with the problem of maladjustment is the outcome of this process of negotiation and conflict and perhaps its most important feature is the key role played by professional groups. Professionals are critical definers of reality for their clients. Major issues such as symptom-classification are not to be regarded as neutral lubricants which have an absolute scientific truth and have as their sole function the satisfying of individual needs. On the contrary, they reflect paradigms or perspectives on the world which help to support the power of particular groups and individuals and thus to buttress the existing institutional arrangements. The implication of this argument is not that needs necessarily remain unmet, but that one cannot satisfactorily explain the workings of the system unless one takes into consideration all those factors over and above the needs of the individual which have tended to be ignored or taken for granted or even treated as irrelevant in traditional studies of maladjustment. Schools and clinics construct labels and categories which channel and delimit our thinking about pupils. Once this is done pupils are placed in these compartments or categories and, because people act out the roles into which they have been cast, schools can be said to create deviancy and maladjustment (see Lacey, 1970; Hargreaves, 1967). Because the process is circular, it can almost be described as a form of self-fulfilling prophecy.

This type of argument has increasingly come to be advanced by sociologists in the study of deviance and such manifestations of it as delinquency and truancy. The suggestion is that in explaining deviant conditions we should move outside the realm of explanation in terms of individual or family pathologies into looking at the way in which labels come to be attached. Thus deviance can be seen in this light, not as a condition pertaining to an individual, but as a product of the social interaction between individual and institution. In summarizing and developing this perspective, Reynolds (1976) has indicated that schools with similar catchment areas display widely different rates of delinquency and truancy. This would appear to suggest that what goes on in schools in some way has an effect in terms of creating deviancy. This chapter has argued that many features of maladjustment can be interpreted as an artefact of the procedures and practices of local authority administrators and it would advance our knowledge if this form of analysis were applied to particular schools. This would greatly enhance our understanding of the condition which we know as maladjustment.

The suggestion, therefore, is that we need to challenge the 'taken-for-grantedness' of the classical model of maladjustment with its medical model of individual illness, symptoms and treatment. In doing so we need not deny that some individuals are maladjusted and need help. However we are better able to provide this help if we recognize that the phenomenon of maladjustment can only be wholly explained if we recognize as a valid field for inquiry the social milieu in which labels are constructed, applied and confirmed. In particular we must look further at the complex structure of roles through which the work of professionals is mediated. If we perform this operation, we find that the social system created to deal with the needs of the maladjusted child represents one attempt at finding a solution, but in no sense is it to be regarded as the only possible one, nor is it self-evidently the right one. By unravelling this taken-for-grantedness, new definitions and models of maladjustment can be exposed to our awareness.

Notes

1   In research studies 'maladjustment' is operationally defined and thus varies with the perspective and objective of the researcher.

2   In the related field of educational subnormality, Williams (1965) points out that it is a commonly held view that the school medical officer carries the responsibility for ascertaining pupils. Segal (1961) found that in 73 percent of a sample of LEAs the final decision was taken by the principal school medical officer. Williams adds, however, that the legal position is made clear in the 1944 Education Act, which indicates that the responsibility for ascertainment and for recommending the appropriate form of special education treatment rests with the LEA itself.

3   Younghusband et al. (1970, p. 202) suggest that, in 1970, nearly 4000 children ascertained as ESN had been waiting for a special school place for more than one year. One does not wish to present this time-lag as necessarily some kind of tragedy. A child's development is continuous, as is the line between adjustment and maladjustment, and the idea of a critical or crisis point is not automatically relevant in every case. Nevertheless the existence of such time-lags should not be treated lightly, precisely because, as pointed out in the text, it tends to lead to the development of a crisis-oriented rather than a preventive service.

References

Berger, P.C. (1965) 'Towards a sociological understanding of psychoanalysis', *Social Research* 36, pp. 26–28

Chazan, Maurice (1963) 'Maladjusted pupils: trends in post-war theory and practice', *Educational Research*, vi, 1, pp. 29–34

Gulliford, R. (1971) *Special Educational Needs*, Routledge & Kegan Paul

Hobbs, Nicholas (1975) *Issues in the Classification of Children*, Volumes I and II, San Francisco: Jossey-Bass

Mills, C. Wright (1940) 'Situated actions and vocabularies of motive', *American Sociological Review* 5(6), pp. 439–452

Ministry of Education (1946) *Special Educational Treatment* (Pamphlet No. 5), HMSO

Ministry of Education (1955) *Report of the Committee on Maladjusted Children*, HMSO (the Underwood Report)

Ministry of Education (1961) *Circular 11/61*, HMSO

Reynolds, David (1976) 'The delinquent school', in Hammersley, Martin and Peter Woods (eds) *The Process of Schooling*, Routledge & Kegan Paul

Roe, M. (1965) *Survey into Progress of Maladjusted Pupils*, ILEA

Szasz, Thomas S. (1972) *The Myth of Mental Illness*, St. Albans, Paladin

Whitmore, Kingsley (1975) 'What do we mean by maladjustment? Then why don't we say so', in Laing, A.F. (ed), *Trends in the Education of Children with Special Learning Needs*, University College, Swansea

Woolfe, Ray (1977) 'An examination of the definition of maladjustment, as reflected in a local authority's administrative procedures for ascertainment', unpublished M.Ed. dissertation, University of Wales

Younghusband, Eileen, Dorothy Birchall, Ronald Davie and M.L. Kellmer-Pringle (eds) (1970) *Living with Handicap*, London, The National Bureau for Co-operation in Child Care

Further reading

Coard, B. (1971) *How the West Indian child is made educationally subnormal in the British school system*, New Beacon

Dale, Roger (1972) 'The career of the pupil', Unit 6 of Open University Course *School and Society* (E282), Open University Press

Hargreaves, D. (1967) *Social Relations in a Secondary School*, Routledge & Kegan Paul

Hobbs, Nicholas (1975) *The Future of Children, Categories, Labels and Their Consequences*, San Francisco: Jossey-Bass

Lacey, C. (1970) *Hightown Grammar*, Manchester University Press

Laing, R.D. (1959) *The Divided Self*, Tavistock

Mercer, J. (1971) 'Socio-cultural factors in labelling mentally retardates' *Peabody Journal of Education* 48, pp. 188–203

White, M.A. and J. Charry (1966) (eds) *School Disorder, Intelligence and Social Class*, Columbia, New York: Teachers College Press

Willower, D. (1970) 'Special education: organization and administration', *Exceptional Children*, 36, pp. 591–594

CHAPTER 9

THE SOCIAL CONSTRUCTION
OF THE ESN(M) CHILD

by Sally Tomlinson

The category of educational subnormality was an administrative category created in 1945, one of (then) eleven possible categories of handicap, and since that time has always encompassed over half of all children designated as handicapped. Indeed the most recent DES statistics (DES, 1979) indicate that ESN children comprise two-thirds of all children currently in special education. In 1945 the category was extended to include children who, prewar, were known as 'defective' but educable, and a larger group of children in ordinary schools, known as 'dull and backward'. Cyril Burt was one of the first to use the term educational subnormality, and to calculate that children scoring between 50–85 on mental tests should be considered as ESN (Burt, 1935). Burt was a member of the Wood Committee which reported in 1929, and recommended the creation of such a category – children with a mental score of between 50–70 to be considered ESN (Report of the Board of Education and the Board of Control, 1929). At this time, of course, 'intelligence' was considered to be a fixed, innate quality, measurable by tests. By 1970 children formerly known as severely subnormal were brought into education and the former ESN became known as ESN(M) (mild or moderate). The Warnock Committee, reporting in 1978, suggested that the ESN(M) and the ESN(S) (severe) categories should be merged with children currently known as 'remedial' in ordinary schools, the whole to be known as Children with Learning Difficulty (mild, moderate, severe). The 1980 White Paper on special educational needs indicated that statutory categories of handicap will be abolished, but descriptive labels, similar to the existing categories of handicap, will remain.

Since the statutory category of ESN(M) is scheduled for disappearance, it might be timely to question the status of the category and the concept of mild educational subnormality. What exactly is, or was, an ESN(M) child?

One initial point that can be made is that it is most certainly a non-normative category. That is, while there can be some external agreement, by relatively objective measurement, about categories such as blindness, deafness or epilepsy, there can and has been disagreement over what constitutes mild educational subnormality. It would seem sociologically important to question the category, since a major feature of children who come to be categorized as ESN(M) is that they are almost entirely the children of manual working-class parentage – and since the arrival of West Indian families in Britain, black children have been over-represented in ESN(M) schools. Sociologists of education have traditionally been preoccupied with the comparative underachievement of working-class children in education, and from the point of view of the acquisition of qualifications and credentials, ESN(M) education can be regarded as total non-achievement. Why is it that relatively powerless groups in society, working-class and black parents, are more likely to have their children assessed as ESN(M)? (And, of course, the creation of the CWLD will encompass even more working-class and black children, as they comprise a majority of children in remedial classes in ordinary schools.)

The criteria by which children are referred, assessed and placed in ESN(M) schools or classes has traditionally been decided on a discretionary basis by groups of professional people (educationalists, educational psychologists and medical officers) using professional judgements and supposedly objective testing procedures. These procedures lead to placement in a non-credentialling type of schooling which leads only to semi- or unskilled employment or unemployment. Moreover, the historical development of schooling for the mildly subnormal, linked in the earlier twentieth century to crime, poverty and moral depravity (Tredgold, 1908), has meant that there is a stigma attached to this type of special education – to be ESN(M) has indeed meant a 'label for life' (Omar, 1971) and a disqualification from full social acceptance.

A study in a large city in 1976–1977 attempted to explore the criteria professionals used to designate children as ESN(M), using both phenomenological and structural perspectives (Tomlinson, 1981). Forty children were followed through the process of their referral and assessment and placement (in 28 cases) in ESN(M) schools, and all the 120 professionals and others who had made a decision about the children were asked how they 'accounted for' (Scott and Lyman, 1968) ESN(M) children. The phenomenological perspective used in this study was that developed most systematically by Berger and Luckman in their book *The Social Construction of Reality* (1966). From their perspective social categories such as ESN(M) are not fixed, objective categories, they are socially created artefacts, which, however permanent they appear to be, may be redefined and changed. The assessment of children as ESN(M), and their being officially recorded as such, creates the category ESN(M). The professionals who refer and assess children, headteachers, educational psychologists, doctors and others, see themselves, quite reasonably, as solely concerned with 'doing a job', but they are also engaged in constructing a 'reality'. The ESN(M) category can be regarded as a social construct which comes into existence through the judgements and decisions of professional people. The construction of the category is influenced by the values, beliefs, and perceived interests of the professionals, who have vested career interests in assessing and defining ESN(M) children. The more children who are candidates for assessment, the more work for the professionals. In addition, if professionals feel they are 'overworked' it becomes a good reason for arguing for the expansion of the profession.

Accounts of educational subnormality

Professionals who make judgements about educational subnormality and profess to distinguish between the normal and the 'not normal' can provide apparently logical, rational accounts of subnormality. Their accounts appear to be natural, because they are held to be grounded in nature – for example, mild educational subnormality is seen by some to be an intrinsic quality – a child 'is ESN(M)' yet at the same time the intrinsic quality is made up of negative qualities – a child 'cannot benefit' from normal education because he or she lacks certain attributes. In the literature on ESN(M) children and between practitioners and professionals, there is actually little consensus as to which accounts are more important in describing an ESN(M) child. In the study of 1976–1977 it was possible, from initial interviews, professional journals, prescriptive books written to assist practitioners, government acts and circulars, etc. to abstract a series of analytic accounts of ESN(M) children. Table 9.1 illustrates the account.

The most popular account of ESN(M) children is in terms of function. An ESN(M) child is unable to perform certain tasks that it is implicitly understood that a 'normal' child of that age can. The key concept in functional accounts is that of attainment – children who cannot obtain a given level of skill or competence in comparison to other children may be subnormal. Functional definitions of ESN(M) children predominate in the literature written for practitioners.

Table 9.1
Accounts of educational subnormality

1 *Functional*	1	Child cannot do X (X may be social, educational, technological, but is usually connected to 'learning' or intellectual functioning).
	2	Child cannot communicate adequately.
2 *Statistical*	1	Child has a 'low' IQ as measured on standardized tests.
	2	Child falls into lowest 1 percent (or 20 percent) of school population in school achievement.
3 *Behavioural*	1	Child is disruptive, troublesome, uncontrolled.
	2	Child exhibits bizarre, odd, non-conformist behaviour.
	3	Child is unable to behave 'appropriately'.
4 *Organic*		Child has:
	1	Genetic disorder or 'innate capacity'.
	2	Prenatal or birth 'damage'.
	3	Organic or metabolic disorder.
	4	Medically demonstrable 'illness' or 'condition'.
5 *Psychological*		Child is 'emotionally disturbed'.
6 *Social*		Child has:
	1	Family with low socio-economic status; father semi- or unskilled.
	2	Family 'disorganized' – poor maternal care, single parent, working mother, etc.
	3	Poor or different socialization techniques
	4	Adverse material factors – poor housing, bad physical environment.
	5	Cultural deficiency – poor cultural milieux; poor preparation for school.
7 *School*	1	Unsatisfactory school conditions.
	2	Normal school rejects child.
	3	Child rejects school, i.e., truants.
8 *Statutory*		Child may be 'certified' as in need of special education.
9 *Intuitive*		Child has 'something wrong with him'.
10 *Tautological*		Child is in need of special educational treatment.

In theory the term ESN(M) could be applied to a large group of children who are very backward in their school work, ranging from those who are barely capable of responding to schooling, to others who apart from their backwardness are capable of following much in the normal school curriculum.
(Gulliford, 1966, p. 40)

Thus, functional accounts tend to be descriptive, depending on the notion that a child cannot perform or attain at a variety of levels.

From 1945 functional accounts have created some confusion by their failure to distinguish between official definitions of ESN(M) (Ministry of Education, 1946; DES, 1972), and children who were known as backward, remedial, or slow-learning in normal schools. The extension of the category into CWLD is a logical solution to a dynamic twentieth-century educational problem – 'what do we do with children who cannot or will not learn?' (Berger and Mitchells, 1978, p. 15). Because functional accounts tend to be descriptive they are usually accompanied by other accounts which purport to be explanatory. One of the most popular accompanying accounts is statistical – a low IQ explains 'ESN(M)-ness'. The assumption is made that IQ tests are accurate, scientific, measuring instruments which can place a child's mental attributes in relation to other children. Teachers, in particular, consider that an IQ score explains a child's attainment (Squibb, 1977), and rely on educational psychologists to confirm this. Statistical accounts of ESN(M) children have popularly followed Cyril Burt's judgement, and the Wood Committee's recommendation, that an IQ score of between 50–70 or 75 'is ESN(M)', and this has given rise to debates over whether children with higher IQs should be placed in ESN(M) schools or classes. This kind of argument demonstrates the ease with which accounts became reified. IQ is itself a very problematic concept – it has often been used to legitimate political decisions (Kamin, 1977; Blok and Dworkin, 1977) – and yet, as the research reported here demonstrated, it is still relied on by a variety of professionals and practitioners to account for children as ESN(M).

Behavioural accounts of ESN(M) children are often presented in conjunction with functional accounts, but there is little consensus as to whether an ESN(M) child is badly behaved or not. Professionals sometimes referred to a 'true ESN(M) child', by which they meant a dull, but conforming child. This mythical figure was sometimes used to invoke the description of a child as 'not ESN(M)'. However, one of the reasons for the creation of special schools in the late nineteenth century was that children who were difficult to teach, and interrupted the system of payment by results, should be removed from normal school classes; and the subsequent history of ESN(M) referral indicates a tendency for schools to refer children who exhibited trouble-some, disruptive or non-conformist behaviour. The artificial simplification attempted by the 1945 Handicapped Pupils regulations – that backward children were to go to ESN schools, and badly behaved children were to go to maladjusted schools – was never very successful. In practice, teachers preferred to get rid of children who were both learning and behaviour problems by ESN referral and it was the ESN(M) category which expanded most rapidly postwar. A decline in referrals during the 1970s was paralleled by the development of a new type of special education – disruptive units – which were a much quicker route to the removal of children with behaviour problems from the normal classroom, and in new legislation children termed disruptive will officially be brought within special education.

Organic accounts of ESN(M) children, which include 'innate' accounts implicitly referring to some inherited attributes, are also used as explana-tions for ESN(M) children. Indeed, the 1946 Ministry of Education guidelines on the handicapped, spoke of 'retardation due to limited ability . . . which was likely to be permanent' (Ministry of Education, 1946). Traditional medical domination in the assessment process for special educa-tion (doctors claiming early on that only they were qualified to detect 'weak-mindedness' – Pritchard, 1963) made it likely that doctors would give organic accounts of ESN(M) children, but interestingly, doctors have been at some pains to stress that mild educational subnormality, or mild mental retardation as the doctors usually put it, seldom has an organic cause (Stein and Susser, 1960; Court Report, 1976). It is the medical profession who stress social accounts of ESN(M) children, and a tautological factor is sometimes introduced in that children ascertained as having other 'hand-icaps' are often also designated as educationally backward.

Psychological accounts of ESN(M) children are not particularly preval-ent in the literature although the 1946 Ministry guidelines did suggest that one cause of educational subnormality might be 'psychological maladjust-ment'. Some writers have suggested that emotional disturbance and/or poor family relationships can account for educational backwardness (Davies, 1961; Hunt, 1975).

The most popular accounts of ESN(M) children have always been social. It was in elementary schools for working-class children that children unsuitable for education in these schools were first 'discovered', and it was in the London School Board's poorest districts that the first schools for special instruction were set up during the 1890s. The influence of the eugenics movement in the early twentieth century linked the lower social classes to a variety of social evils, including crime, poverty, unemployment and mental subnormality (Report of the Royal Commission on the Care and Control of the Feebleminded, 1908) and reinforced popular beliefs that mental subnormality and educational retardation were a prerogative of the lower social classes. Despite some assertions that the middle and upper classes did have dull and defective children, but were able to provide for them privately (Tredgold, 1908), the belief has persisted that there is a natural relationship between the working class and educational subnormality. Postwar research in the sociology of education, while demonstrating the social factors which impinge upon the intellectual development of children, probably also reinforced popular and professional belief in the 'natural' lower educational capacities of lower working-class children. The kind of environmental factors used to account for relative working-class 'failure' at normal schools are also used to account for ESN(M) children, for example, low socio-economic status, cultural and linguistic deficiency and disadvantage, poor socialization techniques and preparation for school, adverse material factors and disorganized families. Much of the literature on ESN(M) children stresses social causation (Stein and Susser, 1960; Williams and Gruber, 1967; Gulliford, 1969). The Warnock Report, which purported to eschew causal explanations for handicapped children, noted that, 'many children with educational deficiencies may suffer from familial or wider social deficiencies' (Warnock Report, p. 4), reinforcing the popular notion that it is largely the 'deficient' working class who produce the educationally backward children. Social accounts have, historically, been so persistent and persuasive that their plausibility as an account of 'ESN(M)-ness' is seldom questioned. It is taken for granted that lower social class attributes are natural factors in accounting for ESN(M) children and that one function of special ESN(M) schools is to help children overcome the deficiencies of their environment (Williams, 1965). The notion that normal schools can be held accountable for a child's educational subnormality is not popular in the literature, nor with practitioners, although again, the 1946 guidelines mentioned 'unsatisfactory school conditions' as a possible causal factor of backwardness. It would, however, seem unrealistic to suppose that practitioners would criticize their own institutions when a variety of other accounts of ESN(M) children are available.

Statutory accounts are likewise seldom referred to but can be discovered in the relevant government acts and circulars. In statutory terms an ESN(M) child is one who can be legally designated as such under Section 35

(5) of the 1944 Education Act and by a 'certification procedure' through which a child can be compelled to attend a special school or class. No change in 'enforceable procedures' is envisaged for children requiring special education, who are 'recorded' (White Paper, 1980).

Intuitive accounts of ESN(M) children are usually offered by parents. The parents 'know there is something wrong' but the intuitive speculations of parents have to be confirmed by professional opinion, whose judgements confirm or deny the speculation (Booth, 1978).

Tautological accounts of ESN(M) children are quite common among professionals and in the literature. The whole concept of 'special educational needs', on which future legislation is to be based, is tautological as far as ESN(M) children are concerned. An ESN(M) child (or a CWLD) is described as a child in need of special education. This presupposes that there is a consensus on how such children can be recognized, but in the literature, and in the research reported here, no such consensus could be deduced. It must surely be logically dubious to prescribe for a 'need' without a causal account of how the need came into existence.

The accounts and explanations of ESN(M) children to be discovered in the literature and from professionals are in fact problematic. They are often contradictory, and they are by no means as 'natural' as common sense would have them be.

Social construction and smooth teamwork

It is, nevertheless, the judgements of professionals, working within the complex referral and assessment processes, which continue to create the category of ESN(M) and to ensure for a particular group of children what Sharp and Green (1973) have called the 'social transmission of ignorance'. At the time of the 1976–1977 study local education authorities were engaged in developing the new referral and assessment procedure suggested in the government Circular 2/75 (HMSO, 1975) and the professionals were beginning to record their opinions and decisions on the new SE (special education) forms, rather than the old HP (handicapped pupils) forms. The 'ideal' procedure envisaged by 2/75 is illustrated in Table 9.2.

The official picture of the construction of the category ESN(M) is that of 'smooth teamwork' – co-operation and agreement between professionals on the 'needs' of particular children. Teachers, headteachers of referring and special schools, educational psychologists, medical officers, and a variety of other people who may be involved – social workers, psychiatrists, assessment centre staff, education welfare officers, etc. are all supposed to work in close co-operation, documenting in writing a series of formal decisions which will produce a consensus on the educational future for particular children. In practice 'smooth teamwork' remains very much an ideology – accounts differ and conflict, and there are a variety of other conflicts, anxieties, and communication difficulties between professionals.

How, in fact, did the various professionals account for ESN(M) children? In order to demonstrate the accounts visually, the percentage of replies given by each group of the professionals in this study were calculated out of the total replies given, and shown in histogram form. In this way it is possible to see at a glance the different kinds of accounts offered by referring heads, educational psychologists, medical officers, special school heads and parents, and to compare the accounts.

Thus, Figure 9.1 shows that headteachers overwhelmingly use functional and behavioural criteria when accounting for ESN(M) children.

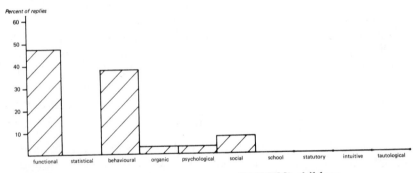

Figure 9.1 Referring heads' accounts of ESN(M) children

The heads are the people who begin the construction of possible ESN(M) children, usually after a class teacher has noted a child: 'the teacher tells one if a child is dull, not talking or reading – we take it from there.' 'Once a year I send a card to all teachers asking about children with problems – down to being backward or smelly.'

In the study, referring heads felt they could make a distinction between ESN(M) children and those who were 'merely backward' on an intuitive basis. However, the selection, by heads, of potentially ESN(M) children did depend to a significant degree on disruptive or non-conformist classroom behaviour. One head, in accounting for his referral of an eight-year-old West Indian boy, said: 'He's disruptive and constantly seeks attention – he makes class teaching a misery.'

Table 9.2

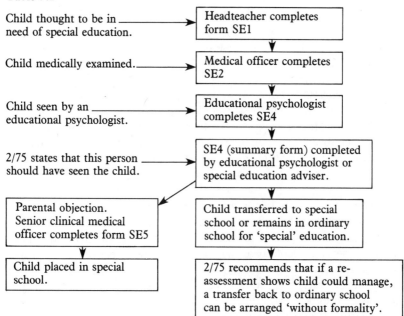

Heads were not particularly concerned to offer causal explanations of their descriptive accounts of learning and behaviour problems; identification rather than explanation, was their most pressing problem. It did appear that the tipping point at which a child became potentially ESN(M), rather than 'remedial', was the behaviour he or she exhibited in the classroom. Heads' accounts of ESN(M) children were very much like the kind of accounts offered by normal schools in the 1890s, when the first candidates for special schools were being selected. Children who cannot, or will not, be 'educated' in a controlled orderly environment may be candidates for a 'special' education.

In the study, referring heads sometimes viewed psychologists with antipathy, regarding them as people with considerable power, including the power to frustrate the initial referral; and indeed, psychologists did seem to be crucial figures in the construction of the ESN(M) child. It is the educational psychologist, working within a 'scientific' testing model, and using skills which the schools do not possess, who may or may not legitimate the schools' judgement that a child 'is ESN'. One potential source of conflict was that the psychologists' accounts of ESN(M) children did differ considerably from the headteachers, as Figure 9.2 demonstrates.

Psychologists did account for ESN children in functional terms: 'The major thing would be attainment – that's what it's all about – intellectual functioning.' But one psychologist qualified this by commenting that 'Our special schools are full of – no, have a percentage of – children who have scored low on some verbal IQ tests – a test which does not put working-class kids in a favourable situation.'

Psychologists also tended to accompany functional accounts with statistical accounts – low intellectual functioning was partly accounted for by a 'low IQ'. But although 36 out of the 40 children in the study had been tested (on the Stanford-Binet revised test) most of the psychologists did not place the kind of reliance on tests that psychologists in the 1930s would have done: 'People think if a child is assessed as ESN he's ESN for ever more . . . we've got to get away from heredity, teachers and administrators are working with a psychology that's twenty years out of date.'

The psychologists did not regard potential ESN(M) children as behaviour problems, and it was here that their differences with head-teachers arose, particularly as they saw themselves as being able to circumvent the referral process. One psychologist remarked that, 'Normal schools often refer children they want to be rid of', and another said, 'In the past schools used to be anxious about children with behaviour problems; there are still a few rogue schools where the children's feet don't touch the floor if they cause problems.' But psychologists do not have to agree with the headteacher's view: 'We may have to say – I'm sorry this child is a nuisance, but what he needs is more appropriate teaching.'

And they do not see themselves as able to turn the referral back and thus not continue the 'construction' of the ESN(M) child.

Psychologists also account for children who do become ESN(M) in social

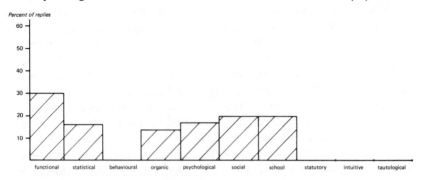

Figure 9.2   Educational psychologists' accounts of ESN(M) children

terms; they may be 'culturally disadvantaged' and *also* partially disadvantaged by organic and psychological problems. But it was the doctors who, interestingly, tended to use social accounts of ESN(M) children the most. Figure 9.3 shows the doctors' accounts of ESN(M) children.

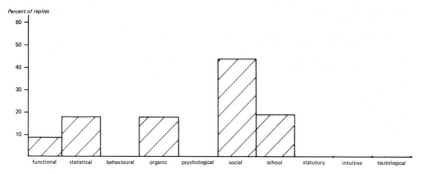

Figure 9.3 Doctors' accounts of ESN(M) children

The doctors thought that ESN(M) children were likely to be of lower social class origins and, as one doctor put it, 'to be a rough child'. They appeared to operate upon the tautological assumption, expressed in the Court Report (1976), that an ESN(M) child is essentially a lower-class child, and that mild educational subnormality (or mental retardation as the doctors tended to put it) is a characteristic of lower social class children. Like the educational psychologists, doctors do not acount for ESN(M) children in behavioural terms; their image of the ESN(M) child is that of the dull but conforming child, who may have 'defects in make-up' or may have been 'failed by his normal school'. Two doctors offered genetic accounts in terms of a child's 'innate dimness' but they did not think that ESN(M) children suffered any particular medical pathologies – indeed the administrative category was regarded almost as a pathology in itself. The doctors also demonstrated that there was some conflict with other professionals during the construction of the ESN(M) child, despite the ideology of smooth teamwork. There was some resentment that psychologists particularly had been 'taking over' what they had formerly regarded as their area of competence – and the autonomy and status of the medical profession conflicted with the notion that they were part of a team.

Headteachers of special schools are also important figures in the social construction of the ESN(M) child, given that the final decision to admit a child to his or her school rests with the head. Indeed, if an ESN(M) child is literally one who has attended an ESN(M) school, the public image of educational subnormality can largely be shaped by the judgements they make on the kind of children they admit, and on what happens in the school. Thus, in one suburban ESN(M) school, a head rejected 'violent' children and the local image of the ESN(M) child was that of a dull, slow child. In an inner-city ESN(M) school, where the head felt he could deal with 'difficult' children, and a high proportion of black children were also admitted, the local image of ESN(M) children was of disturbed children who were also often black children. Figure 9.4 illustrates the special school head's accounts of ESN(M) children.

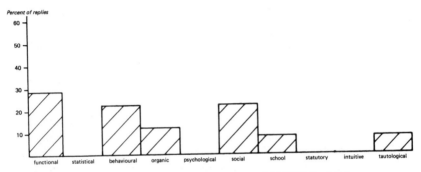

Figure 9.4   Special school heads' accounts of ESN(M) children

Heads of special schools do use functional and behavioural accounts to explain why a child 'is ESN(M)' in their school, but their behavioural accounts are much milder than those offered by referring heads – children are 'deeply disturbed' rather than 'disruptive' or 'vicious'. Some special school heads also accounted for the children in their schools in terms of the rejection by normal schools. One head said, 'My school is a dumping ground for the problem children in the city.' They also used social accounts, stating that ESN(M) children came from disorganized or disadvantaged families. The heads also offered tautological accounts of some children whom they described as being 'not ESN' despite the fact that they had been accepted into an ESN(M) school.

Intuitive accounts of ESN(M) children tended to be most often used by parents. Parents do not, of course, officially 'construct' the ESN(M) child, nor are they involved or consulted too closely in the process, despite official statements that they 'should' or 'ought' to be involved (White Paper, 1980,

p. 7). Parents gave functional accounts of their children: 'He's a bit slow – he doesn't make progress.' But such accounts were often given after the head of the referring school had 'sent for and told them' that their child had learning problems. They then followed this by intuitive accounts, either positive or negative: 'We knew there was something wrong with her,' or a decisive 'there's nothing wrong with him, despite what the flipping school says.'

The parents were very dependent on the referring heads' presentation of what was wrong and how the special school would 'help' and this dependency probably eased the head's self-appointed task of persuading parents to co-operate in the construction of their child as 'ESN(M)'. If a parent does not agree, and is not threatened with legal sanctions, it is possible for the referral to be dropped and the child never officially becomes 'ESN(M)' – (this happened with the one middle-class family in the study). Figure 9.5 illustrates parental accounts of ESN(M) children.

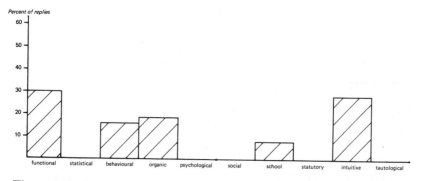

Figure 9.5   Parental accounts of their (potentially) ESN(M) children

Despite the referring schools' preoccupation with behavioural accounts, not many parents accounted for their children 'being ESN' in behavioural terms.

Of the children placed in special schools in this study, the parents had been involved in the process for almost two years. It is difficult to imagine selection procedures in any other area of education taking this length of time, or being tolerated by parents – and it is certainly difficult to imagine articulate middle-class parents accepting a lengthy process where they are 'sent for and told' or 'persuaded' to accept a stigmatized type of schooling for their children.

The notion that only working-class families produce 'ESN(M)' children, or, as the Court Report put it, the 'socially disadvantaged . . . or the socially incompetent are at special risk of having children who are mildly mentally retarded' (Court Report, 1976, p. 24), is thus reinforced during the process of constructing the ESN(M) child. Although Tredgold in 1908 was able to note that 'many of our feeble-minded are gentlefolk . . . able to enter into the social amusements of their class' (Tredgold, 1908, p. 175), the middle and upper classes in the later twentieth century simply do not allow, or need, their children to be socially constructed as ESN(M).

ESN(M) and social structure

While it is possible, using phenomenological perspectives, to ask why and how the category of ESN(M) comes to be socially constructed, it is almost impossible to generate general propositions about education in complex societies from phenomenological perspectives. A phenomenological analysis of the social construction of the ESN(M) child could be accused of doing no more than documenting the obvious – that professionals have social power to construct categories in which their decisions continually place children who are deemed 'less intelligent' or 'in need' of a particular kind of non-credentialling education. A structural perspective is needed to explain what the social uses of the ESN(M) category are and why this form of education is accorded only to lower social class (and black) children. In the study reported in this chapter the structural perspective adopted was that articulated by Bourdieu and Passeron (1973). Their work has attempted to illuminate the subtle relationships between the class structures and the education systems of industrial societies by pointing out that the development of education systems is closely related to changes in the socio-economic structure. Modern societies perpetuate the conditions of their own existence partly through the transmission of varying kinds and amounts of schooling. Education selection has replaced real capital as a seemingly more democratic currency for the reproduction of social class relationships, and educational advancement or exclusion is based on ostensibly fair testing and selection procedures. But Bourdieu and Passeron argue that the education system demands a cultural competence which it does not itself provide. Advantage is given to those who possess cultural 'capital' and can pass it on to their children. The families of children who come to be categorized as ESN(M) have neither cultural capital nor economic capital to pass on. Indeed the 'cultural disadvantage' of the families of ESN(M) children is a recurring theme in the literature. The study reported here suggests that this literature can be turned back to front, since by withdrawing children from normal education and offering them a stigmatized education which fits them only for low status in society, the reproduction of a part of the lower social class is ensured. There is little possibility that children other than those of low socio-economic status will find their way to ESN(M) schools – the upper and middle classes have cultural, and often economic, capital to pass on to their dull children, who do not need to be controlled or legitimated as do those of low status.

The development of this type of special education may have served two functions in society. First, by removing potentially troublesome children who upset the smooth running of the normal education system, order within that system was better ensured. ESN(M) education may have functioned more as a 'safety-valve' of the normal education system than anything else. In the later twentieth century the recognition that more and more children are troublesome to the system has led to more subtle ways of transferring children out. Secondly, the development of ESN(M) education has been one way of solving the perennial problem of social order in class-structured industrial societies, by selecting out and controlling, through a stigmatized type of schooling, potentially troublesome social groups.

The category of ESN(M) is socially constructed by the decisions and beliefs of professional people, but it also serves a wider purpose in the social structure. It is in the interests of all those concerned with special education to be clearer about the categorization of any children out of the normal education system, particularly those in the non-normative categories of ESN(M), Child with Learning Difficulty, disruptive and maladjusted, whether these categories are statutory or merely descriptive. The development of categories must be understood within a wider historical, social and political context than has so far been the case.

References

Berger, A. and G. Mitchells (1978) 'A multitude of sin-bins', *Times Educational Supplement*, July 1978

Berger, P. and T. Luckman (1966) *The Social Construction of Reality*, Penguin

Block, N. and G. Dworkin (1977) *The IQ Controversey*, New York: Quartet Books

Booth, T. (1978) 'From normal baby to handicapped child', *Sociology*, Volume 12, number 2

Bourdieu, P. and J.C. Passeron (1977) *Reproduction in Education Society and Culture*, Sage

Burt, C. (1935) *The Sub-Normal Mind*, Oxford University Press

The Court Report (1976) *Fit for the Future – Report of the Committee on Child Health*, HMSO

Davies, D.R. (1961) 'A disorder theory of mental retardation', *Journal of Mental Sub-normality*, number 7

DES (1979) *Statistics in Education*, Volume 1, HMSO

DES (1972) 'The health of the school child 1969–72', *Report of the Chief Medical Officer to the DES*, HMSO

DES (1975) Circular 2/75, *The Discovery of Children Requiring Special Education and the Assessment of their Needs*

Gulliford, R. (1966) 'Special education for the ESN', HMSO, National Association for Special Education, Conference Proceedings, July, London

Gulliford, R. (1969) *Backwardness and Educational Failure*, Routledge & Kegan Paul

Hunt, S. (1975) *Parents of the ESN*, National Elfrida Rathbone Society, Liverpool

HMSO (1980) *Special Needs in Education*, Cmnd. 7996

Kamin, L. (1977) *The Science and Politics of IQ*, Penguin

Ministry of Education (1946) *Special Educational Treatment*, Pamphlet No. 5, HMSO

Omar, B. (1971) 'ESN children – labelled for life' *Race Today*, January

Pritchard, D.G. (1963) *Education and the Handicapped*, 1760–1960, Routledge & Kegan Paul

Royal Commission on the Care and Control of the Feeble-Minded (1908), 8 volumes, HMSO

Report of the Committee on Mental Deficiency. Board of Education and Board of Control (1929), the Wood Report, HMSO

Scott, M. and S. Lyman (1968) 'Accounts', *American Sociological Review*, Volume 33, number 1

Sharp, R. and A. Green (1973) *Education and Social Control*, Routledge & Kegan Paul

Squibb, P. (1977) 'Some notes towards the analysis of the less-able or backward child', *Journal of Further and Higher Education*, Volume 1, number 3

Stein and Susser (1960) 'Families of dull children', Part III, *Journal of Mental Science*, Volume 106, number 445

Tomlinson, S. (1981) *Educational Sub-Normality – a Study in Decision-Making*, Routledge & Kegan Paul

Tredgold, A.F. (1908) *A Text-Book of Mental Deficiency*, Balliere, Tindall and Cox

The Warnock Report (1978) *Special Educational Needs*, HMSO

Williams, P. and E. Gruber (1967) *Response to Special Schooling*, Longmans

Williams, P. (1965) 'The ascertainment of ESN children', *Educational Research*, Volume 7, number 1

White Paper (1980) *Special Needs in Education*, Cmnd. 7996, HMSO

Further reading

Flude, M. and J. Ahier (1974) *Educability, Schools and Ideology*, Croom-Helm

Tomlinson, S. (1982) *A Sociology of Special Education*, Routledge & Kegan Paul

CHAPTER 10

A RESOURCE APPROACH TO MEETING SPECIAL NEEDS IN A SECONDARY SCHOOL

by *Elizabeth Jones*

This chapter aims to describe an attempt by a local education authority to meet the special needs of pupils within the context of an 'ordinary' secondary school. It outlines an alternative option to existing special education provision, namely that of the 'resources approach', which takes account both of the practical considerations that arise when special education is no longer seen as something set apart from 'normal' education and of changed attitudes towards disability.

The Department of Education and Science expressed interest at the outset in monitoring the progress of such a project. Thus when a special resources department was opened in purpose-built premises in September 1978, in a secondary school in the Midlands, the present author undertook to monitor it for a period of two years, initially on a weekly basis and then on full-time secondment to the Department of Special Education, University of Birmingham.

Monitoring

The process of monitoring embraced a wider concept than that of simple measurement. It was recognized that it is exceptionally difficult to establish what is the 'truth' about the success or failure of any project, or even to establish exactly what happens (limited as one is to one's position as an 'outsider' and the constraints placed upon one by time). In this sense, as a researcher, one's role approximates to that of a contemporary historian whose lot it is to trail some way behind, looking at the consequences of human decisions and relating them to the context of choices in which they were made.

The monitoring tools selected were what Lawton (1980) in *Politics of the School Curriculum* called the illuminative (or anthropological) model and the case-study (or eclectic, portrayal) model. This research approach involves assembling an information profile using data collected from four areas:

observation

interviews (formal and informal)

questionnaires and tests

documentary background sources

Together, these combine to illuminate the problems encountered and the emerging issues and significant features which appear to merit investigation (Parlett, 1972). The course of study cannot be charted in advance, and the actual process of reporting entails description, documentation and summarization.

The aims in monitoring this project can thus be summarized as follows:

1 to document an evolving educational experiment and the controversy surrounding it over a period of eighteen months;

2 to investigate the project in its setting;

3 to record the influence of specific events related to school organization, teacher attitudes, their preference for children with specific disabilities;

4 to record how individual children responded to the project by eliciting *teacher perceptions* on the criteria for success.

Illuminative evaluation and research involve a high degree of interpretative work to be done by the investigator. Critics of the approach claim that this is its major disadvantage, finding it ill-formulated, subjective and anecdotal, or more bluntly 'woolly and vague' (Delamont, 1978).

Information comes in many varied forms – much of it disorderly and incomplete, some of it impressionistic and nebulous. However, it can be claimed that the possible defects of subjectivity are not excluded from more quantative or experimental types of educational research:

There are few, if any, educational 'absolutes'; and curricula, teaching methods, organisational policies, classroom procedures and institutional philosophies have numerous social, historical, political and epistemological determinants. (Jamieson, 1977)

This study unearthed many different levels of decision making in relation to children with special needs and in a variety of contexts. These ranged in shifts from teachers' general thinking about the disabled to the use made of ancillary helpers in ordinary classrooms; from organizational and financial deliberations at county hall level to teacher perception of the social interactions of individual children in their school setting; from questions of curriculum planning and school-based in-service training to the criteria for determining 'success' in meeting the special educational needs of children within a comprehensive school.

The full complexity of the issues raised in the course of this study was not anticipated. In time, the study began to pose questions about the broader issues of education, e.g., mixed-ability teaching, subject choice, open-plan classrooms, size of teaching groups, the roles of form tutors, heads of departments, qualifications, training and nature of previous experience of all teaching staff, the organization and management structure of the school, and its communication network. Definitive answers do not necessarily arise, nor are they sought, but what emerges is another set of questions which appear to merit investigation.

Theoretical issues in special education

A review of the literature of the past decade into research on special education and children with special educational needs shows that, whatever approach to these problems is advocated, philosophical, analytical, managerial or educational, an over-riding consideration is that of attitude towards the disabled. Attitudes towards those who in some way are deviant, in the sense of being different, may be systematized through laws and institutions or they may operate simply as generalized mores of society (Jones, 1980). The history of man is punctuated with incidents of man's persecution of fellow-men of different features, skin pigmentation, size, shape, language, custom and dress. If we examine the ways in which different societies have attempted to handle those who in some way appear to deviate from some societal norm then, according to Wolfensberger (1972), these can be classified in four ways:

1   deviant individuals may be destroyed or persecuted;

2   deviant people may be segregated from normal society;

3   attempts are made to reverse the deviant features by re-education or treatment;

4   methods are sought to prevent future deviances.

The history of the twentieth century shows that in differing ways these strategies are still employed. What is involved here is the wider question of the treatment of minority groups and society's attitude towards assimilating them into an open society. This calls into question such notions as what is normal, abnormal or deviant, and the ways in which such status is accorded to individuals.

The current debate about the integration of children with special educational needs into ordinary schools tends to focus on questions related to resources – teachers, skills, equipment, buildings, support services. When these are provided, the emphasis changes to questions of class size, open-plan teaching, mixed-ability teaching. These are expressed through a discussion of the anomalies between special teachers who have extra allowances and main school teachers who have special children in their classes but without the additional financial inducement. Such focus serves to side-step the issues of (1) what teachers feel about children with special needs; (2) their preferences for or against teaching different categories of disability groups; and (3) how there have grown up 'accepted' ways of responding to children who may be difficult to teach within the institutionalized practices referred to as 'special education'.

The present procedures for identifying, classifying and allocating resources for children with special needs are familiar ones. Attention is focused on some specific need or disability. Historically, those children suffering physical disabilities or mental retardation had special provision made for them. The criteria used in history to determine who should or who should not be responded to and recorded varied in sophistication and application, for example, the ability to count twenty pence, tell one's own name, name your parents, measure a yard of cloth, or name the days of the week (Jones, 1980). The criteria for categorization were extended when scientific psychology began to make an impact towards the turn of this century. Special education began to emerge once compulsory education had been introduced by the 1870 Education Act. There was an increasing recognition that certain children had special needs, resulting in the establishment of the first special schools and classes (Gulliford, 1971). Until the new legislation is enacted there are ten statutory categories of disability for whom local authorities must make specialized provision. This system is to be replaced by one that will recognize children as having 'special needs' but without the automatic outcome that children will be grouped together, according to a range of needs which any child may have, according to one specific classificatory label. The procedure in the past has been to: nominate a category of need; develop methods for its identification; determine the size of the problem and group children together who have a common disability, for example, a class for the ESN(M) or the partially hearing; appoint specialized teachers and require of the local education authority to provide equipment and support services. What emerged from this process was a system of response to children with special needs which derived from a starting point of classification of children and laid an emphasis on placement. The new system will lay emphasis on educational need in the context of individualized learning. By eliminating categories of special need and by attempting to meet these needs in an educational context it is hoped to reduce the handicapping effects of particular disabilities.

Special education

Whatever attitudes prevail about children with special needs and whatever the possible shortcomings of the Warnock Report (Lewis and Vulliamy, 1980) there is little doubt that special education is in a state of change. Many reasons have been attributed to this: legislative action; better understanding of the nature of educational needs; our knowledge of practice in other countries; the availability of staff and material resources; curriculum and pedagogical developments; and pressure from parents and some sections of society at large. It could be said that the response in educational terms has been to set up a task force here, a pilot project there, or a special classroom in the back of the building. It is now apparent that systematic rather than ad hoc changes are urgently needed. The changes that have taken place in society's attitude towards the handicapped have been referred to as

> a social revolution in which their status has altered from discrimination to derogation, through custodial and philanthropic concern and on towards the goal of integration.
> (Thomas, 1978)

Mary Warnock (1979) perceived the relevance of her recent report as not only to bring about a conceptual framework within which educational provision could be made for the handicapped, but also to reflect and change public attitudes. Sabatino (1972) stated:

> special education is a matter for the nation, communities, institutions and individuals.

Speaking with reference to developments in the USA, Blatt (1972) was more precise in claiming that:

> the new heroes of special education appear to be the lawyers, judges and legislators, rather than the educators.

It is perhaps pertinent to observe that in this country, and in relation to the proposals laid out in the government White Paper (1980) on special needs in education, the issues relating to special educational need are not likely to overtax the minds of British lawyers and judges. Nor should they. The debate is likely to centre and remain within the mainstream of ordinary education for that is where new solutions are likely to be found.

Concept of integration

Educational provision for the handicapped in Britain can be viewed as a continuum extending from acceptance and integration within an ordinary school at the one pole, and institutionalization at the other, with special classes, day special schools and residential special schools lying between. This variety serves to illustrate in concrete terms the duality of attitudes towards handicap:

> the desire to create some positive means of assistance and the willingness to separate and confine.
> (Thomas, 1978)

It reflects too what Dunn (1968) referred to in America as 'an expensive proliferation' of special schools and classes which in turn raises serious educational and civil rights issues which require to be faced.

> The overwhelming evidence is that our present and past practices have their major justification in removing pressures on regular teachers' pupils, at the expense of socio-culturally deprived slow learning pupils.
> (p. 6)

Integration as a descriptive term in talking about kinds of schooling is elusive and imprecise. There is a lack of uniformity in its use and much evidence of confused thinking. No single scheme can be considered as qualifying as the paradigm of integration.

Integration can be perceived in numerous ways: as a slogan and battle cry; an educational goal; a social movement in progress; and a rather loose summary description of various educational procedures ranging from occasional *functions* where handicapped and non-disabled children are brought together for social mixing, to the intended complete assimilation of disabled pupils into an ordinary school (Jamieson et al., 1977).

Integration is seen as one aspect of the moves to 'de-institutionalize' handicapped persons; it has an even closer affinity with the North American concept of 'mainstreaming' children with special educational needs into ordinary classes and schools. These trends have their roots in the principle of 'normalization' – a process defined by Nirje (1969) in relation to the intellectually handicapped as letting them obtain 'an existence as close to the normal as possible'.

The philosophy of integration advocates the right of all children

> to acceptance within school programmes regardless of how they may deviate from 'norms' in appearance, performance or behaviour.
> (Meisgeier, 1976)

This is accomplished by making *the school* responsible for adapting its programmes to meet each child's needs rather than requiring the child to adapt to an inflexible programme designed for the hypothetical average child. Approached this way, integration thus shifts the emphasis of special services from *a focus on handicapping conditions* and problems to *a focus on learning needs*.

According to Jones (1978) there are at least three broad concerns behind the 'mainstreaming' movement:

> To reduce the presumed stigma of labelling, to reduce the presumed social isolation and, it is hoped, to increase the effectiveness of educational programming for handicapped children.

Past and present diagnostic procedures are perceived to have done more harm than good in that they have resulted in disability labels, in that they have grouped children homogeneously in school on the basis of these labels. The process of assessment invariably stopped when:

> Something was found to be wrong with the child, when the why has either been found or conjectured, and when some justification has been found for recom-

mending placement in a special education class.
(Dunn, 1968)

Whatever the future holds for education as a whole, it is becoming apparent now that mainstreaming may be the major interim step towards a new special education.

The Warnock Report (1978) recognizes that schools require to make a response to a proportion of children – estimated to include 20 percent of children in *some* schools; and that this response will sometimes be in the form of additional provision which the ordinary school cannot offer:

> These children are likely to include 'those who require a modified or supplemented curriculum, specialist teaching techniques in particular areas of learning, access to some types of specialist apparatus, materials or accommodation, or perhaps simply the occasional enjoyment of the intimate influence of a smaller teaching group.
> (Section 7.12 (ii))

It is with these children that the present project is concerned.

The resource approach

The resource approach to educational provision for children with special needs at present in the process of being developed in Oxfordshire (Jones, E. and Jones, N., 1980) is a concept that has received considerable attention in American literature (Jones and Berrick, 1980). It has been hailed there as a 'renaissance in special education' (Sabatino, 1972) as it is perceived as a middle path between a nearly total reliance on the self-contained special classes and their total disbandment. Although a small number of schools in England are experimenting with this form of special provision, such schemes, according to Cope and Anderson (1977), do not appear to be monitored carefully; if they are, then the findings are not written up.

A 'resource programme' carried out in an ordinary school is usually referred to as a 'resource room'. It is generally used to mean a room or rooms staffed by a teacher or teachers with a specialist qualification and an ancillary helper, and is specially equipped according to the needs of the children. The primary emphasis of the 'approach' is on programming to meet individual needs, rather than grouping children in categories of handicap. The guiding principle is that all children's educational needs should be met *as far as possible* within an ordinary school and as far as possible within an ordinary class. The resource programme is developed as an integral element in the total curriculum and organization of the school. The 'special education' provided is conceived of primarily as an instrument for the facilitation of change and the development of better ways of meeting the learning needs of all children, not only of those who are deemed to be different. As a model, the 'resource approach' requires that special education becomes an adaptive system that is responsive and relevant to the needs of *all* children and not only for those children defined as different by categorized criteria.

There is thus no standardization of the resource room model. Each local authority and school describes the resources departments and their mode of organization, method of operation, and functioning according to local needs and philosophy.

Such an approach calls into question the naive approaches to educational change often associated with the special education debate which focused on a single aspect, e.g., the training of new special educators. It questions whether special education needs to exist as a separate administrative system. Moreover, it highlights what may yet be the fundamental issue of the debate, namely, that the problems confronting both special education and ordinary schools are those which are intrinsic to education in general – one of the major problems being how to educate those who are difficult to teach. The approach recognizes that there are no satisfactory cut-off points in a range of educational opportunities:

> This is as true in the identification of children with disabilities and significant difficulties as it is in the selection at eleven plus. Gifted children and children with handicaps are recognised not as categories but as instances *on a continuum* of ability, performance and special need in this age group.
> (Fish, 1979)

The major task in applying the 'resource approach' has been to find ways of helping teachers, advisers, specialists and administrators to look at familiar problems in new ways which may involve the creation of new attitudes to what in the past have been thought to be simplistic solutions to sometimes insoluble problems, i.e., for the deviant to be 'put away' (Morris, 1969) rather than kept in 'sight and mind' (Burnham and Jones, 1980).

The Burnwood Project

Burnwood is a small town on the edge of the Midlands (population 12,470), overshadowed by a nearby R.A.F. Station which offers employment to approximately 60 percent of the local population. Burnwood School was opened in 1971 as a lower secondary school, catering for approximately 750 pupils from the immediate catchment area. It accepted its first eleven–sixteen age range in September 1978.

The school has four feeder primary schools with a six-form entry in the first year. It has a fairly mobile population because of the nature of the local employment. All tutor groups in Years I and II are mixed-ability, pastoral teaching groups, with the form tutor teaching a minimum of his timetable (25 percent) with his form tutor group. All children, regardless of whether or not they have special educational needs, are members of a tutor group and register there. The school accepts all ESN(M) children who attend the feeder primary schools and also those children who live within an approximate radius of ten miles who are physically handicapped.

The special resources department (SRD) was established in purpose-built premises in September 1978, part of Phase II building of the school, to provide for the all-range secondary intake. The block included several classrooms and science laboratories and was designed to provide easy access and movement to and from subject areas. The amenities provided within the special resources department include an open reception/circulation area, two teaching rooms, each capable of taking a maximum of ten pupils, a smaller teaching room which doubles up as a room available to visiting professionals such as the educational psychologist or the speech therapist, an office with a telephone, a well-equipped art/craft room, a modified kitchen for physically handicapped children, a bathroom and rest/medical room. Typewriters and storage equipment have been provided as well as an array of educational materials required for such a disparate group of children using the special resources department. Capitation is provided through the school's main allocation supplemented by the special education per capita allowance.

Staffing

The special resources department was designed to accommodate thirty full-time children and was fully staffed from the outset. The theoretical ratio for staffing is one teacher to ten children and the department is expected to have its full complement of students by 1982.

Staffing consists of three full-time teachers, two of whom have accepted a teaching commitment in main school, offering their own specialist subject. The head of the special resources department is responsible to the headmaster of the school and has a Scale 3(S) post. The other two staff receive a special schools allowance. There are two full-time ancillary helpers whose primary responsibilities are to meet the physical needs of the children in the department. In the absence of severely handicapped children, the roles of these helpers have been extended to include those of classroom assistants and resource material providers and also to carry out programmes designed by speech therapists and physiotherapists.

The special resources department was opened three months *after* the publication of the Warnock Report. The full implications of the wider concept of special educational needs gradually developed as the work in the special resources department progressed, although in practice county planning appeared to be in line with the philosophy of the report.

From the outset, it was intended that the special education provision was not to be run on 'unit' lines, i.e., children with specific disabilities were not to be grouped together and taught in the 'unit', with 'unit' staff accepting ultimate responsibility for the educational programmes of these 'designated' children. The concept of the resource approach emerged as the project got under way, thus giving it an educational philosophy framework for functioning, with a specific emphasis on adaptability and flexibility, aimed at meeting children's special needs in a secondary school.

Some guiding principles

At the outset, several principles emerged as the result of county/DES recommendations and decisions taken in conjunction with the headmaster and head of the special resources department. Some of these were implicit, others explicit. The result of monitoring was to show how these evolved and changed, or were discarded as irrelevant as the project developed over its first two years.

The stated philosophy behind the planning of the resources department at Burnwood School was that it would adopt a more *flexible* approach to the needs of children who would no longer be so rigidly grouped into ten categories of handicap.

This flexible approach thus ought to enable the school to deal more adequately than was currently possible with the needs of *slow learning children*, their *disruptive* children, or those who for some *other* reason required varying periods of help in a small tutorial group. There was some uncertainty about the actual implementation of such an approach – the notion of a 'multihandicap centre' as opposed to a unit gave some recognition to a wider concept of special education hitherto unexplored in any depth by the county's special resources department. The Burnwood special resources department was thus seen from the outset as an experimental project and as an exercise from which ideas could be used for developments in other parts of the county.

This development was seen as offering one way of keeping together in their home setting children who might otherwise have to attend special day or boarding schools. The idea of providing a 'resource' to the school's local catchment, regardless of nature and degree of disability, was in its infancy.

Within Burnwood School any child with special educational need could be referred to the special resources department. As a principle, no criteria were set out in advance to establish a hierarchy of need. In practice, children designated under the handicap categorization system, especially ESN(M) and physically handicapped, ranked high in order of selection; acting-out 'maladjusted' children were to be ranked low. This partly reflected the decision of the local authority to place a 'resources department' in this secondary school because it had a statutory obligation to meet the educational needs of specific disability groups, notably the ESN(M) and the physically handicapped. In essence it was a resources department to the county as much as to the school. There was a strong acknowledgement from county and teaching staff that the SRD was not to become a 'sin-bin' for those pupils who were 'disenchanted' with school.

The numbers of ESN(M) children admitted to the school would not exceed 40–50 percent; the ideal stated was a ratio of 3:1 in favour of the physically handicapped. In practice, partly as a result of overcrowding in one nearby secondary ESN(M) unit and the lack of similar provision in another, special resources was immediately under pressure to offer 'places' to those children whose *handicap* was defined as ESN(M).

Although it was accepted in principle that the range of disabilities catered for under the special resources department would be wide, it was understood that the degree of disability was not to extend to the severe. This was to impose initial criteria for selection.

All children admitted to the school were to register in normal classes and be retained in main school as far as this was possible. Ultimate responsibility for all pupils was to remain with the form tutor. This implied that children had to be able to spend some time with their normal peer-group; 40 percent was chosen as a criterion for selection. Although designated as a resource to the school, the special resources department's immediate involvement was to be with those children commencing their first and second years. Staffed in advance, the pupil intake was to be built up gradually, thereby enabling staff to explore ways of developing their expertise.

Formal and informal discussions were held with the staff prior to the setting up of the special resources department. There was naturally some uncertainty among main school staff because the vast majority of teachers claimed not to have had previous experience of teaching children designated as ESN(M) and physically handicapped, although in time the special resources department's main intake was to come from within the school. No army of wheelchair children descended upon the school. Few children were 'visibly' handicapped. The special resources department opened with three children already attending main school and known to the county's special services department. At the end of the first year fourteen children were being programmed, three of whom had been admitted during the school year from other local schools. Twelve months later there were twenty-seven children receiving support via the department.

The range of disability presented by these children includes the following: the mildly mentally retarded, severely and mildly epileptic children, a leukaemic child functioning at SSN level, cystic fibrosis, polio, mild cerebral palsy, Hirschprung's disease, deaf and partially hearing, arthritis, minimal cerebral dysfunction, severe learning disability. The majority of the children are multiply handicapped and display symptoms of emotional/social maladjustment; in some instances management is more related to this aspect of need than to medically defined categories of handicap. Children were 'functionally' integrated in main school from 35 percent to 98 percent. No child is in the special resources department full-time.

The roles of SRD staff

In order to provide flexibility and expertise for each child in accordance with his ability and/or disability, the staff have assumed various roles during the first eighteen months.

These relate to and include the following functions:

a   A child may be withdrawn from ordinary classes for specialized help in the SRD. There is no focus on remedial reading as such but rather on perceptual motor skills and similar basic skills, for which the SRD will draw up and implement a detailed and appropriate programme (initial programme planning has been taken on by the head of the SRD). The withdrawal may be for *specialized instruction*, or to reinforce learning in a particular subject, such as a newly acquired numeracy skill. It may be for emotional support and encouragement for the child who, for example, finds it very difficult to return to school after illness or prolonged treatment. The withdrawl may also be an alternative to a particular subject such as swimming in a heated indoor pool, rather than games, for a child with cerebral palsy.

b   A member of the SRD staff may accompany a child into a subject class for a variety of reasons: help in science practical lessons if a child cannot move about freely or keep up with the work pace in the class, or where the alternative would be to withdraw her completely from the subject. As most of the children come from years 1, 2 and 3, it does mean that a member of the SRD staff may be monitoring several children in the same room (science) or, as in humanities, monitoring several children in several adjoining classrooms during the same lessons (years 1 and 2).

c   The SRD may, in consultation with the subject teacher, provide appropriate work which the subject teacher monitors in his own class. Increasingly, the SRD are providing materials for a wider group of children within a teaching group than has been recognized up until now as having special educational needs.

d   The SRD may act as consultants on a particular child within a teaching group. On occasions the head of the SRD has observed a child within his teaching group and offered advice and suggestions as to how to bring out the child's potential within his classroom. Another member of the SRD staff is on a working party attempting to draw up an appropriate programme for 'disenchanted' non-examination fourth- and fifth-year pupils.

e   The SRD attempts to ensure, through the form tutor, that the child has the appropriate equipment/timetable to enable him to join in with his peer-group, e.g., ensuring mobility on ground-floor level for a child who has problems climbing stairs.

f   The SRD offer specialist teaching and diagnostic skills.

g   The SRD staff confer jointly with parents and form/subject teachers and initiate separate staff conferences when needed.

h   The SRD staff initiate the full-time integration of children into the form/subject room and serve as supportive resource teachers until the child has made the complete transition.

i   The SRD staff are responsible for the final evaluation report of each referral and also for a written evaluation of the child's progress in both the classroom and the SRD.

Having assessed 'need' and using 'the resource room model', equipment and personnel are used, not in relation to one or other labelled disability, but to provide a range of special skills and help for a child in need in relation to curriculum planning, the provision of resource material, knowledge of the range of disabilities and their effect on learning, consultation work with teachers and pupils in main school and with parents, liaison with external and supporting agencies.

Emerging issues

This study of a special resources department has illuminated many issues. It seems appropriate to select the following for a more detailed, analytical discussion: teacher attitudes towards children with disabilities; severity of disability and its relation to management; the criteria adopted by staff for determining the successful integration of children.

Teachers attitudes towards disability

Contact with Burnwood staff indicated that all teachers were not equally willing, nor had positive attitudes towards 'integrating' handicapped children. To enable a further exploration of this area, all teachers completed a Likert-type scale (Yuker, 1960, Attitude Towards Disabled Persons Scale) in which they were asked to respond to twenty statements by expressing their degree of agreement or disagreement on a six-point scale. Each statement suggests that disabled persons are either the same as physically normal persons or that they are different. No one obtained scores representing a very high degree of acceptance or rejection of disabled persons. Yet, this was a school which had been 'selected' for its warm and accepting approach to children, a view partly reflected in staffroom discussion.

When investigated further, by asking all staff to rank their hierarchy of preference for teaching children with specific disabilities it was discovered that relative positions of disabilities did exist, in spite of claims by some staff that their knowledge, experience and contact with disabled children was limited. The threshold for acceptance of disability was found to be directly related to teachers' preferences and attitudes towards specific disability groups.

By differentiating between the mild and severe degrees of disability, e.g., the deaf and partially hearing, severe and mild mental retardation, teachers appear to have been forced to differentiate their preferences towards the two groups. The deaf, blind, severely mentally retarded and physically disabled consistently ranked low in order of preference. So too did the maladjusted acting out. The latter is interesting, since it was with acting-out maladjusted children that both the SRD and the main school found themselves in most difficulty (Jones, 1980). They became the test for the viability of the resources department.

Although 'disruptive children' were included in the original brief, there was little discussion in the school about meeting their special educational needs, albeit it was recognized that many of the 'designated' children would require skilled management in this area. There was so much concern not to make the SRD a sin-bin that the issue was shelved.

Twelve months later, the question of specialized provision for maladjusted children was again being discussed. The intervening months had seen the emergence of difficulties related in part to the evolution of an eleven–sixteen school from a middle school. Factors which on investigation appeared to contribute to a greater or lesser degree to this evaluation were the following: 71 percent of staff were appointed to the school during the period of this study (1978–1980), 26 percent of these were probationary staff; the average length of the total teaching experience of staff was *six* years (as opposed to figures in the Survey into Secondary School Staffing (DES, 1980) where the national average is eleven years); no member of staff had received any long-term training in special education; there was no in-service training programme established alongside the project; 16 out of 45 teaching staff were infant/junior trained; 69 percent of staff taught at least one subject for which they had not received any specialized training – one teacher taught *five* specialist subjects for which she had received no training – at a time when subject departments were expanding rapidly and becoming more specialized, with the onset of a formal examination system CSE/GCE.

The principle to retain children as far as possible in ordinary class was upheld by the SRD staff, in relation to disruptive pupils, in what was perceived by main school staff as an inflexible and selective manner. Although this caused friction, it has resulted in open discussions with all teaching staff on the best way to meet the needs of older pupils (fourteen–sixteen), particularly the needs of 'disenchanted' pupils. It is now accepted that the SRD is in too early a stage of development to establish a disruptive unit within its aegis.

The focus is gradually shifting towards more appropriate curricula planning and content for an extended age and ability range. The SRD are attempting to meet the challenge by increasing their involvement in main school teaching and 'curricula planning' by becoming 'resource personnel'.

Severity of disability

An initial guiding principle was that the degree of severity of measured disability was to be a criterion for 'selecting' pupils for inclusion in SRD individualized programmes. All children were to be able to 'integrate' for at least 40 percent of their time. By September 1979, SRD involvement with individual children varied from 5 percent to 71 percent and was not related to any specific disability or handicap. The average percent of withdrawal to the SRD was 13.7 percent. In time, the school had admitted, on a trial and error basis, several severely handicapped children, e.g., a fourteen-year-old deaf girl who had previously been at a school for the deaf full-time, and an eleven-year-old severe leukaemic boy, functioning at an ESN(S) level, who was considered by staff to be coping well.

What the study seems to indicate is that the special acceptability of all the children studied was not related per se to severity or degree of disability, to mobility or more tenuously to educational attainments. What did appear to influence children's acceptance by teachers was related to a greater or lesser degree to the children's own personality characteristics, their level of social adaptability and more particularly to their level of educational attainment *associated with* severity of behavioural difficulties.

A conclusion accepted by the main school staff is that admissions do require to be made on a trial-and-error basis, with an emphasis on whether the school can meet the individual child's needs, taking into consideration the above factors. Approached in this way, the total staff – pastoral and academic – were gradually involved in planning individualized programmes for children, and accepting responsibility for pupils across subject departments. The task of the SRD to persuade teachers to 'take in' children into their subject lessons diminished, and they were enabled to become more effectively involved in a subject content. Their focus is moving towards meeting the learning needs of children, regardless of the nature or degree of their disability, and is seen as the task of all departments and all staff. This is reflected in the recent working party established to look at the curricula needs of children, and in the subject departmental meetings. The central discussion is now about how we teach those who are hard to teach, and less about where these 'difficult' children ought to be taught.

Criteria for determining success

An increase in the school's resources did not in itself produce an improvement in the quality of a child's performance. A problem experienced by the majority of staff was in determining the demands which legitimately could be made on children. If they were unsure, there were signs that they resorted to the natural tendency to 'play safe' and lower expectations. This tended to take several forms and was usually left to the SRD staff to determine, main school staff claiming lack of expertise with 'these' children:

a   not expecting work of a high quality.
b   excusing a child from certain academic tasks, e.g., end of term exams.
c   excluding him from certain aspects of work, e.g., science practicals.
d   taking it for granted that certain subjects are not appropriate, e.g., French/German for slow learners (ESN(M)).

An identified source of tension was the choice staff felt they were forced to make between wanting to normalize the child's presence in school, by not extensively modifying his environment or programme, or separating the child off in any way, and wanting to ensure that the child did receive requisite attention and that proper allowances were made. Several illustrations may clarify these points.

Kathleen, a third-year epileptic girl, was refused admission to cookery on the grounds that she was a liability in the classroom due to frequent fitting – the reason for her total exclusion from her last secondary school was that she fell over a stove during a cookery demonstration. When investigated at closer range, one finds that the girl could not keep up with the rest of her class (she is heavily sedated); as she could not finish in time no one wished to partner her. In a less stressful environment, she controls the extent of her fits. One has to ask whether more could have been done to reassure her class teacher – or modify the work of the class.

Mark, a second-year student, virtually a non-reader, was excluded from science on the grounds that his behaviour was so disruptive that the nature of the subject in practical sessions made him a liability in class. In accepting his exclusion, no one questioned the ability of the class teacher to effectively control the whole class, although it was known that the teacher was experiencing serious management difficulties. Mark was 'taken in' by the SRD because he was one of their 'designated' children, being retarded in reading skills. The following September he was returned to science which was to be taken by another member of staff. There, the boundaries were clearly spelt out in relation to 'expected' behaviour, lesson content was meticulously planned to meet the educational needs of this mixed-ability class. Mark was still there at the end of the year, and apparently coping with his work.

Patrick was a second-year pupil who had been in the school a year prior to the opening of the SRD. He has multiple disabilities – spinabifida, a slow learner with considerable behavioural management problems. He had thus followed a normal timetable, apart from minimal withdrawal for remedial help, and was retained in his French lessons with his peer-group. His teacher was his form-tutor with whom he got on well. She insisted that he ought to be allowed to continue his French as he was coping in class (he got 50 percent in his last termly exam and will probably sit CSE). On closer examination, it was found that the class is following a specially designed county programme for low achievers in modern languages, which is appropriate for his level.

However, all slow-learning children admitted to the school since September 1978 are withdrawn from French. This is not a reflection of that department's policy to refuse to teach slow-learning children a foreign language. A more likely reason put forward by one staff member is that it is easy to rationalize such withdrawal. 'After all, slow-learning children have all got reading difficulties. Time must be found to withdraw them in order to increase their basic skills. What other subject can you withdraw them from if their programme is to be balanced?'

During a careful study of the individualized programmes of children attending the SRD it was discovered that all slow-learning third-year pupils had been withdrawn to the SRD during history lessons, yet they were retained in geography. There was no evidence that the history department had requested this formally – it would appear to have been a 'silent agreement' that these children could spend their time more profitably in the SRD. The geography teacher, although verbally expressing doubts about the viability of being competent to teach such a wide range of mixed ability, devises worksheets, materials and even examination papers for different levels of ability within the same class.

Teachers differed in their criteria for determining successful integration, tending to relate to the child's ability to mix with his peer-group and to participate in the learning process in a normal environment. These criteria were subject to change – e.g., the epileptic child who was integrated 92 percent of her time in main school (having been excluded from her former school and placed on home tuition) was seen by several teachers as failing to integrate successfully. A close study of a child with cystic fibrosis showed that with increased support his attendance improved, but his presence caused new classroom difficulties related to his attention-seeking behaviour. No member of staff offered any evidence to suggest that the amount of time 'integrated' per se had any impact on the way other children felt about SRD children.

This study did not set out to measure whether children who received help in the SRD learn better or even as well as similar children in traditional special classes, or in the remedial department, or even with children in ordinary classrooms who do not receive SRD support.

What did emerge was that integration per se was not of paramount importance. Staff were forced to look more searchingly at the academic performance of their pupils. The existence of extra resources in the form of staffing and physical facilities did not eliminate the difficulties they were experiencing with children, whether these were of an educational and/or behavioural nature. Where they did accept that individual children were making progress via the SRD (in all instances but one, where the child eventually went to a residential maladjusted school), staff immediately cited numerous other children who required extra support and more effective teaching.

It would appear from this study that Burnwood has gone some way towards meeting the special educational needs of some of its pupils. But it does seem that the degree to which it can continue to do so is related directly to the ability and power of the whole school to respond to all its children in all curricular areas. Perceived in this way, the focus of meeting the needs of children is related to the renewal of the entire educational system. It may be that the comprehensive system of education will only become meaningful when each school accepts that each child in its catchment area is entitled by right to attend their neighbourhood school. A naive approach which focused only on a single aspect of special education, e.g., the resource room model, does not bring about the fundamental changes required to serve all children.

References

Blatt, B. (1972) 'The legal rights of the mentally retarded', *Syracuse Law Review*, 991, pp. 991–994

Burnham, M. and N.J. Jones (1980) 'Keeping the handicapped in sight and mind', *Education*, 4 July

Chalk, J. (1975) 'Sanctuary units in primary schools', *Special Education* 2, number 4, pp. 18–20

Cope, C. and E. Anderson (1977) *Special Units in Ordinary Schools*: An Explanatory Study of Special Provision for Disabled Children, Studies in Education (new series) 6, University of London, Institute of Education

Delamont, S. (1978) 'Sociology and the classroom', in Barton, L. and R. Meighan (eds), *Sociological Interpretations of Schoolings and Classrooms – A Reappraisal*, pp. 59–72, Studies in Education Limited, Nafferton, Driffield

Department of Education and Science (1978) *Special Educational Needs*, Report of the Committee of Enquiry into the Education of Handicapped Children and Young People, Cmnd. 7212, HMSO

Department of Education and Science (1980) *Special Needs in Education*, White Paper, Cmmd. 7996, HMSO

Dunn, M.L. (1968) 'Special education for the mentally retarded – is much of it justified?' *Exceptional Children*, 35, pp. 5–22

Fish, J.R. (1979) 'Children and students with special educational needs', *Trends in Education*, 3, pp. 3–8

Gulliford, R. (1971) *Special Educational Needs*, Routledge & Kegan Paul

Jamieson, M., M. Partlett and K. Pocklington (1977) *Towards Integration, A study of blind and partially sighted children in ordinary schools*, NFER

Jones, E. (1980) *The Carterton Project: a monitored account of the way a comprehensive school responded to children with special educational needs*, unpublished M.Ed. thesis, Birmingham University

Jones, E. and S. Berrick (1980) 'The Carterton Resources Department', *Special Education*, Volume 7, number 1, pp. 11–14

Jones, E. and N.J. Jones (1980) 'Special education in Oxfordshire in the 1980's', unpublished policy document: OCC

Jones, R.L., J. Gottleib, S. Guskin and R.K. Yoshida (1978) 'Evaluating mainstreaming programmes: models, caveats, considerations and guidelines', *Exceptional Children* 44, pp. 588–601.

Jones, Neville J. (1971) 'The Brislington Project at Bristol', *Special Education*, Volume 60, number 2, July

Lawton, D. (1980) *The Politics of the School Curriculum*, Routledge & Kegan Paul

Lewis, I. and G. Vulliamy (1980) 'Warnock or Warlock? The sorcery of definitions: the limitations of the report on special education', *Educa-*

tional Review, Volume 32, 1, pp. 3–10

Morris, P. (1969) *Put Away: A Sociological Study of Institutions for the Mentally Retarded*, Routledge & Kegan Paul

Meisgeier, C. (1976) 'A review of critical issues indulging mainstreaming', in Mann, L. and D.A. Sabatino (eds), *The Third Review of Special Education*, Philadelphia: J.S.E. Press, pp. 245–269

Nirje, B. (1969) 'The normalisation principle and its human management implication', in Kugel, R.B. and W. Wolfensberger (eds), *Changing Patterns in Residential Services for the Mentally Retarded*, Washington: President's Committee on Mental Retardation

Parlett, M. and D. Hamilton (1972) *Evaluation as Illumination: A new approach to the study of evaluating programmes*, Occasional Paper Nine, Edinburgh: Centre for Research in the Educational Sciences

Sabatino, D.A. (1972) 'Resource rooms: the renaissance in special education', *The Journal of Special Education*, 6, (4), pp. 335–347

Snowdon Working Party (1976) *Integration of the Disabled*, Report of the Snowdon Working Party, National Fund for Research into Crippling Disease

Thomas, D. (1978) *The Social Psychology of Childhood Disability*, Methuen

Tringo, J.L. (1970) 'The hierarchy of preference towards disability groups', *Journal of Special Education* 4, pp. 295–306

Warnock, M. (1979) 'Children with special needs: The Warnock Report', *British Medical Journal* 1, pp. 667–668

Wolfensberger, W. (1972) *The Principle of Normalisation in Human Services*, National Institute of Mental Retardation, Toronto

Yuker, H.E., J.R. Block and W.J. Campbell (1960) 'A scale to measure attitudes towards disabled persons', *Human Resources Study*, number 5, Alberton, N.Y. Human Resources Foundation

Further reading

Codd, J.A. (1975) 'The resource room concept in special education', *Delta* 17, pp. 2–17

Gickling, E.E., and J.T. Theobold (1975) 'Mainstreaming: affect or effect?' *Journal of Special Education*, 9, pp. 317–328

Haring, N.G., G.G. Stern and W.M. Cruickshank (1958) *Attitudes of Educators Towards Exceptional Children*, Syracuse University Press

Lynas, W. (1980) 'The hearing-impaired child in the ordinary school', *Journal of the British Association for Teachers of the Deaf* (4), 2, pp. 49–57

Stephens, T.W. and B.L. Braun (1980) 'Measurement of regular teachers' attitudes towards handicapped children', *Exceptional Children*, Volume 46, number 4, pp. 292–294

Wedell, K. (1975) *Orientations in Special Education*, John Wiley

CHAPTER 11

LABOURING TO LEARN?
INDUSTRIAL TRAINING FOR SLOW LEARNERS

by Paul Atkinson, David Shone and Teresa Rees

Introduction

The growth in youth unemployment has been matched by an increase in state intervention to manage the 'social problems' thought to be an inevitable and direct consequence. One aspect of this has been intervention in the process of work socialization of young people now no longer necessarily experiencing work itself straight after leaving school. This chapter examines one such intervention measure which has as its client group slow learners. The project is overtly attempting to increase the students' life-chances by preparing them for working life: this involves not only the inculcation of certain industrial skills designed to make them more marketable, but also the instilling of a range of social skills seen to be appropriate in a 'good worker'.

Slow learners, along with the mentally and physically handicapped generally, experience special difficulties in competing effectively in the labour market. Their position has long been recognized as needing some form of positive discrimination policies. However, these policies have been singularly impotent. The Disabled Persons (Employment) Acts of 1944 and 1958, which established a quota system whereby employers of more than 20 persons were to ensure that 3 percent of their workforce were registered as disabled, have been widely disregarded and are in any case virtually impossible to enforce. As Hudson suggests 'a total of five prosecutions between 1970–75 makes the maximum penalty of £500 an ineffective deterrent' (Hudson, 1977, p. 1703).

If the quota system has been ineffective, it seems unlikely that the initiative from the Manpower Services Commission and the National

Advisory Council on Employment of Disabled People in publishing a guide to employing disabled people can have materially effected their competitive edge either. The document, *Positive Policies* (1977), was sent to all employers with 20 or more staff (about 55,000); it was both supported by the CBI and TUC and welcomed by the Warnock Committee on Special Education Needs.

These strategies, focusing as they do on the employers, seem unlikely to make much of an impact on the job prospects of those young handicapped capable of working in open employment. During the current high levels of youth unemployment, when employers can pick the more attractive candidates from the dole queues for even the most menial of tasks, clearly a different approach is required if the handicapped school-leaver is to have any chance of a job at all.

The National Society for Mentally Handicapped Children has for many years attempted to enhance the life-chances of the mentally handicapped school-leaver by paying their wages for the first twelve weeks of employment and recruiting a foster worker to oversee and advise the young person at the place of work. The Pathway scheme thus introduces employers to handicapped workers on a no-commitment basis, thereby ensuring even if the employer does not then take on the young person permanently, he or she has at least had the benefit of work experience.

The initial response by the government to high levels of youth unemployment was also to provide some form of work experience so that school-leavers were not hopelessly penalized in the labour market. Of the revamped schemes operated by the Manpower Services Commission (MSC) since 1978, it is work experience which accounts for the majority of places under the Youth Opportunities Programme (YOP). And, according to one source at least (Gregory, 1980), specialist career officers for the handicapped have been able to do a 'deal' with employers, persuading them to take a handicapped young person as part of a job lot. Employers have apparently expressed surprise at their employability and kept them on; the capacity of some mentally handicapped young people to tolerate extremely boring work has been cited as one reason.

Under YOP there are also a variety of courses aimed at preparing young people for working life (Working Introduction Course, Short Training Course), including one specifically aimed at young people with mental or physical handicaps – the Young Persons Work Preparation Course. In addition, while, nominally at least, a further input has always been an integral element of YOP, including those on some form of work experience, its emphasis and role has become more significant. The MSC is no longer simply concerned to provide work experience, it is now concentrating more and more on aspects of work socialization.

Gregory and Markall (1982) refer to MSC's:

> *transformative* attempt to intervene culturally, ideologically and materially in the sphere of education, training, work induction and the identification and transmission of 'skills' which not only carry meanings about the nature of work and wage labour but which also attempt to structure and delimit other understandings and definitions available to and entertained by the young.

The MSC is now in the business of enhancing life-chances, instilling skills, further education, remedial literacy and numeracy, and, most significant of all perhaps, providing the young unemployed with 'social and life skills'. That includes, as the MSC instructional guides on teaching social and life skills illustrate, how to have the 'right attitude' to work and to employers. Increasingly, then, rather than just offering young people work experience to improve their marketability, MSC is intervening to a far greater extent by moulding young people to the 'needs' of industry.

Industrialists have for many years bemoaned 'declining standards' and illiteracy and innumeracy among young workers. With greater horror complaints have been lodged at the *attitude* of young job-seekers. Indeed in one survey, 43 percent of employers claimed to have turned down applicants because of their attitude and personality, 29 percent because of their appearance and manners, compared with 24 percent because of their 'lack of a basic education' (DE *Gazette*, October 1977; see also MSC, 1980). The concentration of MSC on aspects of work socialization can be seen as a response to the desire by industry for workers with the 'right' attitude.

Clearly the transition from school to work is not simply a linear process with MSC and other agencies acting as 'bridge' between the two worlds by equipping young people with appropriate experience and social skills. The two worlds overlap in multifarious ways – parents and friends are known to play as important a role in shaping the work socialization of handicapped young people as all the official 'gatekeepers' (careers, specialist education services) and voluntary agencies. Nevertheless, increasingly such interventions have shifted in emphasis from allowing the experience itself to be the formative factor in work socialization to more overt instilling of 'right' attitudes.

The rest of this chapter is based on an ethnographic study of one institution designed to ease the transition from school to working life for adolescents who are 'educationally subnormal' or 'slow learners'. (We shall not enter into any discussion at this stage as to the precise definition of the young people involved, since in practice there is no single educational, psychological or social characteristic which delimits the client group.) We shall describe some features of the working of an industrial training unit in industrial South Wales. We shall make no claims as to the 'typicality' of this one institution: indeed, we have reason to believe that in some respects it is rather unusual. On the other hand, we do wish to claim that the issues *raised* by this 'case study' are of more general relevance. In particular, we wish to highlight some aspects of the training and socialization for work that goes on in the training unit, and some of the ways in which the young people there are evaluated and assessed.

The industrial training unit: an introduction

The unit is part of a college of further education, but is physically distinct and self-contained. It is located on an industrial site, rather than the college campus. The unit consists of a workshop, with woodwork and metalwork machines, an industrial sewing room, a canteen and staff facilities. It can accommodate up to twenty-one students at a time. It is staffed by a manager, whose background is woodwork craft teaching, one other lecturer specializing in woodwork, two lecturers in metalwork (all male), one sewing teacher, one part-time machinist/nurse, and one part-time tutor in literacy and numeracy (all female).

Broadly speaking, three components can be identified in the training provided: specific 'industrial' tasks and skills, 'social and life skills', and remedial numeracy and literacy. We shall not comment on this last aspect in this chapter. In practice the former two aspects are not sharply differentiated. At the time of our observations, the unit's day-to-day work was not organized in accordance with a preset curriculum in the normal sense of the term. Rather, the pace and content of the work was framed by *production* processes. The 'philosophy' of the unit reflected a belief that students should engage in and be responsible for 'real' work, and most of the tasks they perform are aimed at the completion of contracts placed with the unit by local firms. The range of tasks performed by the students is also determined largely by the sort of machinery available, which in turn constrains the range of contracts that can be attracted by the manager and his staff. The 'curriculum' of the unit, then, is embodied in its physical plant, the contracts which are placed, and the production processes which these imply.

Most of the machine tasks performed by students are simple and repetitive. They require students to conduct a simple set of sequenced activities which form a complete cycle which is then repeated. A typical task of this sort on the metalwork side would include drilling components – placing them in a vice or jig, lowering the drill and raising it again, by simply pulling a lever. While it is more difficult to preset the woodworking machinery, similarly repetitive tasks, such as sawing or planing lengths of timber, are undertaken. The sewing tasks involve the operation of industrial sewing machines, a button machine and a hand-operated press.

The unit takes male and female students. There is a degree of gender differentiation in the allocation of tasks in the unit. Most of the girls are allocated work in the sewing room, except those whose ability is regarded as too low to cope with industrial sewing machines. When the sewing room is not in operation, the girls are usually provided with the more simple tasks in the workshop.

Over and above the routines of productive work, the students also receive more general instruction, through talks and lectures. These arise out of particular incidents that crop up in the course of the day's work.

Lectures on workshop practice

Certain general principles of workshop practice are communicated to the students as a group, through a lecture. For example, breaches of the safety procedures have been occasions for a lecture on the potential danger of machinery. Such lectures are used to emphasize the necessity of safety procedures and they underline the precept that the students must 'do exactly as you're told', in order to avoid danger.

Other problems which occur, such as continual faulty workmanship, may form the basis of a lecture of this sort. These lectures reinforce the procedures and safety rules of the workshop by demonstrating the potentially dangerous, and sometimes expensive, consequences of failure to obey them. Thus students are enjoined 'always stack materials tidily and correctly'; 'no smoking in the workshop'; 'always switch off machines when leaving them'; 'do as you're told'; 'inform staff if you see something going wrong'.

It is a common ploy of the lectures to include dramatic and vivid demonstrations of matters of danger and safety precautions. For instance, on one occasion the observer noticed the manager hurrying over to where one boy, Dennis, was using a circular saw.

He switched off the main power and called everybody to 'gather round'. He said something to Dennis which I couldn't hear[1] and then he asked if anyone would put their hand on the bench while he picked up a piece of wood and waved it up and down aggressively.

Someone replied 'No', then the manager said 'Why not?' I was at the rear of the assembled group and as I shuffled forward I saw that it was Tina who was replying to the questions. 'Well this saw blade is travelling at 120 mph and it cuts this wood. What do you think it could do to your fingers?' (Rhetorically). The telephone rang and then the manager asked another lecturer to take over and to 'show them the other display'.

He moved over to the edge planer machine and selected a long length of wood about 6 feet and said something to the effect that 'imagine this was a finger'. He then pushed it against the rotating cylindrical blade of the planer, and in a matter of a few seconds it was reduced to about 18 inches in length. Stuart said, 'You've proved your point' (sarcastically).

The lecturer then said that the saw travels at 120 mph which is 'the same speed as the high speed train . . .'

The lecturer then pointed out that putting their hands near the unguarded saw was as dangerous as standing in front of the high speed train. Then the students were directed back to work. The impression here is of a well-established 'routine' to make the safety point: and the point was certainly well made. Our field notes contain numerous examples of such teaching episodes.

Given the nature of the workshop, the machinery in it, and the nature of the youngsters who work there, safety must be a major preoccupation for the staff. The following extract from our notes may convey something of the urgency with which staff members attempt to instil safe workshop practice in the students. The workshop is noisy, and staff have to gain students' attention above the roar of the machinery.

The manager then entered the workshop just after a lecturer had called lunch. Then he shouted everyone to gather round. But some had already left for the canteen. The manager said 'C'mon will you all gather round.' Just a few students who had been in the immediate vicinity remained. Someone asked if they should fetch the others. The manager said, 'If you could, if it's not too late.' Then he said 'I'm bringing in this machine. It's a very dangerous machine. It may not look it but that blade can cut your fingers off. If I ask a lecturer which is the most dangerous machine in the workshop he'll say "this one" ,' as the lecturer pointed to the cutter. 'You only have to have the handle slip down and it can take four fingers off. We've got machines working fast in this workshop but they're not nearly so dangerous as this because you can see how dangerous they are. I was once working with this and the handle slipped, and the blades are very, very sharp and it took the skin off the top of all my fingers'. The girls went 'eugh'.

'They were only little cuts though but it was painful. Now I'm going to put one of you on this machine this afternoon and whoever it is I don't want you to put your fingers through there. Keep well clear of it. And the others, I don't want you to go anywhere near the one who's using it. Do you hear me, you've got to keep well away from whoever it is 'n I don't want to see anybody near it.'

Understandably, such warnings are not sufficient to eliminate dangerous practices altogether. Like many factory workers, the young people in the unit take dangerous short cuts when dealing with the machinery, or they are simply forgetful or careless. Staff supervising the workshop must therefore be on the lookout for this, and as we have already indicated, may treat any such incident as the occasion for a general lecture in an attempt to reinforce the basic safety message. The lectures and demonstrations about workshop practice are often concerned with more mundane aspects of work, such as tidiness. Such lectures deal not only with the particular event or action which sparks them off, but may also include more general advice on good workmanship and relations with future employers. For instance, in the following example, the operation of a simple task like sweeping the floor can become the occasion for general advice on employers:

> The cleaning up operation began and one of the charge-hands, Rhian, went around collecting the ear protectors. Apart from that particular piece of work the two charge-hands were doing nothing different from the others. Most were busily brushing down benches, stacking timber and two were sweeping the floor. The manager then stopped the cleaning up operation and asked everybody to gather round Colin who was sweeping the floor. He stated to everyone: 'I have shown you how to sweep up haven't I? Look what I just saw this boy, Colin, doing.'
>
> He proceeded to sweep in a straight line from one point to another, he then went back and swept in a straight line adjacent to the one he had just swept. He then finally demonstrated the correct way of sweeping, i.e. all around a particular spot. The manager concluded by pointing out that 'An employer wants to see results. He wants to get value for money. Employers don't like people who insist on time wasting. They're not worth paying', or words to that effect. I happened to be standing next to one of the other lecturers at this point who stated to me, 'I don't know what's the matter with that boy. He always works untidily and I can't get him to work any better.'

This last example from the field notes illustrates how a topic of workshop practice can be expanded into a talk on 'good workers', and how students should behave in order to impress or please their future or potential employers. This is a central theme to a good deal of the more formal teaching which goes on in the unit. There is a good deal of instruction which is concerned with general matters of social and personal behaviour, and much of this is directed at how students can 'make the most of themselves', and hence make the most of their employment opportunities. We describe this component of the training as 'social and life skills'.

This aspect of the unit's work is not designated 'social and life skills training' as such by the staff, but it seems useful to describe some of the teaching that goes on under this heading. The description is that given to a major component of a great deal of comparable work training and experience for young people. As with most of the teaching, this is not necessarily a prescheduled part of the work but staff members normally capitalize on particular occurrences to make some general point to the students as a group. All the workshop staff contribute to teaching of this sort. The teaching normally takes the form of lectures to the students; the topics covered include issues relevant to students' work and employment prospects and to general social and personal behaviour.

Training for working life

The sort of topics that have been taken up include: 'motivation', 'attention span', 'confidence', 'appearance', and 'smoking'. By and large the staff identify personal attributes or habits among the students which they regard as undesirable for working life.

Often a particular student is singled out to exemplify the undesirable trait, and his or her 'shortcomings' are generalized upon. A common strategy is for the lecturer to suggest that some supposedly undesirable characteristic is liable to give employers, or potential employers, a poor or false impression of the student. They therefore attempt to point out the undesirability of such behaviour and exhort the students to adopt more acceptable characteristics. In tone, then, these lectures are partly punitive, in drawing attention to a particular student and 'showing up' him or her. They also have the air of moral homilies and exhortations to self-improvement.

The following extract from the field notes exemplifies a lecture of this sort:

> The machines had been switched off four times that morning for the manager to cite an incident that he had noticed, and to indicate the things that had been going wrong. Once more the manager walked over to the main power switch. 'Will you gather round,' he called. Students wandered halfheartedly from their respective positions in the workshop towards the place where the manager was now stand-

ing. The manager turned to Clive and said: 'Will you Clive walk over to the door and then walk back.' Puzzled looks appeared on students' faces and one or two voiced the complaint: 'What for?' The manager said: 'You'll see in a moment.' Clive looked up at the manager and then walked over to the door and back. The manager then asked Stuart to walk over to the door and back. Stuart arrived back and was asked to repeat the procedure. One further student was asked to complete this procedure.

The manager made a joke about the slovenly way in which the students walked about.

Several students laughed at this remark. The manager continued: 'I particularly noticed you, Stuart, walking earlier, you were straight. You looked as if you were going somewhere, as if you knew what you were doing, but you didn't do it then. Most of you slouch around, all down and out as if you couldn't care a damn. When I saw Stuart walking straight I thought to myself, he's got a purpose; he knows what he's doing. Most of you look as if you don't know what you're doing. An employer would think that you were a good worker if you were walking straight. Yes, you may know this, people can only judge us on appearances and the way we walk is very important. Don't you agree?' At this point Geraint entered into an argument with the manager:

Geraint: 'People don't just think of the way we walk.'
Manager: 'Well how else can an employer tell what we're like?'
Geraint: 'Not just by the way we walk though' (laughing as he said it).
Manager: 'People do make these impressions on the way we walk and our general attitude when we first meet.'
Geraint: 'But that's not right.'
Manager: 'You're deliberately misunderstanding me you are. Does anybody think that I'm talking through the back of my head?'
Geraint: 'Yes.'
Manager: 'What about the rest of you? Do you think that I'm talking through the back of my head?'
Stuart: 'No.'

This question was then posed to most of the students in turn. Only three students actually disagreed with him.

This particular lecture is a typical instance of how the staff members take a particular youngster's personal characteristics as the starting point for more general homilies and maxims. It is also characteristic of this teaching approach that the students are allowed, even encouraged, to 'answer back' and agree or disagree with the points that have been made. These lectures are a particularly characteristic feature of the teaching strategy and training content of the unit.

In such ways the students were exhorted to mind their demeanour and appearance so as to create the most favourable impression with employers. In various ways, images of the 'good worker' are presented to the students, who are exhorted to behave in a manner which conforms to such a view. This is amply illustrated in the following extract from our notes:

The manager then went over to the main power switch and asked everyone to 'gather round'. He stood at the top of the workshop by the barrier which separated most of the metal working jobs from the woodworking machinery. He asked: 'What do we need to get by in life, what are the basic necessities?' One boy, Dennis, said 'food'. Another one, Stuart, said 'shelter'. A further one said 'money'. The manager then said: 'What about sex, do we need that?' Someone shouted that 'it makes you feel tired'. The manager said, 'It doesn't do that for me', at which there were a few approving giggles from the kids. He then said: 'What about this one, not many people realize this but we all like to be important: you may not have thought of it before but it's true. Everyone needs to feel important in some ways. The point is there are all sorts of ways of being important.'

The manager then mentioned people wearing 'punk' clothing such as chains, earrings and rubbish bags to make themselves feel important. He went on:

'What they don't realize is that the only people they impress are children and others who do the same. Most people just laugh at them. An employer wouldn't give them a job if they came to an interview like that, he'd think they were loonies.'

'Well what I'm saying is that we all like to feel important but there are some ways of feeling important or trying to be important that are better than others. The outrageous ways, such as wearing black rubbish bags, are not going to get you a job nor help you keep that job. But you can be important by being a good worker, and that is better because you're then important to the man who pays your wages.'

'Anyway that's all I wanted to say. Jeremy when are you going to get your hair cut?'

Jeremy: 'I don't know' (laughing as he said it).

Manager: 'You need to buck up a bit my lad.'

On such occasions, some students' personal habits will be commented on adversely, and general maxims on their 'self-presentation' offered. In the following example, the stress on 'importance' seems to be carried through, in the lecturer's choice of 'role models' for the students to emulate:

At this point Geraint noticed the manger writing on the board. He indicated that

I should look. I laughed with him. He then shouted across to Daniel, 'look what he's writing'. On the board the manager had written:

How do you know if someone is an idiot?
Harold Wilson
Raquel Welch

Esther Rantzen

The manager gathered all the students together again and said something to the effect that: 'C'mon this is a serious question. How do you know if someone is an idiot? Well, from the way they behave. Are Harold Wilson, Raquel Welch or Esther Rantzen idiots?' Someone answered 'No'. 'We tell that by the way they behave, by what they do. I bet you've never seen any of these on the television biting their nails or leaving their mouths hanging open. That's one way that people will definitely know you're an idiot. We only know people are idiots if we see them acting like idiots.' (Geraint gave a glance across to Deirdre, accusing her of being the nail-biting culprit.) 'These people don't bite their nails on the television'. Geraint commented, 'They could do', but the manager ignored the remark and concluded. He said 'I bite my nails sometimes but I don't do it where anybody can see me. I make sure nobody's watching and I do it in the car. So if you have to bite your nails make sure you do it when nobody can see you and then they won't think you're an idiot. Go on have your lunch.'

As they all filed past to go to lunch the manager said to Tina, 'Did you know who I was talking about then?' (jokingly). Tina said, 'Me.'

It is noticeable in this example how the lecturers use colloquial speech forms to produce an informal, relaxed atmosphere. These lectures to the students exhorting them to self-improvement also include injunctions to improve their general attitude, their concentration and motivation.

Social training

Again, these lectures arise as specific responses to particular incidents in the workshop. In such cases the students concerned are particularly likely to be singled out and named in the course of the lecture to the whole group. The lecturer will often attempt to demonstrate the negative consequences of the behaviour in question and provide advice on how to avoid such behaviour in the future. These lectures are particularly concerned with the students' social relationships and their general behaviour. As the manager has put it, it is a matter of 'teaching them how to get on with each other'. Clearly there can be no hard and fast distinction between such general 'social' skills, and the work-related concerns mentioned above. It is not a distinction made by the staff themselves and the two are necessarily closely related. Both kinds of lecture have to be delivered amid the machinery for lack of a classroom.

The following report provides a representative example of this sort of intervention by a member of staff and of the sort of lecture it can give rise to.

> The manager had observed Geraint and Frank arguing as they were returning to the workshop after loading a van. The manager asked everybody to assemble together at the front of the workshop in readiness for a lecture. The manager began: 'Before I start I want you two to shake hands and make friends. Will you do that now?' Frank moved forward to shake hands with Geraint who was sitting on a milk crate opposite to him. Geraint's head was held low and he looked up at Frank approaching and immediately looked down again. The manager continued: 'Did you notice that gesture? He's adult enough to say, "let's forget it". There's nothing worse than walking around with poison in your stomach which is what you two had. And he's not adult enough to shake hands. If you have a bit of difficulty with somebody, if they're getting on your nerves, you just go up and tell him. It's terrible if you can't get on with the people you work with. So if you have to have a row you'll have to remember to make it up. You two, each of you had poison in your stomach. When you get older you just can't do that, because what happens, you talk to somebody and then you call then names, and then you go and talk about how horrible he is to somebody else. Then that person thinks you're a great bloke and then you get on his nerves. . . .'

The moral here was that quarrelling led to loss of friends and hence loneliness.

The following incident is very similar, in that an event relating to workshop practice and discipline is turned towards a concern with interpersonal relationships:

> Geraint had been instructed to plane down some wood on the planer. He began to run the machine and Tony noticed that some dust was blowing out of the air bags of the waste collector. From where he was working on the rear circular saw he shouted to a lecturer who was standing just in front of the bench saw, and indicated the blowing dust. The lecturer ran and switched off the planer and shook hands with Tony for the deed he had performed. The lecturer then instructed Dennis and Geraint to repair the canvas bag. The air has been seeping from the seal between the bag and the machine. Presumably the metal band which was fitted to the bag like a belt with saw teeth fastenings had worked loose, allowing the bag to ride up. The lecturer instructed them how to unleash the band. . . . The two boys then replaced the band and went over to switch on the machine again. However, the bag began to leak again and Geraint turned the planer off, and he and Dennis raced over to the bag. As they began to ply the metal band and pull at the canvas in order to replace the broken seal, the lecturer approached them. He said to Geraint, 'Oh you've put it back on wrong haven't you?' Dennis then answered 'No, it was me.'
> The lecturer then shouted everybody to gather round and began to relate what Dennis had just done. He said: 'Y'know what he just did? I accused Geraint of

making a mistake and Dennis said to me, "No, it was my fault". It takes a brave man to admit when he's in the wrong.' At which point the lecturer beckoned Dennis nearer and held his hand out for him to shake it. As they shook hands he said 'congratulations'.

Sometimes these incidents are basically matters of 'telling off' students who are misbehaving in some way. One day the lecturer called everybody together and said:

'I've just overheard Stuart telling Rhian to shut up. That's not the way to get on with each other, it's a childish way to talk. What happened?' he said to Rhian. She said, 'He was throwing things at me.' The lecturer's eyes returned to Stuart who said with his head held down, 'She started it.' The lecturer said 'There's no need for you to sulk, stop sulking and tell me what happened.' He said, 'I'm not sulking, she started it.' The lecturer went on, 'I was praising you for being so grown up this morning and now look how childish and stupid you are. This calling each other names and saying "she started it" and telling people to shut up is not the way to get on with each other. Honestly it's just so stupid and childish. Get back to work, and you two stop fighting.'

In addition to the lectures we have just described where working relations are stressed, general topics of demeanour and self-presentation are sometimes emphasized:

Immediately on returning to the workshop the lecturer began with a lecture on swearing. He proceeded to say something to the effect that you've got to be careful when you're swearing. 'I don't mind swearing at all. But don't do it in public where other people can hear you because they might not like it. You might get done for obscene behaviour. The other thing is, don't swear in front of girls because they may not like it either. Don't swear on buses and other public places.'

Training for adult life

This training is less concerned with changing students' immediate behaviour, and is more informative in character. Lectures are aimed at providing students with knowledge which the staff regards as potentially important for adult life in general. These lectures, unlike the first two types, are not necessarily triggered by particular incidents of poor behaviour or workmanship. In fact, unlike the other training, they are routinely provided at fixed points during the day – before students begin work in the morning, or immediately after the lunch break.

It did appear, however, that as with other components of 'social' training, the content of these talks was rather ad hoc. There was little evidence of any preplanning or sequencing of topics and so on. The result was a somewhat disparate series of topics. Over the fieldwork period, the topics covered were: 'capitalism'; 'democracy'; 'advertising'; 'literature' and 'classical music'; 'mortgages'. In style and tone these sessions differed little from those we have already described. They tended to take the form of 'improving' lectures from members of staff. The students had little or no active part to play, and the presentation of the topics was not always grounded in the students' own immediate experiences. The students were not involved in any practical activities, and no attempt was made to make use of such techniques as role playing and so on.

We reproduce here the notes on just one session of this sort. The first example shows how the students were introduced to topics 'out of the blue'. It is also revealing about some of the distinctive social and political views of the staff members themselves. The emphasis on self-help and the moral virtue of work is a theme which runs through a good deal of the unit's work. It is a recurrent theme in what we can only describe, metaphorically, as 'homilies'.

The capitalism lecture

Everybody had just started back to work and Jeremy was leaning on the bench with eyes half closed. The manager had looked over towards him, and that seemed to spark off the lecture he gave. He switched off the machinery and invited everybody to stand over by the blackboard. He began by saying something like, 'Did you know that we live in a capitalist society?' (as he wrote the word *capitalist* on the blackboard). 'What that means is that machinery and factories are owned by capitalists. This is not just one person, it's a lot of people, and they run factories to make a profit. Most people are workers and the trouble is we depend on each other for a living. The worker gets his pay at the end of the week and the capitalist gets his profit. But when workers are lazy or continually make high pay demands a lot of employers go broke and then the workers lose their jobs. Like British Leyland. So employers can't afford to carry lazy workers as passengers. Now, you're all passengers now, and you've depended on your parents for most of your lives. People on the dole, they are passengers, they take their living from people who are working. If you're very lucky you may go to college and become a passenger for a lot longer. But you'll all hopefully get a job and you won't lose it for laziness, with one or two exceptions.' The telephone rang and he instructed another lecturer to continue.

The lecturer began by saying, 'What he was saying about passengers is that when you leave here and get a job you won't be a passenger any longer. There are too many people today who think they're owed a living. So you've got to try to be independent, to look after yourselves and stop being passengers.'

Staff evaluations of student ability

In organizing the day-to-day activities of the unit, and in assessing the suitability of students for particular tasks, the staff members base their decisions on evaluations of students' ability and motivation: these are based on their observation of the students rather than the use of standardized tests. It seems that the staff feel themselves qualified to make such assessments of students' skill, character and personality.

During the early period of fieldwork it became apparent that the students were being evaluated according to two basic dimensions. The first of these reflected the assessment of a given student's relative intelligence; it boiled down to whether they were seen as 'bright' or 'dull'. The second evaluative dimension reflected their ability and orientation with respect to work; that is, whether they were 'good' or 'bad' workers. In addition to these two basic categorizations, students were characterized in terms of their personal characteristics – sometimes their personal or social shortcomings, sometimes their more 'endearing' qualities. Examples from the field notes include:

> She's ever so dull but she's a very nice kid though.
>
> He's a nice kid but he's so shy.
>
> He's a good lad this one only he lets himself go.

The informal assessment of students' abilities is of considerable importance for the running of the unit, and it seems to be the case that the identification of students as 'bright' or 'dull' (able or unable) is reflected in the tasks they are given and in the way they are treated. As we have just suggested, some jobs – such as the use of the woodwork lathe – were reserved for students who were regarded as 'good workers'. The evaluation of a student as a 'good worker' does not rest on *ability* alone. In practice, a major criterion of 'good work' is a student's willingness to conduct tasks for relatively long periods of time, on his or her own, without disruptive contact with other students. A good worker, then, can be left to get on with his or her work, without needing constant supervision, and without upsetting the work of other students.

Since 'good' workers are given 'good' jobs, and may be left to get on with it, there is an inbuilt bias against any systematic attempts to introduce students to progressively more demanding tasks, or to rotate students through a large range of available jobs. Rather, there is a tendency for students to be allocated to their perceived level of competence, and then for them to stop there. Of course, we do not wish to suggest that there is absolutely no fluidity and movement between jobs. Nevertheless, there is a tendency for students to spend long periods of time at the same task, and hence to work constantly at the same level, in terms of the demands made on them, intellectually and manually.

The staff's impressions of students not only have some bearing on the training they receive, but also on the types of employment they are considered suitable for. In general they are considered to be destined for manual and semi-skilled work. Occasionally, when a student shows 'promise' he or she may be steered towards a particular skill in the hope that employment in that line of work may become available. It does appear that the students so assessed and selected have a passive role, although they occasionally object to the work they are steered towards. Such objections may be that they 'want to work with their friends' or that they have unrealistic expectations of wages elsewhere. It was also suggested to us that students might object to particular sorts of employment by virtue of inaccurate assessment of their own abilities (as lower than the staff's evaluations of them).

There were, for instance, two boys who were regarded as exceptionally 'bright'. They were routinely given relatively skilled carpentry jobs to perform, and were eventually channelled into relatively skilled employment of this sort. After 'proving' their ability in routine work they were rarely allocated to repetitive tasks. In contrast, two of the girls were assessed by the staff as particularly 'dull', and as likely candidates for the adult training centre. They were provided with what the staff themselves regarded as simple, routine, uninteresting work. The manager has pointed out to us that he regards such work as necessary, in that it closely approximates the kind of work the least able students would be likely to find in open employment.

As we have already remarked, the most obvious categorization of students is on gender lines, and this overlaps with the assessment of student ability. Most of the girls are allocated work in the sewing room, except those whose ability is regarded as too low to cope with the sewing machines. When the sewing room is not in operation (approximately eight hours a week, because of timetabling problems), the girls are allocated to the more simple tasks in the workshop. Only rarely do they operate woodworking or metalworking machinery, although in theory they may do so if they wish. The manager attributes the gender differentiation to the girls' preference for the more 'congenial' atmosphere of the sewing room. There is a consensus among the staff that certain of the metalworking jobs – simple drilling and tapping operations – are safe and simple, and therefore particularly suitable for the less able student. When the girls have to leave the sewing room for varying periods of time they are given such metalworking jobs, along with the least able boys. One of the boys who was regarded as one of the 'least able' and was also seen as 'troublesome' spent most of his time conducting simple metalwork operations. He frequently complained that he would be 'dreaming of these brackets' in his sleep.

The criteria on which staff opinions are based appeared to include: attendance, timekeeping, and evidence of working ability (e.g., judged by the number of components made). But these aspects are mediated by a global impression of less tangible matters, such as aspects of students' personality. Guidelines for student assessment are explicitly included in a *Readiness for Work Chart*, which forms part of the student's record. But staff rarely articulate their assessments in terms of these explicit criteria, but rather in terms of students' personal idiosyncracies and characteristics. Thus those students who seem unable to conform to the standards expected, or who appear to possess less favourable or likeable attributes are often those who benefit least from their stay at the unit, in that they will not be considered for placement if a work vacancy arises.

Although many of the students may have extremely low IQs they may not be regarded as exceptionally dull or relatively bright unless their performance at the unit confirms or disconfirms such an impression. Thus, attempts at training on tasks and at inculcating work speeds may prove to be difficult, and may thus reinforce prior categorizations. In other words, IQ is not considered to be particularly important in itself. Appearance, demeanour and a willingness to accept subordinate roles and discipline have a far greater influence on staff impressions, and may be influential in obtaining jobs for these students.

More important, however, is the implicit notion of 'work readiness' which the staff adopt. Unless jobs are actually sought after for particular students, who are thought to have 'shown improvement', it seems to be the case that most of the student body are regarded as 'not ready' for such work. Of course, the seeking out and finding of jobs does not necessarily depend on their being 'work ready', but more importantly on other factors such as the availability of work, the geographical location of students' homes, their length of stay at the unit, and the point at which their course terminates. In other words, there are various contingencies involved in finding jobs for students, the most pressing of which is the need to find work at the end of a course or before long college holidays.

However, categorization of students as outlined above is rarely articulated fully. The staff seem to glean their impressions of who are the better students from conversations between each other. Thus, one student was regarded as particularly annoying and the following was heard during a break-time conversation in the staffroom:

> 'Oh she gets on my nerves she does. She's always wanting to organize everything.'

It would appear that others concur in this particular evaluation of the student: we have learned that the employers who subsequently took on this girl have found her unsatisfactory, not least because of her 'attention seeking'.

Perhaps the most illuminating area in which these non-articulated categorizations are elicited is in connection with job opportunities that arise. In such instances the staff would suggest particular students as suitable for that employment. Thus, the following exchanges occurred:

> A: 'I've got these two apprenticeships at ——— joinery.'
> B: 'But what are we going to do about the interview?'
> A: 'Oh I'd forgotten about that, we could put somebody else in.'
> B: 'What about Stuart?'
> A: 'Oh that would be an improvement.'

and also:

> A: 'They've got a vacancy up there for a good lad, one like they had before. But I told them I don't think we've got anybody ready.'
> B: 'What about ———?'
> A: 'He's not been here long enough.'
> C: 'His attitude's not right.'

One student was found a job and the staff kept him back because they were afraid that he might 'mess up another student's chances'. Thus, when the decisions finally had to be made two members of the staff consulted:

> A: 'What are we going to do about Geraint?'
> B: 'He'll only mess up James's chances.'

In this case the staff members felt that while one of the boys would work well, together they could be 'troublesome'.

Another example relating to the problem that students present is as follows:

Staff: 'What would you do with somebody like that?'
Researcher: 'Well he works alright doesn't he?'
Staff: 'But there's a communication problem somewhere. You can't just get through to him.'

In other words, the students are categorized as having particular problems which mitigate against their consideration as 'work ready'. It seems to be the case that the problems which the students present during early training are either reinforced or not according to the problems they present on a daily basis. Although the staff may operate an implicit conception of work readiness this is subject to shifting criteria in response to day-to-day contingencies. Thus, the age of students, the imminence of their course termination, their length of stay at the unit, are all aspects that may be taken into account when decisions as to finding employment are made.

Some of the features of the staff evaluation of student ability can be illustrated by the following case study of one student, Tina. Tina was regarded as particularly dull and immature. She was normally allocated to the most simple and undemanding of tasks: drilling and tapping, and sorting springs. (This last job involved unwinding tangled springs – something which was also being done by adult workers in a nearby factory.) She was often referred to as being suitable for the adult training centre, and was given tasks which did not involve her in any potential danger. Unlike most of the other girls she was not allowed to use the sewing machines, except on rare occasions under close supervision.

Of course Tina was assigned to other tasks during her long period at the unit, but during the fieldwork period she was only provided with the opportunity of attending for one interview. This was for sheltered employment at Remploy, and she expressed considerable antagonism at this chance of employment.

Although Tina did not seem to present the staff with any particular problems that were required to be discussed among them, she was consistently allocated to the most simple tasks and was sometimes reprimanded for particular misdemeanours. The most common of these misdemeanours was that if she was assigned sitting next to Kevin, they would spend considerable periods of time telling jokes and hence Tina would end up in prolonged spasms of laughter. This laughter led on several occasions to a lecture by the manager on 'not speaking up above the machines since that may indicate that an accident has occurred'. It also led to members of staff having to instruct her to 'get on with her work'. (It seemed to be the case that often most of the misdemeanours Tina committed could be regarded as petty and in no way antagonistic.)

It would appear that the manager's view of Tina's abilities was not wholeheartedly shared by other members of staff who claimed that despite 'immature' behaviour, she had 'work rhythm', which might enable her to survive in selected open employment. The manager regards admittance to the ATC as a 'backward step to be avoided if at all possible'. During one incident during the early fieldwork, Tina was heading for lunch; she jumped down the last four stairs to the locker room and shouted 'Geronimo'. The manager turned to the fieldworker and remarked that she was likely to wind up in the ATC. It seemed to be the case that most of the tasks that she was assigned to reflected this estimation of her. That is to say, there was no conception of her progressing or improving and she was destined for sheltered employment.

There may be something of a paradox in the way in which most of the students are found jobs. That is, jobs are often found by the manager of the unit, using the network of informal relationships he has built up in local firms. As we have suggested, students are selected for vacancies which arise in line with the staff's evaluations as to their 'readiness' and suitability. Hence there is a built-in bias against the students looking for jobs themselves. It is also apparent that they are not usually aware of the nature of the staff assessments of them (although they may be made aware of particular areas of perceived 'weakness'). The resulting overall impression is that jobs are 'rewards', allocated by the manager, on the basis of compliance, good behaviour and hard work. This is not necessarily a matter for criticism in itself. The process may well be a reasonable approximation of how such youngsters might find work anyway: through the intervention of a parent, relative or elder brother or sister, rather than through formal agencies. Nevertheless there does seem to be a tension between the way jobs are found and allocated, and the professed aim of the unit's training, in fostering a degree of self-reliance and competence in the students when it comes to the world of work. Our strong impression as a result of the fieldwork so far is that the students are very *passive* in the process whereby they are channelled towards jobs. They rarely object to jobs which are found for them and are generally acquiescent.

Conclusion

In this chapter we have been able to touch on just some aspects of the organization and working of an industrial training unit. As we remarked at the outset, we advance no claims as to the 'typicality' of the unit we describe. It does, however, exemplify a number of themes which are generic to contemporary programmes to ease the transition from education to working life.

The work of the unit interweaves 'formal' and 'informal' components. At the level of its overt, official aims and objectives, the unit is intended to provide the young people with specific skills and competencies which will enhance their chances of finding and keeping a job in a shrinking labour market. At a more informal level, the day-to-day training is couched in terms of the model 'good worker' and the values of 'good work'. The unit's activities are pervaded by a distinctive work 'ethos' or 'ideology'.

As we have described, the industrial training unit is not run in accordance with a set 'timetable' or 'curriculum', in the sense usually used in educational settings. The work is organized primarily in terms of the production process of the unit's contract work. Many of the instructional episodes we have exemplified stem directly from threats to production, or 'failures' of workshop practice. Other types of instruction stem from staff members' perception of students' failure to live up to the model worker, in terms of deference and demeanour.

For the most part, it is not at all clear that the students' skills are significantly changed, in terms of their competence with industrial machinery. There is little or no sense of their progressing through graded tasks, and of measurable improvement in performance. Rather, the students find a level at which they work satisfactorily, and stick to it. There is also little to suggest that the actual skills and tasks mastered in the workshop correspond to those most appropriate for the available sectors of the labour market. Training in carpentry may be unlikely to produce directly marketable skills.

As high levels of youth unemployment persist, the number of projects of the kind described here appear to be increasing sharply. Those directed purely at the needs of the slow learner are in the minority, but share with other innovations a concern with work preparation in the broadest sense. Evaluations of such projects abound; in particular the Manpower Services Commission is concerned that its schemes be scrutinized. What such studies appear to lack, however, is a questioning of the aims and objectives of the schemes themselves. In this chapter we have attempted to draw out into the open some of the implicit assumptions that projects set up to ease the transition process for slow learners appear to make.

Acknowledgements

The handicapped were identified by the Council of Ministers as being particularly at risk when youth employment rates rose throughout the European Community in the early 1970s. The Industrial Training Unit described in this paper, which was set up to prepare slow learners for working life, is an associated project of the European Community Action Programme on the Transition from School to Work set up in 1977. It is one of many such innovative projects throughout the Community being evaluated for the Commission. We are grateful to IFAPLAN, the social research institute in Cologne coordinating the evaluation of the Community Action Programme, for funding the work reported here through Professor Alan Little of Goldsmith's College, London, the UK evaluator.

We are also indebted to numerous organizations and individuals in Wales for their support and cooperation, in particular the manager, staff and students of the unit. Finally our thanks are due to Dr. Sara Delamont of the Department of Sociology, University College Cardiff, for her comments upon an earlier draft.

Notes

1 The observer was later told that the manager was seeking the boy's permission to use the incident as a teaching example.

References

Department of Employment (1977) 'Attitude and personality lose young people jobs', *DE Gazette*, October, p. 1127

Gregory, D. (1980) 'Current trends in the local labour market of Mid Glamorgan', Report No. 6 of Evaluation of Industrial Training Units, Sociological Research Unit, Department of Sociology, University College, Cardiff

Gregory, D. and G. Markall (1982) 'State intervention – assumptions and programmes', in Atkinson, P. and T.L. Rees (eds) *Youth Unemployment and State Intervention*, Routledge & Kegan Paul.

Hudson, B. (1977) 'Time to rethink policy for forgotten jobless', *Health and Social Services Journal*, pp. 1702–1704

Manpower Services Commission (1980) 'The Sheffield and Rotherham Labour Market Survey', MSC

Further reading

Lane, D. (1980) The work needs of Mentally Handicapped Adults, published by the Disability Alliance (1 Cambridge Terrace, London NW1)

Jackson, R.N. (1978) 'Are we unrealistic about jobs?' in *Special Education – Forward Trends*, Volume 5, number 1, pp. 11–13

Rogers, J. (1979) 'The Prospects for ESN(M) School Leavers', in *Special Education – Forward Trends*, Volume 6, number 1, pp. 8–10

The ESN(M) School Leaver – Transition to What? Report of a Joint Conference of the National Elfrida Rathbone Society at the Centre for Educational Disadvantage, July 1980, Manchester

CONCLUSION

Sociology is concerned with understanding and explaining the social world. The contributions to this book represent an attempt to understand and to clarify some of the issues, policies and practices in special education, starting from the assumption that special education must be understood and evaluated in terms of the social conditions within which it developed and functions. As such, the book represents a departure from familiar ways of thinking about this subject.

What then, are some of the general issues in this book has sought to bring into the open?

Firstly, we wanted to stress the ways in which beliefs and practices are often based on largely unexamined or taken-for-granted assumptions. The ideology of benevolent humanitarianism (special education as 'doing good' to children) and the assumption that it was a spontaneous, natural development is very strong. At the 1980 conference of the National Council for Special Education (NCSE, 1980) the chairman referred to special education as an 'historical accident'. We hope that this book is seen as presenting a counter-argument to such a view, because in the case of special education it developed as a way of dealing with large groups of children whom the normal educational system could not or would not cope with, and a variety of groups have come to have vested interests in its continued growth. If we examine the processes of development and the assumptions on which special education rests, we will be in a better position to understand the recent changes more clearly and, hopefully, influence change in the direction which will be of maximum benefit to all those in or who may move into special education.

Secondly, we have tried to generate some understanding of the inter-relationship of the practices which make up special education. The system has become immensely complex; introducing the concepts of 'special need' and 'integration' may appear to simplify issues, but in fact they beg many questions and introduce more complex problems. We wanted to generate an interest in the question *why* the system has developed in this way, and in doing so to point out that there is an important distinction to be made between ideology and practice, between rhetoric and reality, between the official view and what the clients may feel and understand. There may be a 'verbal smokescreen to the unadmitted and often unpleasant mainsprings of action' (Berger, 1966, p. 55), which must be blown away to provide a clearer view of what special education is all about, who is benefiting and whose interests are being served. Special education is an area where confidentiality is the rule rather than the exception. This stems partly from the medical involvement, but the majority of children in special education have few medical 'problems' and their education and welfare should be a matter for free and open debate in a democratic society.

Thirdly, a recurring theme of the book has been that an adequate understanding of special education must be based on the realization that it is a political issue. This necessitates a concern with the nature of power and social control, how these are experienced by people in different contexts and the personal and social consequences involved. From this perspective, analysis of special education must be located within a wider examination of the kind of society in which such policies and practices are permitted and legitimated.

Finally, although all the contributors would not claim to be sociologists, and some of those that are represent, or are influenced by, different perspectives, they all share the belief in the important and distinct contribution that sociology can make to our understanding of this significant area. As our knowledge and understanding of the daily experiences of those people in special education is very limited, we hope that this book will in some small way stimulate more creative and constructive research and debate within the field.

Some contributions to this book are polemical and contentious and we make no apology for this. There is, as we noted in the introduction, a general demand for more openness and accountability on the part of those involved in all the education and welfare systems of society and special education should be no exception to this. Social justice, the quality of the lives and experiences of those deemed 'in need' of special education, as well as ultimately the kind of society we want, are the crucial issues.

References

Berger, P. (1966) *Invitation to Sociology: A Humanistic Perspective*, Penguin

NCSE (1980) Annual Conference Proceedings, Cleveland, Middlesborough

CONTRIBUTORS

Paul Atkinson
   Lecturer, Department of Sociology,
   University College, Cardiff.
Len Barton
   Senior Lecturer, Education Department,
   Westhill College, Selly Oak, Birmingham.
Elizabeth Jones
   Teacher, Banbury School, Oxford.
David Lane
   Professor, Department of Sociology,
   University of Birmingham, Birmingham.
Ian Lewis
   Lecturer, Department of Education,
   University of York, York.
Ian Macdonald
   Research Fellow, Institute of Organisation & Social Studies,
   Brunel University, Uxbridge, Middlesex.
Susan Moody
   Teacher, Bettridge ESN(S) School, Cheltenham.
Teresa Rees
   Research Officer, Sociological Research Unit,
   Department of Sociology,
   University College, Cardiff.
Geof Sewell
   Lecturer, School of Education,
   University of Durham, Durham.

David Shone
  Research Assistant, Sociological Research Unit,
  Department of Sociology,
  University College, Cardiff.

Janet Strivens
  Lecturer, School of Education
  University of Liverpool, Liverpool.

Peter Squibb
  Head of Department of Humanities,
  Ilkley College, Ilkley, West Yorkshire.

Andrew Sutton
  Honorary Lecturer, Faculty of Education,
  University of Birmingham, Birmingham.

Sally Tomlinson
  Lecturer, Department of Educational Research,
  University of Lancaster, Lancaster.

Graham Vulliamy
  Lecturer, Department of Education,
  University of York, York.

Ray Woolfe
  Staff Tutor, Educational Studies,
  The Open University in Wales, 24 Cathedral Road, Cardiff.

AUTHOR INDEX

Bibliographical details will be found on those page numbers printed in **bold**

SUBJECT INDEX

Main references are given in **bold**

The Harper Education Series has been designed to meet the needs of students following initial courses in teacher education at colleges and in University departments of education, as well as the interests of practising teachers.

All volumes in the series are based firmly in the practice of education and deal, in a multidisciplinary way, with practical classroom issues, school organisation and aspects of the curriculum.

Topics in the series are wide ranging, as the list of current titles indicates. In all cases the authors have set out to discuss current educational developments and show how practice is changing in the light of recent research and educational thinking. Theoretical discussions, supported by an examination of recent research and literature in the relevant fields, arise out of a consideration of classroom practice.

Care is taken to present specialist topics to the non-specialist reader in a style that is lucid and approachable. Extensive bibliographies are supplied to enable readers to pursue any given topic further.

Meriel Downey, General Editor